ISRAEL'S PRAISE

WALTER BRUEGGEMANN

ISRAEL'S PRAISE

Doxology against
Idolatry and
Ideology

FORTRESS PRESS   PHILADELPHIA

Library of Congress Cataloging-in-Publication Data

Brueggemann, Walter.
  Israel's praise.

  Includes index.
    1. Bible. O.T. Psalms—Criticism, interpretation, etc. 2. Sociology, Biblical. 3. Pastoral theology.
  4. Liturgics. 5. Idolatry. 6. Ideology. I. Title.
  BS1430.2.B78 1988   223'.2067   86–46419
  ISBN 0–8006–2044–5

2987H87   Printed in the United States of America   1–2044

For
John A. Hollar

Contents

Preface

[handwritten notes:] Gunkel — Sitz + Origin
Mowinckel — cultic use

❦ ━━━━━━━━━━━━━━━━━━ ❧

In this book I seek to explicate the convergence of three factors in current theological conversation. First, I attempt to reflect and to advance our current situation in Psalms studies. After the magisterial work of Hermann Gunkel and Sigmund Mowinckel and the important advances of Claus Westermann, critical study of the Psalms seems to be resting on a plateau. Other than an attempt at "intratextual" interpretation, we do not seem to be prepared for any new steps.[1] I believe the reason for this dormancy is that we have forgotten that Gunkel's program, even without Mowinckel's departure, was not simply a literary analysis but also a sociological study. Gunkel's understanding of *Gattungen* was integrally related to the "life-setting" of the literature.[2] For him *Sitz im Leben* did not refer to a vacuous literary fantasy but the real relationships of human persons to each other in societal patterns.[3] Here I have tried to take up the sociological question of the Psalms, to suggest that the Psalms can only be understood and used rightly if we attend to their social interaction and function, not only in their origin but also in their repeated use. My suggestion is that the intent and use of a psalm is never only transcendental (e.g., as praise to God), but that it functions characteristically and inevitably in the deployment and legitimation of social power. Thus I have returned to Mowinckel's cultic use as a way of reconsidering the question of social use for the deployment and legitimation of social power.

ix

Second, I have wanted to be attentive to the central task of the pastor within the Christian congregation, and within a culture that continues to draw heavily from and rely seriously upon theological claims and assurances. After two generations of the splintering "professionalism" of ordained ministry,[4] we are at a moment when ordained ministry is being refocused on the pastoral, liturgical task of nurturing a communal, intentional, and often alternative imagination. This means that the pastor, in his or her pastoral-liturgical functions, cannot avoid the sociopolitical "surplus" of that work.[5] It may be done knowingly or unknowingly, but it will be done. That is, pastors are willy-nilly engaged in "world-making," a task that is much more elemental and urgent than the "therapeutic" and "managerial" tasks often acknowledged.[6]

Third, the social reality of the Psalms and the social enactment of reality done by the pastoral office meet, I propose, in the act of liturgy—an act of resymbolizing community experience.[7] The resymbolization of experience as "world-making" or as "social construction" is an activity now under scrutiny in many scholarly disciplines—in the sciences as well as the humanities—and undertaken by many different agents in society. Because there are competing and conflicting programs of resymbolization available to us, we are engaged in a battle for the mind, heart, and imagination of our society.[8] It is not yet clear which liturgy will prevail in the postindustrial, post-Christian West. But it is clear that the outcome of the liturgical conflict will be decisive for policy formation and public values in our society as concerns politics, economics, and law.

Thus I have pursued the question of how the sociology of the Psalms, the work of the pastoral office, and the competing symbolizations converge in our present circumstance—in church and in society. The convergence of these three agendas reflects, I believe, our new post-Enlightenment epistemological situation. It is no longer tenable to imagine that there is a "given" world into which we may fit, and which we have only to describe, and to which we may bear witness. That easy "givenness" is now seen to be theologically unconvincing and sociologically naive. Whatever one may think about the ontology of faith and world, in a dramatic, experiential, and political sense, we are indeed world-makers. It remains to be seen if we have the courage to do world-making honestly and faithfully. For us in the Jewish and Christian traditions, it remains

to be seen not only if our world will be faithful to our memory, but
also how the text will function to discipline, legitimate, and energize that world construction.

It is my hope and belief that in addressing these three issues as
part of a single concern, I have been faithful to the intent of the
Sprunt Lectures for which the material in this book was originally
prepared. That distinguished lecture series at Union Theological
Seminary in Virginia expects, as I understand it, a treatment of the
theological tradition, a focus on the pastoral task, and responsible
reference to the intellectual currents of the day. Those factors
were in my awareness in making preparation for the lectures.

The title of this book, *Israel's Praise: Doxology against Idolatry
and Ideology,* reflects the way I have shaped the argument. First, I
consider in a formal way the possibility and burden of "world-
making" (chap. 1), and then in a substantive way the peculiar
world the Psalms of ancient Israel make available under the rubric
of the "Kingship of Yahweh" (chap. 2). In chapters 3 and 4, I have
considered how the proposed world of Yahwistic faith, marked by
righteousness, equity, and truth, becomes skewed by royal management. The Psalms then are distorted to symbolize a god (idol)
who cannot act, and a social system (ideology) that cannot change
or be criticized. After that critical investigation, which I hope is
pertinent both to ancient royal Israel and to our own cultural
context in the American church, I have explored the ways in which
praise may be free of idolatry and ideology (chap. 5). The way I
have proposed is to read and sing the psalms of praise "back down"
to pain, where hope lives; to hurt, where newness surfaces; to
death, where life is strangely given.[9] In the end, I intend this
statement about the Psalms to be neither literary analysis nor sociological criticism, but a statement of an evangelical sort that the
God of Israel, the faith of Israel, and the singing of Israel make
available a very different world. It is that different world which is
entrusted to the pastoral office, a world for which the whole human community deeply yearns.

It remains for me to give thanks. I am grateful to President
Hartley Hall III and the faculty of Union Theological Seminary,
Richmond, Virginia, for their invitation to be the Sprunt lecturer
and for their gracious hosting. During the lectures, I enjoyed the
generous and supportive hospitality of many faculty colleagues

and friends, especially the graciousness of Professor and Mrs. James L. Mays. I am grateful, moreover, to Kevin Andrews, my former student who assisted me in concrete ways during the lectures, and Donna LaGrasso who patiently typed, and retyped, and typed again.

Only those who struggle to complete a book know the importance of a faithful, attentive, evocative editor. It is a remarkable editor who listens well enough to know what the next words will be before they are written, who knows how to be present in the indecision and fatigue, who can wean one from words he has come to love too much. John A. Hollar is all of that for my work, and so I dedicate this to him with thanks and thanksgiving.

Beyond these acknowledgments I am the recipient of great gifts of courage, honesty, hope, and grace from colleagues who share this scholarly, pastoral concern.

Columbia Theological Seminary   WALTER BRUEGGEMANN
February 18, 1987

1

Praise as a Constitutive Act

❧ ────────────────── ❧

Praise is the duty and delight, the ultimate vocation of the human community; indeed, of all creation.[1] Yes, all of life is aimed toward God and finally exists for the sake of God. Praise articulates and embodies our capacity to yield, submit, and abandon ourselves in trust and gratitude to the One whose we are. Praise is not only a human requirement and a human need, it is also a human delight. We have a resilient hunger to move beyond self, to return our energy and worth to the One from whom it has been granted. In our return to that One, we find our deepest joy. That is what it means to "glorify God and enjoy God forever."

As praise is appropriate to human community, so praise is appropriate to the character of God, for our praise is a response to God's power and mercy. Nothing more can be said to God. Nothing more can be added to God. Nonetheless God must be addressed. It is appropriate to address God in need, by way of petition and intercession. But address in need occurs in a context of lyrical submission in which God is addressed not because we have need, but simply because God is God and we are summoned to turn our lives in answer to God.[2] It is appropriate that we should address God in submission. It is inappropriate that God should not be addressed. This is a God who evokes address of gratitude and awe, simply because of who God is.

Our delight and duty in praise corresponds precisely to God's sovereignty and compassion. This positioning of the two parties in a reciprocal but not symmetrical relation requires and permits praise. This relation acknowledges both that God must be addressed, and that nothing need be done or dare be said. Where something must be said, but nothing need or dare be said, speech of celebration, wonder, and surrender, of enhancement and abandonment, is our appropriate practice.

This vocation of praise is embraced as an ecumenical reality. It is precisely the children of John Calvin who are so clear about God's majesty, who understand praise best. That is why we are able to say boldly that our chief concern is "to glorify and enjoy God forever." Glorification and enjoyment, the first serving God, the second including us, are the final purpose of humanity.

When we seek a voice in the tradition of Calvin to say what praise signifies, we of course will not do better than Karl Barth:[3]

> It is in his spoken word that man, like God, comes out into the open, making himself clear, intelligible and in some way responsible, venturing forth and binding and committing himself. In his word man hazards himself. And it is demanded of him that in his word he shall continually hazard himself to God's glory, coming out into the open as a partisan of God.[4] . . . Pure, childlike, disinterested and unpremeditated witness may and should sometimes be an eloquent fact in this disputation to God's glory. This is the meaning of the command that man with his word shall continually be God's witness. The meaning of this command lies in the fact that man may be and speak as God's partisan.[5] . . . And if we know who we are, how can we answer from the infinite disquiet which we create for ourselves unless we call on His name, on His merciful and saving name? What else can we say to what God gives us but stammer praise of this gift and Giver? What else can our praise of this gift and Giver be—always assuming that we know who and what we are—but a single petition and supplication, a spreading out of empty hands to the One who, so long as we are on our way, must always fill them afresh, that we may be able to live in the midst of work with the freedom at which we can aim in our work only as we do it aright?[6]

I had always assumed that this articulation of the place of praise was a discernment peculiar to the tradition of Calvin. I preached on Psalm 100 at the ordination of the Episcopal bishop of Milwaukee several years ago, asserting that the bishop must nurture the diocese in praise, and that such praise is a bold, political act. I thought I had sounded the best sounds of Calvin as I understood them. After the ordination liturgy, Bishop Rembert G. Weakland, that great and courageous Roman Catholic shepherd from Milwaukee, said, "That was excellent Benedictine theology." I took him at his word, but such an act can be gladly Benedictine without ceasing to be gladly Calvinist. Calvinists and Benedictines and all of those who live toward this majestic, merciful God know a central duty and ultimate delight in the praise of God.

Here in this book I want to articulate the full importance of that vocation which is both duty and delight. To be sure, praise is addressed to heaven. That is central to Barth and the tradition to which I refer. But it is equally true that praise is spoken by human voices on earth. The address to God indicates that praise is a theological act of profound dramatic importance. Praise is spoken on earth. Inevitably then, praise is not a pure, unmitigated impingement in heaven. The act also impinges on earth. That is, praise is not only a religious vocation, but it is also a social gesture that effects the shape and character of human life and human community.[7] Inevitably praise does its work among human persons as much as it does in the courts of heaven.

I want to pay attention to the social reality of praise, so that we might discern more fully its theological risk and benefit. I do not minimize the genuinely theological character of the act of praise, but I want to approach it critically in order that our practice of worship and our commitment to ethical responsibility should be intentionally related to each other. My argument is based on the conviction that the church has acute problems concerning ethical responsibility because our worship has not been critiqued or understood as a social act. As a result, we find ourselves embracing realities about which we are not intentional. Worship in which heaven and earth commune is worship in which our deepest religious acts and our boldest worldly commitments may be brought under a common discipline.

THE PSALMS AS CREATIVE ACTS

When we become specific about praise of God in the biblical tradition, we arrive quickly at the Book of Psalms, which is the central resource for praise in the Bible. Gerhard von Rad[8] and Claus Westermann[9] have seen that the Psalms are *responsive* to the reality, power, and activity of God. Indeed, in von Rad's *Old Testament Theology*, the Psalms are identified as part of "Israel's answer" to God's action.

In this book, I want to pursue the notion that in addition to being responsive, praise is also *constitutive* of theological reality. It not only addresses the God who is there before us but also is an act of constructing the theological world in which we shall interact with God. Because praise is *constitutive* as well as *responsive*, practitioners of praise would do well to be critical, knowing, and intentional about the enterprise of construction.

The magisterial hypothesis of Sigmund Mowinckel is the beginning point of our study. In 1921–24, Mowinckel wrote six fascicles of *Psalmenstudien*, which have never been translated into English.[10] In 1951 he published *Offersang og Sangoffer*, which in 1962 was translated with revisions into English as *The Psalms in Israel's Worship*.[11] The latter work is more of a handbook, which is neither as imaginative nor as important as his *Psalmenstudien*, in which he laid down programmatic proposals that continue to occupy scholars. Of the six fascicles of his original work, it is the second which concerns us. The formal title is "The Festival of the Enthronement of Yahweh and the Origin of Eschatology."[12] The title indicates Mowinckel's concern for the relation between worship and eschatology.

In this fascicle Mowinckel broke new ground that I suspect has not yet been fully appropriated. His teacher, Hermann Gunkel, is responsible for putting Psalms study on a completely new basis by the form-critical categories he articulated.[13] After Gunkel, Mowinckel has done the most important work on the Psalms.[14] He argued that the various literary genres Gunkel identified are reflective of actual cultic use, not imitations as Gunkel had proposed. Because the Psalms are reflective of actual cultic use, one can then reconstruct from them the liturgy in which they were used.

In an incredibly imaginative act, Mowinckel proposed that in the early days of the Jerusalem Temple, the king sponsored and supervised a festival. In the festival Yahweh was once again enthroned as sovereign for the coming year. The regularized and routinized liturgical sequence of the festival provided for a ritual combat among various gods, all of whom wanted to be king. Thus the premise of the hypothesis is a vigorous polytheism. Yahweh, the God of Israel, was victorious in combat and so warranted the throne. There was then a celebrative procession in which Yahweh ascended the throne and was acclaimed king. The other gods promised to serve and obey this God for a year. Seated upon the throne, Yahweh gave something like a "state of the union" message, in which the condition of life was decreed for the coming year. It was characteristically a decree of health, peace, and *shalom.* Mowinckel proposed (and Aubrey Johnson reinforced) the notion that the Davidic king played a crucial role in the festival.[15] The king, according to the hypothesis, played the role of Yahweh and was enthroned on his behalf. That is, the enthronement of Yahweh as God carried with it important implications for the legitimacy of the Davidic monarchy, which was also liturgically renewed in the festival.

That Mowinckel's title also concerned eschatology has gone largely unnoticed among scholars. He proposed that eschatology is a projection of hope into the future out of a cultic enactment that never fully met expectations. Because present realities were short of expectation, Israel's hope was delayed and increasingly displaced by the future.[16] That projection into the future, according to Mowinckel, is not inappropriate to the cultic act itself. That is, the cultic act, which is an act of liturgic imagination in and of itself, opens to a future that was in tension with "business as usual." In that context, the very enactment of the narrative (*mythos*) of the cult is itself an assertion of an alternative world that permits a basis for hope.[17] All such liturgic activity, and especially praise, is an act of embracing an alternative future. Scholarly categories which separate cult from eschatology artificially divide what belongs together in the act of worship in Israel. Cult and eschatology together mediate an alternative which critiques the present world and invites liberation from it.

Two widespread and conflicting reactions to Mowinckel's magisterial hypothesis are equally important. First, the hypothesis has been subjected to important criticisms.[18] It is urged that Mowinckel relied too much on nonbiblical parallels from patterns in the Babylonian parallels. It is widely thought that Mowinckel relied too much on later materials, which he unconvincingly projected back into the early period. The hypothesis is also criticized as too comprehensive, too imperial, so that too many psalms are claimed, and there is a tendency to fit everything into a single scheme. This reaction reflects a general disease among scholars with any hypothesis that is too massive, so that it monopolizes all the data and precludes all alternative understandings. Moreover, scholars with a historical-critical inclination are resistant to a dynamic, creative understanding of cult because such a way of thinking precludes historical analysis and requires a different mode of thought. As a result, scholars have largely missed the point of the proposal. By asking only historical questions, the hypothesis has been misunderstood and distorted. Everything in the hypothesis depends on the creative, generative function of the cult. But scholarship, largely liberal Protestant, is reluctant to credit cult with that much power or significance and that has led to caution, if not resistance, of Mowinckel.[19]

Second, while scholarship has been cautious and critical, it is also fair to say that the hypothesis continues to dominate the discussion. Even scholars who are not in sympathy with the proposal appeal either to the hypothesis itself or to some derivative form of the hypothesis.[20] Mowinckel's comprehensive proposal accounts for a great deal of data, and no alternative that is so satisfying has been forthcoming. Johnson[21] and J. H. Eaton[22] have enthusiastically embraced it and have pressed matters even further. In the more sober and historically oriented modes of German scholarship, Artur Weiser and Hans Joachim Kraus have offered different festival hypotheses more firmly rooted in historical memory, but they are largely dependent on the insights of Mowinckel for their basic paradigm.

THE CONSTITUTIVE POWER OF PRAISE

I suggest, however, that Mowinckel's hypothesis has not yet been fully considered because attention has been focused in the wrong place. Criticism has attended to questions about kingship and evidence for the particulars of the festival, but that is mostly to miss the point. What counts is that the cult (and therefore, praise, which is our subject) is understood by Mowinckel as *constitutive* and not merely *responsive*. It is not as important to focus on the substance of kingship as on the claim that in public worship Israel is engaged in constructing a world in which Israel can viably, joyously, and obediently live.

If the cult is creative, then what was done in the cult is constitutive. What was done in the cult was praise. Praise not only celebrates God but portrays the world given us by this God now received as sovereign. From this celebration of God and portrayal of world, we may ask, *in what sense is praise constitutive of the world?* I am aware that, theologically, such a view is problematic, because it smacks of synergism, wherein the community, or at least the king and priest, share in God's creative work, or indeed, do God's creative work. I do not minimize that problem. But that theological question notwithstanding, the constitutive power of praise is anthropologically and sociologically a most plausible, attractive, and finally, important idea.[23] In Psalms study generally, Gunkel was highly resistant to such a notion of creative cult, and Westermann, who after Gunkel and Mowinckel is most important for critical Psalms study, has simply disregarded the issue of cult.[24] Yet without the cult, that is, a viable community that actively processes the claims of the Psalms, they are only dormant literature.

I take up this question of creative cult and constitutive praise (that is, the view of Mowinckel, which Gunkel and Westermann largely dismissed) because I believe the matter is of interest and importance to the exercise of the pastoral office. My interest is not speculative, but intensely practical. To the extent that praise, and worship more generally, is constitutive, awareness of this constitutive element will permit greater intentionality and will permit the agents of the liturgical drama—priests and pastors—to be more knowingly critical of what they themselves do. As long as cultic acts of praise are taken to be only responsive and not constitutive, the agents of the drama are likely to be neither intentional nor critical. Lack of such awareness in itself, however, will not prevent the inevitably ongoing work of construction.

Thus I begin with Mowinckel's notion of *worship as world-making.* Such a focus places the more particular question of kingship in the dramatic context of public worship. Recent scholarship has tried to interpret Mowinckel on kingship without that more comprehensive dramatic context. Such a loss of context denies Mowinckel a serious or fair hearing.

Informed by the anthropological work of Wilhelm Groenbeck, Mowinckel had a clear grasp of this issue, even though it opposed the dominant historical tendencies of his day, and indeed of our day. Mowinckel is generally credited with bringing together the anthropological study of Groenbeck and the literary analysis of Gunkel.[25] While Gunkel's work has been readily embraced by scholars, the anthropological studies represented by Groenbeck

have been found less convincing. The fact that we now return to
the issue of dynamic of the cult perhaps reflects a shift not only in
scholarship, but in the categories of knowledge to which we are
now responsive. The shift away from historical-critical methods as
we have practiced them in scripture studies is to be understood
as part of a much broader shift that is under way in the epistemological foundations of our culture.

Mowinckel's introduction to the question of creativity in cult
may be summarized in his own words:

> Cult (*'abodah*) was for ancient Israel, as for primitive men generally,
> the festive, holy activities through which the divine power, the bless-
> ing (*berakah*) of the society, the community, and through it, individ-
> uals was obtained.[26]

The operational word "obtained" (*erwerben*) is crucial. The cult
effects that which would not otherwise be effected. Or again,
Mowinckel asserts:

> The cult is not only originally, but everywhere and always, drama.
> Cult is a holy enterprise, but it is at the same time a holy reality. It
> is not merely a playful drama, a play, but an effective and reality-
> generating drama, a drama which actualizes with real power the
> dramatic event, a reality which shows forth real power, or in other
> words, a sacrament.[27]

Mowinckel's rhetoric leaves no doubt of his intention. In this one
paragraph, the word *Wirklichkeit* ("reality") occurs three times as
a noun, once more as an adjective, and once as a verb. The action
of the sacramental drama is "real." It effects something.

Mowinckel continues:

> These are the holy actions of cult. At the same time these actions
> maintain (*erhalten*) "the world," the cosmos. The tribal sphere or the
> national state of the "world" are originally and properly identical.[28]

Two matters are of interest in this statement. First, the verb "maintain" is a strong verb, again suggesting effective action. Second, the
term "world" is in quotation marks, but the word "cosmos" is not.
The last sentence indicates that Mowinckel means the creation and
maintenance of a life-world and a socioeconomic-political order
that makes public life possible and sustainable. That formation of a
viable life-world happens through the work of the cult. The identification of world and cosmos with a social life-world will be important for our argument.

Mowinckel's more recent work contains the following reflection on his general claim:

> What the congregation wants to achieve through the cult, and what the "power" for God is to create, is *life* —in the most comprehensive sense of the word, from the fundamental material needs: rain, sun, and fertility, the continuation of the race, the strength and victory of the tribe, and so on, up to the spiritual, religious and ethical values that are the lifeblood of the society—life for everything that belongs to its "world." . . . The Israelites expressed the same idea by the word "blessing." Blessing is to be created, increased and served through the cult.[29]

Again the term "world" is in quotation marks, but it is clear that Mowinckel means the social life-world in its most comprehensive sense. It is the world created in cult that mediates the blessing of God.

Finally, one more direct quote from Mowinckel:

> That life is *created* through the cult means salvation from the distress and destruction which would befall if life were not renewed. For existence is an everlasting war between the forces of life and death, of blessing and curse. The "world" is worn out if it is not regularly renewed, as anyone can see by the annual course of life and nature. Thus it is the "fact of salvation" which is actualized in the cult. . . . This actualization of the fact of salvation is repeated as often as necessary.[30]

Notice that Mowinckel here places "world" and "fact of salvation" in quotation marks, and "created" is italicized.

Mowinckel wants to resist the notion that world-creation in cult is simply a subjective reading of the world that in fact exists apart from the cult. To such a notion Mowinckel would say, "No, it does not exist apart from the cult." Mowinckel surely knows about the danger of a primitive "realism" in the cult that imagines that priests form rocks and trees by their rituals. Mowinckel urges a mode of thought and language which escapes this split of subjectivism and rational positivism. It is my urging that we also must escape both subjectivism and rational objectivism if worship is to have the centrality that we claim for it and which is promised in our theological tradition. It is not a matter of saying that we are in fact subjective rather than realistic, or that we are realistic rather than subjective, but that insisting on such a distinction is a major part of the problem. In the language of our time, one might say that Mowinckel wants to understand in the modes of praxis and not in a speculative way that divides what cannot be divided. The cult has a realism that is more than subjectivism, but is not the kind of realism that caters to the technological modes of modernity. What happens in cult is realistic, but it is not the realism of technique.

Notice that Mowinckel is not suggesting that cult *ought* to do this creative work, nor indeed that the cult *ought not* to do this. It simply does. It does indeed, as every serious pastor knows. Every serious pastor knows as she listens to parishioners that what happens in sacramental activity has a reality that the outside world does not understand, but that nonetheless is a reality. The problem is not in the character of the cultic act, but in our poor language that can scarcely say what it is that we do and in our poor epistemology that can scarcely know what it is that we do.

Taken as an anthropological statement, Mowinckel's analysis may be simply descriptive: This is how the cult operates. Taken as a theological statement, one may claim that cult, as a gift from God, is granted as a means through which God's creative power is mediated. That is what we mean when we say a sacrament is "instituted." Mowinckel would, I believe, say that the dramatic work of worship is instituted, that is, authorized and legitimated, by the power of God to do world-making work which is God's work, but which is processed through intentional, disciplined, obedient human action and human speech. It is the process of the authorized word and the legitimated action that decisively shapes and articulates the world.

If the subject of liturgy is kingship—of Yahweh, of David, or derivatively, of Jesus—then the liturgy serves to authorize, recognize, acknowledge, coronate, legitimate the ruler and the order that belongs to that ruler. The liturgy is the festive act of enthroning and the obedient act of submitting more and more areas of life to that newly wrought sovereignty. The world may think this is subjective self-deception, but the assembly which credits the speech and action knows that the reality of God is not a reality unless it is visibly done in, with, and by the community. That is what we know, even if that knowledge flies in the face of our cynical modernity. That is what we know and attest to as professionals who preside over this action for the sake of the others, and what we know as participants as we sense our own world shaped and reshaped, maintained, renewed, transformed. What we know and see happen there we know will not happen anywhere else. Everything, therefore, is at stake in world-making here.

The categories for this assertion are elusive. There are of course problems, if this argument be taken as an ontological statement, because it suggests on the one hand that God's creation is precarious and depends on ritual activity and, indeed, that God's sovereignty depends on such actions. On the other hand, along with jeopardizing God's standing, it suggests an efficacy that assigns more to liturgy than is intended, a kind of uncritical *ex opere operato*, as if it is effective in itself. If the language of Mowinckel be taken as dramatic (not denying the ontological, but simply bracketing it out for now), then more is happening in liturgy than remembrance and response. In the liturgy, world-making is indeed effected. The making of this world would be impossible without this dramatic enactment of liturgy. Implicit in this argument, then, is the provisional claim that social reality (and here we dare say religious reality) is a dramatic reality, always to be enacted again. The claim of reality makes no sense unless its dramatic character is understood. It is the claim for reality for this particular world that the critics of Mowinckel have largely missed, because historical-critical methods of investigation simply cannot make contact with that dangerous and elusive point. When questions are posed historically, categories pertaining to the dramatic character of the cult are precluded.

I wish then, if I have correctly understood Mowinckel, to suggest that the praise of Israel—or more broadly, the human vocation of praise—is to maintain and transform the world, obtain a blessing that would not be obtained, maintained, or transformed, except through this routinized and most serious activity authorized by God and enacted by human agents. "World-making" is done by God. That is foundational to Israel's faith. But it is done through human activity which God has authorized and in which God is known to be present. Thus it is commonly agreed that Gen. 1:1—2:4a is a liturgical text in which the community "remembers" God's creating event, but also reenacts and participates in it in order to give pattern to present experience, presumably in the exile. Praise is not a response to a world already fixed and settled, but it is a responsive and obedient participation in a world yet to be decreed and in process of being decreed through this liturgical act.

no room for fundamentalism ! *Good intro for parables*

WORLD-MAKING AS AN IMAGINATIVE ENTERPRISE

An important epistemological shift that is happening in our generation[31] is evident in the shift of scholarly investigation generally, the shift in scripture study from *historical* to *literary*,[32] and the shift from the valuing of *facticity* to the celebration of *imagination*. These shifts are all of a piece. They reflect the failure and loss of confidence in Enlightenment modes of knowledge, which were aimed at technical control. We are coming to see that conventional modes of historical-critical investigation—our excessive preoccupation with facticity—are congenial and subservient to an Enlightenment notion of reality that assumes that the world is a fixed, settled object that can be described, characterized, analyzed, and finally controlled in an objective way. This objective settlement of reality has left very little for us to do, except to get it right. And we have been able to assume there was a way to get it right.

It has become increasingly clear, however, that reality is not fixed and settled, that it cannot be described objectively. We do not simply respond to a world that is here, but we engage in constituting that world by our participation, our actions, and our speech. As participants in the constitutive act, we do not describe what is there, but we evoke what is not fully there until we act or speak.[33] The human agent, then, is a constitutive part of the enterprise, which means that the shape of reality in part awaits our shaping adherence. Or, as a chemist has put it concerning his research, "The world is not a crossword puzzle to be solved, but a symphony yet to be written."[34]

good

Such a discernment moves our understanding of reality away from a settled absoluteness. That, to be sure, is an awareness that theologians have affirmed for a long time, arguing that God continues to create the world.[35] This affirmation of the dynamic character of creation asserts:

- that God is still operative and exercises choices along the way;
- that the world is still open and we are not fated;
- that human agents, as creatures in God's image, share in God's imaging activity.[36]

I can identify four facets of current intellectual reflection that illuminate the proposal that praise is constitutive and not merely responsive.

Sociological Understandings

We are able to see that the social world in which we live is not an inevitable arrangement. It is a chosen or contrived arrangement, chosen or contrived according to someone's initiative and/or interest. This social world could therefore be arranged differently, if different choices were made according to other initiatives and interests. The most accessible reading of this notion is by Peter L. Berger and Thomas Luckmann, in their illuminating phrase, "The Social Construction of Reality."[37] All three terms of the formulation are important. "Reality" refers to a structure, system, and arrangement of social life that is known, perceived, relied upon, and judged to be true. Reality par excellence—paramount reality—is everyday life, which is always experienced as "prearranged in patterns."[38] It is the patterning or order that is definitional for daily life.

The second term, "construction," indicates that this pattern or ordering is constructed. It is not a given. The fact that it is not a given is evidenced in the harsh conflict that arises over the rearrangement of patterns of life and power, and the rearrangement of the symbols that legitimate those patterns. Berger and Luckmann say it tersely: "man produces himself."[39] This patterning is not simply "there," as is evidenced by the fact that the life-world is patterned differently in different societies. It is chosen, guarded, justified, defended, maintained, at least partly, with intentionality. While a society can greatly prize a certain ordering of experience, the world never needs to be ordered the way it is. It could be ordered differently or the ordering can be abandoned, so that there is only disorder.

The third term is "social." "Man's self-production" is always and of necessity a social enterprise of the community.[40] Human agents together purpose a human environment. Thus the formula means that the legitimation and patterning of experience, which in daily experience is reality, is produced and arranged in active ways by the society itself. This special operation is mediated to and appropriated by individuals who live in that society and regard that constructed world as a given.

The process of "world-building" requires that society assert its world as authoritative, accepted as a given without a doubt or reservation, and without any entertainment of a plausible alternative.

That process of world construction, as Berger has said so well, depends on adequate and trusting appropriation. On the one hand, there must be externalization, so that the ordering is perceived in the community as objectively true. On the other hand, there must be internalization so that individuals receive this ordering of experience as "mine." When this reality is accepted as objectively true and personally mine, it becomes a norm (*nomos*) by which all else is tested.

Sociologically, this process of social construction is not simply a response to a world already given. Rather, it is constitutive of a world now and always being constructed. Those who sponsor the constructive act regard that constructed world as given. Nonetheless, much energy is put into the construction, especially by those who want it experienced as given, and into compelling others to accept the construction as given. When "world" is understood as a legitimated and ordered patterning of experience, we are very close to Mowinckel's definition of world and world-creation. For Mowinckel had written, as we have seen, that "world" and the sphere of the tribe or of the national state are originally identical.

Thus Berger and Luckmann, I suggest, use the notion of "world" in the same way as Mowinckel does.[41] Moreover, by speaking of world-construction and world-maintenance—that is, active intentional processes of legitimation—Berger and Luckmann are very close to Mowinckel's understanding of cult. Indeed, Berger mentions worship in relation to legitimation.[42] Insofar as Berger is correct, notice that he does not urge that this process ought to be so, but observes that it inevitably is so. Mowinckel's understanding of the Psalms, and of praise, is a specific case in point of Berger's general argument. Israel's hymnic worship is an act of world-construction.

Literary Understandings   *Good sites for Parables*

A second dimension of human activity which is constitutive of reality is reflected in the current interest in narrative particularly, and in literature more generally.[43] (More broadly, one might say in all of the arts, but we will stay with the primary focus of current interest.) The shift from history to literature in scripture method, now documented and embraced by a host of scholars, is pertinent to our theme. Focus on historical questions served positivistic notions of reality in which we could recover what was really there as an objective, given reality which only awaited description. Indeed, much discussion about the authority of scripture, as James Barr has argued, wrongly appealed to historical objectivity to establish its case.[44]

The shift to literary analysis is related to the abandonment of this historical pursuit of objectivity. It is clear that literature not only reports or describes reality, but good literature that is imaginative mediates and redescribes reality. In such literature, the reality that is carried in this particular form did not exist until it was articulated and rendered in exactly this way. That is, speech leads reality, and until reality is spoken, we did not know reality, perceive it, or embrace it. This capacity to lead reality to where it has not yet been is of course the basis of preaching in a sound theology of the Word. Imaginative speech not only describes, but constitutes reality.

The more theoretical basis for this new effort in scripture study is heavily informed by the work of Paul Ricoeur, but along with Ricoeur attention may be paid to Hans-Georg Gadamer and, foundationally, to Martin Heidegger.[45] It is Ricoeur who has been most helpful in making the case that imagination (the offer of images which are open, inventive, and energizing) lies behind our conceptual reality.

More immediately helpful for our work is the contribution of Amos Wilder, who has not been so concerned with the theoretical discussion, but has helped us to see the ways in which the words of scripture work to constitute reality, or better, constitute a reality alternative to the one conventionally assumed.[46] Only such construction through imagination permits the prospect of an alternative. The themes of Wilder's distinguished research have been drawn together recently in a summary article, "Story and Story-World."[47] He asserts that the listener or reader "should feel himself or herself a tacit interlocutor in the performance, a participant in the world-making that is going on."[48] He continues, "myths and rehearsals [i.e., von Rad's recitals] were evoked in the first place like shelters to provide us with a habitation in whatever homelessness may attend the mortal creature. . . ."[49] The reference to homelessness may be taken as a primordial condition of humanity, but it may also suggest social chaos in which there is no ordered or patterned experience which is accepted as normative.[50]

I suggest that Wilder's discernment of the function of literature relates directly to Mowinckel's hypothesis. First, Wilder has proposed that storytelling begins in myths and rehearsals,[51] exactly Mowinckel's view of myth as the story which the liturgy enacts. Second, Wilder's view of "world" is close to that of Mowinckel. Wilder writes,

> There is no "world" for us until we have named and languaged and storied whatever is. What we take to be the nature of things has been shaped by calling it so. This therefore is also a story-world. Here again we cannot move behind the story to what may be more "real." Our language-worlds are the only worlds we know![52]

In saying this sort of thing, I have an uneasiness which may reassure you, for Wilder's statement suggests that matters are excessively subjective. Wilder is of course aware of that uneasiness. Following Samuel Beckett, he asserts,

> The fact is that there is a prior sense for the real which pervades and tests all language and all stories. The clue to the relation between story-worlds and real world is to be found in that motif of "interest" on which I have laid such stress. In all those features of storying which exert their spell on hearer or reader we can recognize the bridge between fiction and life itself. Stories would not even exist or be heard through if human nature did not look to them avidly for illumination of its homelessness in time and circumstance. It is just because life is a labyrinth that we follow eagerly for clues and traces, the impasses and detours and open-sesames of a myth or tale. The world of our story is our own world in a higher register.[53]

I am not sure "higher register" is the best way to put it. I should say that story mediates the real world in a direct, peculiar, and concrete way, so that it is available for appropriation in, with, and through our experience. Such mediation is not secondary activity. It is elemental to having any world at all which we may appropriate as a home in our homelessness.

This programmatic notion of Wilder has been given concrete exegetical form in two brief but discerning studies by David J. A. Clines. In 1976, he published an innovative and suggestive study of Isa. 52:13—53:12, the familiar fourth Servant Song.[54] He observed that the pronouns in that poem have no obvious or unambiguous references or antecedents. Thus his study is entitled *I, He, We, & They*. His argument is that this absence of clear reference is a deliberate strategy in the text, with the result that the text has multiple meanings, in which each new reading and interpretation may be freshly heard.

The text creates a world in which participants in the world of the text get to know their way around, and come to be able to say with Wittgenstein, "Now I can go on." . . . That is, that it [the poem] exists to create another world, a world indeed that is recognizably our own, with brutality and suffering and God and a coming-to-see on the part of some, but not a world that simply once existed and is gone for good. The poem's very lack of specificity refuses to let it be tied down to one spot on the globe, or frozen at one point in history: it opens up the possibility that the poem can become true in a variety of circumstances—that is its work. . . . The language becomes more than a tool for the conveyance of information or even emotion: it creates an event; it destroys a world and replaces it by a new one which it brings into being.[55]

Two points are important in Clines's understanding. First, it is evident from the sustained appeal to this fourth Servant Song in the church's tradition that it is the text which makes this world of redemptive suffering available. Without this poem, we would be hard put to find textual rootage for such a world in the Old Testament. Second, Clines suggests that the ambiguity of the poem is not a riddle to be resolved by criticism, but is an intentional strategy to make the world repeatedly available. To solve the riddle of the servant would be a distortion of the intent of the text.

In a more recent study, Clines has considered the Pentateuch as a literature of promise not yet fulfilled.[56] He asserts of this promissory literature,

What is offered in a story is a "world"—make-believe or real, familiar or unfamiliar. To the degree that the hearer or reader of the story is imaginatively seized by the story, to that degree he or she "enters" the world of the story. That means that the reader of the story, when powerfully affected by it, becomes a participant of its world. One learns, by familiarity with the story, one's way about its world, until it becomes one's own world too. The Pentateuch as a story therefore performs the function of creating a "world" that is to a greater or lesser extent unlike the world of the reader, and that invites the reader to allow the horizons of his own world to merge with those of that other world.[57]

No awkward historical questions about the material of the Pentateuch stand in the way of its efficacy in creating "world" or in drawing its readers into participation in its world.[58]

So it is a particular decision about reality, a particular judgement about the shape of human existence, that is presupposed by story. . . . Story creates order out of the flux of happenings by arranging them in (or, discerning in them—let the question remain unresolved) such a chain of connectedness that leads one to speak of the end as the goal and the middle as directed movement.[59]

Clines concludes:

> The Pentateuch becomes such a source of life, not by being fed
> through some hermeneutical machine that prints out contemporary
> answers to contemporary questions, but through the reader's patient
> engagement with the text and openness to being seized, challenged,
> or threatened by the "world" it lays bare.[60]

Clines's point is freshly and helpfully made. It is nonetheless worth
noting that his views are fully congruent with the credo proposal
of von Rad[61] and the social analysis of Norman K. Gottwald.[62] Both
von Rad and Gottwald argued in other language that the purpose
of the recital is to create a people with a different reliance and a
different mandate, a reliance and mandate which make sense only
in a different "world."

What Berger and Luckmann present in sociological categories,
Wilder and Clines have seen in the literary process. The social
community constitutes reality by its authoritative restatement of
consensual language. The normative literature mediates a world
that would not be available or embraced, as a basis for action,
unless mediated by this literature. Both these sociological and the
literary approaches take up the central themes of Mowinckel. The
social community does not respond to a world that is there, but it
awaits a world now to be given, and it constitutes that world
through its consensual speech. The literature does not simply comment on a world that is there. It generates a world that would not
be there apart from the work and words of the literature. Like
Mowinckel, Wilder and Clines speak of the "world" in quotes. By
"world" they also refer to a set of social relations, perceptions, and
gestures which bring order, sequence, and sense to the flux of
disordered experience. Those social relations, perceptions, and
gestures fashion normlessness into a reliable order. They fashion
homelessness into a stable and reliable habitat for humanity.

Psychological Understandings

More recently, the constitutive act of the human agent has been
important for personality theory and the psychological disciplines.
The awareness that the human person is not a given, but is an
ongoing work of freedom, at least to some extent, is found in various theories of personality formation. The human person is an
agent who in some part decides and chooses who she or he will be.
That person makes those choices in the midst of a community

which, along with the person, makes choices, and legitimates or precludes some choices the person may make.

Robert Kegan argues at length that the individual is an active meaning-maker:

> Before long the reader will find the expression "meaning-making organism" redundant; what an organism does, as William Perry says (1970), is organize; and what a human organism organizes is meaning. Thus it is not that a person makes meaning, as much as that the activity of being a person is the activity of meaning-making. There is no feeling, no experience, no thought, no perception, independent of a meaning-making context in which it *becomes* a feeling, an experience, a thought, a perception, because we *are* the meaning-making context.[63]

Kegan comments on the small infant in the categories of object-relations theory:

> The capacity to hold the mother with a recognizing eye is as fundamental to our development as the prehensile capacity to hold a physical object.[64]

In speaking of the infant's growing capacity to "hold reality," Kegan asserts:

> But there are a number of similarly primordial experiences that begin in the infant's *societal* world. . . . In creating for the first time an "object world" or "other world" which the infant, too, sees as "other," the infant begins the history of successively joining the world rather than incorporating it, of holding the world while guaranteeing its distinct integrity, which is the history of its development.[65]

In his comment on the fourth stage of Lawrence Kohlberg's moral stages, Kegan writes,

> We should not imagine, however, that in constructing the stage 4 balance we become cowardly conformists. We do not so much submit to a system as *create* it.[66]

Note that his use of "create" is in italics.

A second theorist contributing to this dynamic understanding of world-making, with a more intentional psychoanalytical frame of reference, is Roy Schafer.[67] In his book *Language and Insight*, Schafer understands linguistic transactions with the therapist as a moment of speech and listening when reality is being constituted, not simply as a report on reality. The two terms—"language" and "insight"—are crucial for Schafer, because he asserts that each

fresh linguistic act gives new meaning, shape, and organization to
the disturbing and distinctive present. Thus he makes his most
helpful statement on the therapeutic encounter:

> The analyst is studying the making of psychic reality as well as the
> product. Thus one analyzes the disturbed and disturbing past-as-
> the-present and seeks to construct a present that encompasses the
> past recognized as such. . . . The psychoanalyst sees in these de-
> fects and strategies the analysand's attempts to achieve and maintain
> personal discontinuity, both historical and in present psychic reality,
> and also to impose this discontinuity on others, denying them their
> own life histories and present worlds. The analysand does not tolerate
> the idea that the present can only be some comprehensive, even if
> modified, version of the past—in the end, one hopes, a less frag-
> mented, confining, anguished, and self-destructive modification of
> that version. Through interpretation, one helps the analysand to
> abandon the goal of radical discontinuity, of rejection and oblitera-
> tion of personal pasts and of major features of present existences.[68]

Schafer then suggests that the goal of the therapeutic transaction is to permit the client to participate actively in the process of
world-making:

> Thus, when psychoanalysts speak of insight, they necessarily imply
> emotionally experienced transformation of the analysand, not only as
> life-history and present world, but as life-historian and world-maker.
> It is the analysand's transformation and not his or her intellectual
> recitation of explanations that demonstrate the attainment of useful
> insight. The analysand has gained a past history and present world
> that are more intelligible and tolerable than before, even if still not
> very enjoyable or tranquil. The past and present are considerably
> more extensive, cohesive, consistent, humane, and convincingly felt
> than they were before. But these gains are based as much on know-
> ing *how* as on knowing *that*. Insight is as much a way of looking as it is
> of seeing anything in particular.[69]

I understand Schafer to mean that the analyst, in her role as
interpreter, is to help the person understand the constitutive
power of the conversation. It is for this reason that a therapeutic
conversation can be transformative, because the speech-event
constitutes a new person in a new world that did not exist until or
apart from that linguistic transaction. The person creates himself
in this moment of speech. It is perhaps interesting that Schafer
does not use quotation marks when he speaks about world-
making. There is a kind of realism here that is more scientific

than the liturgic playfulness we have seen heretofore, but the argument is congruent with the other dimensions of world-making I have mentioned.

The third theorist we mention is Paul Pruyser, who has been particularly attentive to the work of pastors.[70] His recent study of play and playfulness, in his book entitled *The Play of Imagination*, suggests that the playful, imaginative, illusionary function of the person is an act of hope concerning who the person may yet become and what the world may yet be.

Pruyser is aware of the basic psychoanalytic duality of the autistic and the realistic worlds. The autistic world is one turned inward in unmitigated desire. The realistic world is one of social demand which requires renunciation. With particular appeal to D. W. Winnicott and his notion of the transitional object, Pruyser draws this most helpful, programmatic conclusion:

> These two sources—Winnicott's idea and the realization that natural man is a fiction—lead me to replace the basic psychoanalytic duality of the autistic and the realistic worlds with a tripartite scheme. To these worlds I shall add another; one I shall call, following Freud's usage, the *illusionistic world* (Pruyser, 1979). The impact of this enlargement is, among other things, a modification of the forced choice that the classical psychoanalytic duality puts to the individual: Do you remain autistic or will you become realistic? A third choice is not only possible, but is in fact made by most civilized people: engagement in illusionistic activities, abounding in imaginative processes and entities that are not only shareable, but are in fact institutionalized in the social order.[71]

He then characterizes these three worlds. First, the autistic world is a private one whose essence is difficult to convey. Those who live there are out of touch. Their verbalizations make no sense to others. The realistic world is a public one whose features are open to inspection and verification by all. This is the world of common sense, which must be taken with great seriousness.

Pruyser then offers a third world, the illusionistic world, which he correlates and contrasts with the other two worlds. This world is an alternative to the other two and the coercive assumption that one must choose between those two. This third world is marked by these phrases: "tutored fantasy," "adventurous thinking," "orderly imagination," "inspired connections," "verbalizable images," "transcendent objects."[72]

The remainder of Pruyser's book characterizes the process of living in this third world, which he calls the "illusion processing," by which he means tutored, disciplined, public imagination. He then reviews how this process is operative in the visual arts, literature, science, religion, and music. In his chapter on religion, he makes some remarkable suggestions about how crucial the play of religion is for society. In speaking of this third world, which he positions between autism and realism, Pruyser concludes:

> Though I am dissatisfied with the special imagery attached to such words as "sphere," "displacement," "world," or "domain," I can as yet find no better terminology . . . in which to articulate my point. Tying in with Winnicott's choice of "sphere" (which happily connotes emotional and ideational atmosphere) and without limiting the meaning of "world" to "orb," I persist in raising the question: Two or three? My answer is three . . . or more—and its thrust runs parallel to William James' aversion to monism and dualism. I join him in opting for a pluralistic universe (James, 1909).[73]

All three—Kegan, Schafer, and Pruyser—reflect on the world of creative possibility which in the life of the individual is as yet unfinished. Kegan speaks of "meaning-making," Schafer of "worldmaking," and Pruyser of "the illusional process." In the moment of speech and imagination, the person evokes, embraces, and experiences a new world.

The three agree:
- that the human person is not a given, but an unfinished task;
- that the human person is not fated, but has options and exercises freedom;
- that the exercise of freedom is a constitutive act whereby the person becomes who he or she was not;
- that the essential work of the person is to organize experience in alternative ways (a comment that echoes Berger);
- that reorganized reality is the person's "world," which shapes, authorizes, and requires actions and possibilities; and
- that this reorganization is creative of a world that happens through speech.

It is clear that these categories of understanding are remarkably congruent with Mowinckel, only they are cast in personal and interpersonal terms which ignore the possibilities belonging to public (liturgic) acts of constitution.

Theological Understandings

The fourth and final dimension of the constitutive act of "world-making" that is present in current intellectual reflection is a fresh understanding of theology as it is presented by Gordon Kaufman. Kaufman has concluded (more firmly than perhaps most of us) that the old categories of theology have lost their power to evoke and mediate faith.[74] Responsible theology must therefore be a constitutive act, in which our discernment of God must be reconstituted in wholly new ways.

The language Kaufman uses is not without problems. He clearly intends to come very close to the language of the "reconstitution of God" through theological articulation. Taken ontologically, that is obviously a hazardous claim. Taken practically and dramatically, which is in fact how we do theology, each theological articulation intends to render God in a more faithful and more available way.[75] So far as the church is concerned, each such rendering of God offers to the church a "new God" who must be reckoned with in new terms. Clearly the new God in theology that is faithful and disciplined is identified with and congruent with the God always known in our memory. New speech about God done in the theology and proclamation of the church is never only reiterative, but constructive in some sense for the faith of the church.

Kaufman states—probably overstates—his conviction that the crisis of modernity requires a reconstruction of God, that God should be articulated in ways other than has been done in the tradition. On the one hand, he is deeply impressed with the crises of humanness, which he sees most drastically and dangerously in the nuclear threat.[76] On the other hand, he is aware that much traditional theology "has often nourished and authorized massive historical evils: western imperialism and colonialism, slavery, unrestrained exploitation of the earth's resources, racism and sexism, persecution of those thought of as heretics or infidels, even attempts at genocide."[77] It is of course easy to say in response that such spin-offs are distortions and caricatures, but it is precisely because of distortions and caricatures, Kaufman would say, that God needs to be rearticulated in ways more intentional, disciplined, and carefully nuanced.

The other methodological urging of Kaufman, which we may note, is a distinction between the "real referent," the holy God in actuality who is always unknown and unavailable, and the "available referent," our imaginative construct of God. Since the real referent, in the very nature of God, is unavailable, the available referent is always imaginative and always a construct.[78]

I do not wish to pursue this aspect of Kaufman very far, because I do not agree with his argument concerning theological reference. Those of us who are more fully embedded in the tradition (which he judges to be inadequate) would affirm that in Jesus Christ, the available referent, the real referent is precisely disclosed. The man of Nazareth is the available referent and gives access to the real referent. And this Jesus ultimately is not an imaginative construct. Kaufman is deficient in the christological focus of his understanding of revelation, or as we might say, he is "soft" on the *homoousia* ("of like substance") formula. This deficiency is evident in his statement, "Hence, if we are to understand the meaning and importance of Christ, we shall first have to get clear what is meant by 'God'."[79] Precisely the opposite is true. We affirm the centrality of Christ, and in so doing, we get clear on what is meant by "God."[80]

Nonetheless, we can learn from Kaufman's argument that theology is constructive and not merely reiterative. Even for one who accepts the particularity of Jesus as the clue to the real referent, the practical truth is that, even in our discernments of Jesus, we are dealing in important ways with imaginative reconstructions. This is true also in the gospel narratives, which are constructions and not descriptions, and much more is it the case that our own articulations are imaginative constructions.[81]

When Kaufman gets down to specifics, however, his argument is not as radical or as much a departure from the tradition as we might expect. After he has dealt with his three central categories—God, world, and human experience—he comes to the fourth category, Christ. He concedes that Christ is not a category like the other three, but a category which permeates and reshapes the other three. When he tries to characterize this fourth category, he asserts that Jesus was "essentially self-giving."[82] That definitional characteristic serves to *relativize* all human pretensions and to *humanize* us by the power to transform.[83]

It is my judgment that Kaufman is not as radical as his introductory rhetoric suggests,[84] but he is honest in characterizing what we do in theology. We do in fact, by our words, reconstruct the religious reality which we seek to praise and obey. If one were to say it less radically than Kaufman, we might only say that we continue the ongoing construction of the tradition. Whether one says it in Kaufman's radical rhetoric or in more conventional language, over time the speech of the church shapes the world of faith in which we live. I do not for a moment suggest that such speech-construction finally reshapes the ontology of God, but that it does decisively shape the life-world in which we encounter God. Kaufman's intent is to reshape the life-world in which we live so that our response to the danger of nuclear threat is faithful, responsible, caring, and obedient. Perhaps Kaufman's extreme rhetoric is commensurate with the extreme situation in which we find ourselves. Kaufman's candid methodology seems to be congruent with Mowinckel's, for Mowinckel did not claim that liturgy creates God, but creates the world.[85]

I have cited four lines of intellectual investigation which reflect the intellectual mood of our post-Enlightenment, postpositivistic situation.

- Sociological understandings of the ways in which a community constructs its life-world.
- Literary understandings, which suggest that good literature creates alternative worlds of imagination to provide a home in which we may live and act differently.
- Psychological understandings of human personality, which suggest that the individual person is an active agent in choosing self.
- Theological understanding, which suggests that the religious world in which we live is an imaginative construct, to mediate the whence and whither of our common life.

The tendency of all of these approaches is to insist and assume that the "world" in which we live is not a flat, frozen given, but is a particular formation of reality that is established on the basis of trusted speech and gesture. That speech and gesture impose a certain pattern, shape, and legitimacy on our shared experience that could have been patterned, shaped, and legitimated in other ways. Because of the choices that are made in world-construction, however, it *is* this way and not some other way in this community.

It is the act of praise, the corporate, regularized, intentional,

verbalized, and enacted act of praise, through which the community of faith creates, orders, shapes, imagines, and patterns the
world of God, the world of faith, the world of life, in which we are
to act in joy and obedience. I do not resist the traditional theological claim that praise is response to the God that is already there.
But dramatically, liturgically, functionally, the world is as it is
when we give it authorized speech. The act of praise is indeed
world-making for the community which takes the act of worship as
serious and realistic.

CONCLUSION

My review of four contemporary intellectual explorations in various disciplines permits a recovery of Mowinckel's basic insight.
From these explorations, I draw three conclusions, which I will
explicate in the subsequent chapters.

1. I suggest that Mowinckel is essentially correct to assert that,
at a dramatic level, the act of worship does *create a world*. On one
hand, we are not so naive as to imagine that there is no world there
until the moment of praise. That already-existing world is either an
unshaped world waiting to be invested with shape and meaning
(i.e., making creation [cosmos] out of chaos), or, more likely, it is a
world that has already been created by some other liturgy so that
it has had some other meaning imposed upon it. To say that there is
a world already there is congruent with what the Bible says of
creation. The main tendency of the Old Testament is to say that
creation is not "out of nothing" (*ex nihilo*), but it is an act wrought
on chaos that is there—formless and void (*tōhû webōhû*), not yet a
world.[86]

On the other hand, experientially, we may say that the world
created by the community is the only world that is there, that is
available for me and to which I may gladly and trustingly respond.
Sociologically, the life-world of my community is the only world
that I credit. Literarily, when I am addressed by a good piece of
literature, I am required and permitted to suspend all other
worlds and commit myself to this world alone. That is the prerequi-
site of all serious literature. Psychologically, the self I present and
construct is the only self I know. The counselor may already perceive another self for me, but that perception is fundamentally
irrelevant to me, so long as I am an occupant of this self. That is,

the created, constructed world which I inhabit is the only real world, and therefore the task of world-formation is a life-or-death matter.

There are other modes of world-creation in which we participate and to which we are subject. They include advertising, ideology, propaganda, education, and child-nurture. For the community gathered around Jesus, however, it is precisely the act of worship that is the act of world-formation!

2. It is clear, as Wilder has seen, that the life-world created in biblical worship is one among many theoretical worlds, and therefore such worship is not only constitutive, but inevitably polemical.[87] Praise insists not only that this is the true world, but that other worlds are false. World-creation also includes world-delegitimation of other worlds. The church sings praises not only toward God but against the gods.

That polemical function is easily discerned. The polemic is evident in the hermeneutical quarrel we have about the meaning of our traditional language and its interface with and impingement upon public and political reality. The interpretive quarrel will not normally be expressed explicitly. The response to polemical world-making is more likely to be expressed in anger at the door of the church after the service, "I don't see why the church does not stay with religion and stay out of politics and economics." In the categories of my book chapters, this response means that the world-construction of the gospel-oriented community has begun to delegitimate other worlds which we had thought to be compatible with or existing alongside this world. When our other worlds are threatened, it evokes resistance and hostility.

More obviously, the quarrel about sexist and feminist or inclusive language is not an argument about language. It is an argument about the world that is there, about the world we shall inhabit, about the ordering of experience that we take as real, reliable, and normative. It is clear that words matter enormously, for words give us worlds in which to live. The particular words of this tradition are crucial, as is attested by both the zeal for new inclusive language and the zeal for conventional masculine language.[88] By the use of our words we construct worlds! It is clear that the words with which we praise God shape the world of legitimacy in which we shall live.

3. Finally, the pastor, the priest, the manager of the liturgy is a

key agent in the process of world-construction. In her recent book
on professional ethics, Karen Lebacqz has discerningly characterized the power entrusted to professionals. About professionals in
general, she writes:

> Professionals have the power to define reality. . . . The profes-
> sional defines how some aspect of society is to be thought of and how
> policy is to be formulated around it . . . "a new social reality is
> created by the professional."[89]

Then, more precisely about the minister as a professional,
Lebacqz asserts:

> The minister does not simply heal or help or console. She defines
> reality by offering a new language, a perspective on hidden mean-
> ings, a transformation of ordinary symbols, a hope in the midst of
> seeming hopelessness. . . . The social construction of reality is at
> the heart of the minister's vocation.[90]

Lebacqz's account, rooted in a sociology of symbols, is surely
correct. It is correct, moreover, for ministers who may not recognize their powerful function and who may do this work without
self-awareness or intentionality. Lebacqz's insight from sociology
is reenforced and deepened by our theological awareness of the
ministerial office. It is precisely the task of ministry (professional,
but also called) to convene, evoke, form, and re-form a community
of praise and obedience.

Every aspect of the pastor's work is aimed at this function of
ministry. But the pastor's work happens in the context of and as a
function of the "work of the whole church," which we call liturgy.
In its liturgical life the church, led by the Spirit, engages in praise
and obedience and so constitutes and is constituted as God's people. Thus, the discernment of social science which I have explored
in this chapter helps us to see what in fact is under way theologically and liturgically in the church. What is under way is the
formation of an alternative community. This work of the church is
of course in response to the command of God and is indeed human
work. It is at the same time, however, in inscrutable and undeni-
able ways, a moment when the voice of God is enacted "who gives
life to the dead and calls into existence the things that do not exist"
(Rom. 4:17).

2

The "World" of Israel's Doxology

In the first chapter I sought to establish the formal reality of liturgy as world-construction. On the grounds of sociological, literary, psychological, and theological understandings, I argued that world-construction is what persons and communities do in various ways, inevitably and inescapably. The act of world-construction may or may not be intentional, but it happens nonetheless. The biblical community has no monopoly on the work of world-construction, but it is also not exempt from the enterprise.

Here I want to move from formal factors to substantive claims, from the recognition that world-construction is a common and unavoidable activity to the particularity of Israel's faith. Israel constructs a very particular world that is different from and in direct tension with other available worlds. This very particular world is shaped according to the particular character of Yahweh, who convenes this world and who presides over it. That means, of course, that the functional activity of world construction is never far removed for Israel from the reality and identity of Yahweh.[1]

The modes and practices of world-construction in ancient Israel have much in common with the same modes and practices elsewhere in the Near East. The distinctiveness of Israel's world-construction is derived from the distinctiveness of Yahweh. For that reason I here turn from the general practice of world-construction to the particular and peculiar world Israel constructs, a world appropriate to and congruent with the character of Yahweh.

The process of world-construction, in Israel as elsewhere, is a liturgical process. It is conventional to define liturgy (*leiturgia*) as the "work of the people," and that is correct.[2] Such a phrase recognizes world-construction as human work. But it leaves us with the question, what work is done in liturgy? I submit that the work of the people in liturgy is to process shared experience through the normative narratives, images, metaphors, and symbols of that community. Shared experience from one community is not unlike experience that is found in other communities. What is distinctive is the range of symbols through which the experience is processed. In its liturgy, Israel is engaged in processing its shared experience through its normative symbols and narratives.[3] As the community does this work, it finds mediated to it energy, power, authority, assurance, and mandate that are available nowhere else. That "work of the people" makes Israel the distinctive community that it is.

Sigmund Mowinckel has proposed that Israel's central liturgic act is the enthronement of Yahweh as king. Israel's preeminent act of world-construction, then, is that liturgy, the outcome of which is a world over which Yahweh rules. Here I will consider that particular act of world-construction and the particular character of that life-world over which Yahweh presides.

THE GOSPEL OF ENTHRONEMENT

As is well known, Mowinckel places the six enthronement psalms at the center of his thesis on world-making: Psalms 47, 93, and 96—99.[4] He finds in these psalms a liturgic sequence of combat among the gods, victory for Yahweh, entrance and enthronement of Yahweh, and establishment of Yahweh's rule for the period of kingship proclaimed.[5] That sequence is well established in the common liturgies of the Near East and is appropriated liturgically and affirmed theologically in Israel.

Psalm 96

I will begin with Psalm 96, because it is the most telling for the theme of world-making that I wish to explore.[6] The psalm is highly stylized and is not unlike the other enthronement psalms, but its particular wording is important in several regards. The initial summons to praise is an invitation to participate in world-construction.

The praise centers around six imperatives. The first three are "sing":

- Sing to Yahweh a new song,
- Sing to Yahweh all the earth,
- Sing to Yahweh.

Verses 1–5

The fourth imperative is "bless." The fifth one is anemically rendered in the RSV: "Tell of his salvation from day to day." (The sixth verb continues the summons with "declare.") It is the fifth imperative which concerns us. The verb translated "tell" is actually *basar,* "proclaim the news." It is the word which in its nominal form has become the word "gospel," and which in this psalm the Septuagint (LXX) renders *euaggelizesthe.*[7]

In its verbal form, it is difficult to render *basar* in English so that the allusion to the gospel is evident. The verb *basar* in Psalm 96 occupies a midpoint between two distinct clusters of occurrences. To begin with, there is a series of occurrences in the Books of Samuel which reflect an ordinary, uncritical use of the term in Israel's early narrative articulations. In these narratives, *basar* is used without intentional theological reflection (see 1 Sam. 4:17; 31:9 [= 1 Chron. 10:9]; 2 Sam. 1:20; 4:10; 18:20–31; 1 Kings 1:42; 7:9). The word *basar* functions to report the outcome of a battle, or specifically, to report the death of someone in battle, for example, Abner or Ishbosheth. The episode reported in 2 Sam. 18:20–31 is a good example of this function for *basar.* Two messengers run: one the son of Zadok, who runs against the will of Joab; the other a Cushite, a foreigner who is permitted to carry bad news. David speculates about the messengers, imagining that he can determine the message by the appearance of the runner (vv. 24–27). The second runner brings good news that the rebellion is squelched (v. 31). In v. 32, he reports the death of Absalom, thinking that also is good news. But of course it is not. David is "deeply moved" and begins his lamentation. Obviously David's lamentation does not begin when Absalom is killed, but only when the message is delivered. It is then that the fact of the death takes on power and social reality.

Thus the word *basar* refers to a message brought from the place of happening to a place of reception. The news communicated may be good or bad. Our word *basar* refers to the substance of the message, the articulation of the message, or the messenger who

brings the news. The word *basar* refers to speech which transfers
the significance of an event from one place to another. The reported action carried by the verb is received as significant and
effective in the place of hearing, even though it happened in another place, that is, on the battlefield or at the death scene. The
verb functions to show how the community of Israel actualized
the event in a second setting. One did not need to be present at the
battle to celebrate and benefit from the victory. One did not need
to be present at the death to grieve the death upon hearing the
news, because functionally the death "occurred" for the listening
community when the fact was announced.

The second cluster of uses in the Old Testament is in the Isaiah
tradition, in texts which are well known to us (see Isa. 40:9;
41:27; 52:7; 60:6; 61:1). In these uses, *basar* has now been
claimed for theological purposes. It reports a victory of God
wrought elsewhere that has decisive effect on the situation in
which the reported outcome is spoken and heard. In Isa. 41:25–
29, Yahweh asserts that he dispatched to Jerusalem a messenger
announcing the summons of Cyrus, "one from the north." For
Jerusalem who hears the announcement, the Cyrus movement
takes on social significance in the effective moment when the
word telling what Yahweh has decreed elsewhere is spoken in
Israel. The event happened earlier when Yahweh acted without
aid from the other gods, but the moment of social reality is in the
moment of announcement.

Basar functions in Second Isaiah as in Samuel, to bring a message
from one place to another, except that it now has a theological referent. Now matters of victory and defeat, of life and death, concern
the action of the gods, who are not present here but whose actions
elsewhere are reported as effective. It is in the moment of speech
that the interactions of the gods become real and operative.

Psalm 96 stands at a liturgical moment of new linguistic usage
between the old narrative usage which reports military events,
and the intentional theological use of the Isaiah tradition.[8] Between these two kinds of uses, Psalm 96 may mark the usage
whereby *basar* has been claimed and transformed for the parlance
of Israel's faith. This psalm, like the old Samuel narratives, reports
on an event which happens elsewhere but which has a decisive
effect here in the present, where the news of the outcome is
spoken and heard. In the speaking and hearing, the content of the

message takes on social reality. The gospel of Yahweh, which is to be sung and recounted among the nations, is that Yahweh is to be feared above all the gods. In Yahweh's presence the other gods are deabsolutized and delegitimated. Yahweh's triumph over the gods is negatively articulated by the statement that "the gods are idols" (v. 5), that is, empty of power and incapable of doing anything. Yahweh's victory is asserted positively by the lyrical affirmation that Yahweh is the maker of the heavens, the place where the other gods allegedly abide.[9] Yahweh can do something visible and decisive and is to be acknowledged to be a serious power in the world, from which the other gods derive whatever they claim of life.

The six imperatives with which Psalm 96 summons to a new world are followed in vv. 4–5 by two motivational statements, one positive and one negative:

> For great is the Lord, and greatly to be praised,
> he is to be feared above all gods.
> For all the gods of the peoples are idols;
> but the Lord made the heavens.

The language in vv. 1–5 reports on what happened elsewhere, not in the sanctuary. Verse 6 moves from the field of action to the resultant situation in the sanctuary where the news is announced:

> Honor and majesty are before him;
> Strength and beauty are in his sanctuary.

The verse draws conclusions about the context of Yahweh's governance, expressed without any verbs. Now there is no action. The action has been completed. Now the psalm describes the new situation resulting from the action of the verbs. There is a new mood, situation, and atmosphere in the throne room resulting from the news: honor, majesty, strength, and beauty. The announcement evokes a situation of honor and majesty. The gospel is news from elsewhere that changed things in the sanctuary. The change is wrought by the authoritative assertion of what happened prior to the meeting in the sanctuary.

In vv. 7–10a the psalm presents eight imperative verbs which command present, responsive action on the part of the community. Derivative from the claims of vv. 4–5, these imperatives are more powerful and more intense than the initial summoning imperatives of vv. 1–3. The verbs now are: "ascribe, ascribe, ascribe, bring,

come, worship, tremble, say." The initial imperatives in this cluster are a quote from Ps. 29:1–2, an older, less specifically Israelite
psalm.[10] The eighth imperative, "say," moves beyond Psalm 29.
With this verb Israel at worship is not simply to celebrate in its own
life, but to reach outside its own celebrative circle to circulate the
news, which concerns non-Israelites as much as Israelites.

This announcement to the nations has been anticipated earlier
in the Psalms. In Ps. 96:3 the sixth imperative is to "declare"
among the nations. In v. 5 the motivation is that "the gods of
the peoples" are overcome. These verses summon Israel to tell the
nations that the gods in whom they trust are not worthy of trust
because they are defeated by Yahweh. Now, in v. 10, the gospel is
to be said "among the nations." The gospel to be announced to the
nations is that Yahweh governs and judges the peoples with equity.
Thus in the imperative sequences of vv. 1–3 and vv. 7–10, the poetry builds to the climactic point of linking the rule of Yahweh with
the life of the nations. The news announced is about Yahweh and the
gods, but it also concerns the nations, who must now redirect their
loyalty, so that they are not aligned with gods who have already
been defeated and delegitimated.

A great deal depends on this phrase, *malak Adonai*. It may be
variously rendered "Yahweh rules," "Yahweh has become king,"
"Yahweh has always been king," "Yahweh has just now become
king."[11] In the question of this translation, we are here at the
difficult point between an ontology which wants to say what always is, and a dramatic claim which wants to assert what is just
now happening in this moment.[12] Mowinckel's argument (which I
support and urge) is that the ontology need not be denied, but
must be bracketed out if we are to understand the intent of the
psalm, which focuses on the action in this moment. Such bracketing out of ontological matters is in fact what we do if we are serious
about liturgy. Liturgy is not an appeal to any enduring ontology,
but is an enactment of a fresh drama in this moment.

Dramatically, experientially, realistically, this liturgic formula,
"the Lord reigns," is not a remembering, but is an enactment, a
making so. If this moment of announcement is not a real enactment,
then in fact there is no news, but only reiteration, the unveiling of
what has always been.[13] Reiteration is not the intent of Israel's
liturgy, nor the effect, and it cannot be the intent or effect of our
liturgy when we stand in this tradition. The liturgy of biblical faith is

to be practiced among us as a genuine newness. The intent of liturgy, and its only real importance among us and claim upon us, is that the news is enacted in this moment so that the claim is real as it has never been real before this moment of articulation.

The fact that the formula "Yahweh rules" is *news*, a message, creates a decisive, dramatic recognition. The messenger (evangel) must give the message because an event has happened elsewhere which matters to those who now listen. It has happened on the battlefield, among the gods, but it is told here. And if it is not told, it is not real, effective, or powerful. It happened elsewhere, but its effectiveness is in the moment of its retelling. It is the moment of retelling that is the moment of dramatic actualization. When known, the victory of Yahweh over the other gods is received, affirmed, celebrated, acted upon. And it is not known or acted on until it is retold. Such a "there-here" construct gives the dramatic reality of the news considerable flexibility. Thus Israel may understand that the news is "worked" in heaven among the gods (as in Psalm 29), or in a distant encounter with the empire (as we shall see in Second Isaiah), but in either case the social power and reality of the occasion is in the message "worked" here among us.

The "there-here" dynamic of news is exemplified in our experience in the death of a loved one. The death may occur at a time and place unknown to us, but the death has no social reality or social significance until the news of the death is told among us. Until that moment of announcement, we proceed on the unreflective assumption that the person is alive and well. Not having the news, we take as reality the old, unexamined (and also unconfirmed) social fact. When the news is announced, then the death is a social reality evoking new responses and new patterns of conduct.

As the news of death changes reality, so also the news of birth changes reality. In Jer. 20:14–18, where the prophet laments the fact that he was born, his rage is not against the God who "formed" him (cf. 1:5), but against the man who brought the news (20:15). The news of birth is what gave the newborn baby social reality. Until the moment of the news, there was no rejoicing over the birth. For the community, the baby did not exist until the announcement of the news.

In a religion of historical memory, the "there-here" reality of news can also be paralleled temporally. It happened then, but its

retelling makes it effective now. It is the very announcement that
lets the news be received, affirmed, celebrated, acted upon. The
liturgic assertion of news ("tell it") is here and now. The participating congregation does not really ask about then and there, because
the reality and its future is so powerful here and now. When my son
was eight years old, his friend was the poorest player and so, predictably, in right field. His mind wandered and he always looked
everywhere but toward the diamond. The coach spent much energy
shouting to him, "The game's in here, the game's in here." I submit
that this strange dynamic of news enacted and news announced
turns on the claim that the game is in here, now and not then, here
and not there. The reality of Yahweh's new rule is effected in this
moment when the news is asserted.

That, of course, is how the church engages in the liturgic act of
asserting the news which makes a new world and which makes
the world new. In its great festivals of Christmas and Easter, the
church's liturgy dramatically enacts the new world here and now.
In Christmas we do not celebrate the world of ancient Herod, but
we sing, "Joy to the world, the lord is come. . . . Joy to the earth,
the savior reigns." The lord who is come, the savior who reigns, the
one who is to be received is the one who comes, reigns, and is
received in this moment of the message. In the festival of enthronement we call Christmas, it is the celebration of the king who has just
in this moment come to power. It is not a remembrance, but an
enactment.[14] In Easter we do not celebrate an ancient resurrection,
but we sing, "Christ the Lord is risen today." That resurrection
today gives freedom and energy and courage.

This dramatic enactment is not game-playing. It is the necessarily and inevitably imaginative, interpretive enterprise of world-
making which is the only way a historical religion can make and
sustain a world for the faithful. The liturgic message is rooted in a
memory, but it is the fresh announcement itself which causes kings
to celebrate, peasants to dance, governments to tremble, troops to
be given R & R. The liturgic act is the moment of announcement in
which old claims are made present realities, in which victories
won in other places are made available as victories in this place
now. Through such speech the world is changed. The world is
changed because the news is that Yahweh reigns, Yahweh has become king. The power of destabilization is overcome and the world

is safe. The power of enslavement is overcome, and the world is free. The world is safe and the world is free. It was not and could not be so until that news-making moment.

In the drama a messenger breathlessly comes to say, "We won." The messenger might have brought a very different message. We might not have won. The news then is a surprise. Such news causes rejoicing like the crowd welcoming the American armies into Paris, or like the dancing that happened when it was announced that Ferdinand Marcos had indeed taken the plane out to Guam. The event itself caused no rejoicing until the official announcement came. Marcos left earlier than the announcement, but we did not know. What counted in Manila was the announcement. It was the message of his departure that evoked the dancing. Then, and only then, the world of Manila was changed.

It is the same in the drama of Psalm 96. The whole world, according to this drama, received the news of Yahweh's surprising victory with joy (vv. 11–12). The world had been under threat, unsure, made to conform to purposes not truly its own. The world had cringed under alien sovereignty and foreign rulers that did not honor its true character, but the streets are now crowded with creatures who have come to celebrate, to rejoice, to receive, to acclaim.

> Let the heavens be glad, and let the earth rejoice;
>   let the sea roar, and all that fills it;
> let the field exult, and everything in it!
> Then shall all the trees of the wood sing for joy.

All creatures rejoice, because finally they have permission to be who they really are. When the real king rules, the fraudulent rulers who have distorted reality are nullified. When the king rules, the world can be truly the world. Until then the world can only be distorted, never its true self. For now life can be lived without distortion, fear, undue deference, terror. To be sure, the adherents of the defeated gods were not dancing and singing in the streets. But they are a pitiful minority, now to be dismissed. They had committed themselves to a loser and have lost with him and are now socially discounted. But the liturgy is not for them. The liturgy is the work of the liberated people, articulating and receiving a new world for those nearly destroyed by the old world. The liturgy is for the ones who for so long seem to have lost, but hope and care and wait. Now "their time has come." Their joy is beyond bounds, needing words, but beyond words. Their joy is full and it must be brought to celebrative speech.

The new world now to be enacted reflects the character of the new king. The king is one of mercy, righteousness, and justice. Like an effective chief executive officer (CEO) changing the character of the corporation, very soon the world reflects the character of the new sovereign. The world soon takes on the same characteristics of mercy, righteousness, and justice. The real ruler remakes the world in his own image.

> He will judge the peoples with equity. (v. 10)

> He will judge the world with righteousness,
> and the peoples with his truth. (v. 13)

The new world is marked by equity, righteousness, and truth. The world is relieved of the terrible distortions of infidelity. All the social practices of inequity, unrighteousness, untruth are not only dysfunctional; they are banished. Nobody need act any longer in unrighteousness and injustice. Such action is now inappropriate. All those who sponsored injustice fled when their legitimating gods were defeated. In their place comes the massive practice of fidelity, not only between human persons, but between God and world, between various elements of creation. All the elements of creation become faithful and reliable. The abrasive cacophony has now become a unified rendering, a new symphony, for all sing together.[15]

All who share the dramatic moment of announcement and celebration are energized to live in this new world with these fresh possibilities. This is indeed the work of evangelism, of telling, of world-making, of life offered imaginatively under the rule of and in response to this One who, in this moment of invasion, does indeed make all things new. The new God makes possible a new world. At the moment when the rule of the new king is asserted, in that moment the new world emerges, not gradually, but abruptly, for the whole of creation has been waiting for this moment.[16] The pivotal point in Israel's liturgic life is the continued reassertion of the astonishing claim that the gods are defeated, Yahweh rules, and therefore the world can act out its true character as God's creation.

THE LITURGY OF LIBERATION

Israel's enthronement liturgy is very old, very deep, very weighty, very authoritative. For members of the community, the liturgy is simply present at the outset. It was there before us. New members of the community are born into a liturgy already under way. It is a dramatic, experienced given. The liturgy grew out of events which were powerfully originary. Now these primal events are carried by the liturgy on which we rely unquestioningly. We always went to church. We always went to temple. This liturgy of enthronement, as Mowinckel has shown, is mostly borrowed by Israel from other cultures. The liturgic form has been appropriated.

The appropriated liturgy of enthronement has been transformed so massively, however, that it is peculiarly ours. It has been made a vehicle to mediate what is most precious in our shared memory. It is liturgy, which means that it can move from time to time, from place to place. Because it is stylized imagination, the liturgy moves from there to here, from then to now. The enthronement liturgy has specificity but it is capable of more than one embodiment. It waits to be used by this community, and it can always be used in fresh, imaginative ways.

This capacity for fresh, imaginative embodiment is what makes hermeneutics so critical in the utilization of liturgy. When the liturgy of enthronement is taken up by Israel for concrete use, the interaction between the liturgy and historical concreteness moves in two directions. The liturgy is changed, shaped, and nuanced by its new historical reference. But Israel's historical memory is also transformed by the power of liturgy. The liturgy has a way of making a historical memory theologically, cosmically, dramatically, grandly significant, so that all the hopes and fears of Israel, from generation to generation, are mobilized, gathered, made present and available in this particular concrete liturgical event. The glimpse of reality in the memory of Israel is now mediated as a world in which to live. Without liturgic processing, the specific memory would be mere memory. The liturgy imposes a pattern of meaning on experiences so that Israel's world is shaped as this world and not some other. This liturgy shapes the world so that the old world of inequity, unrighteousness, and falsity is always being defeated, and Yahweh's new world of equity, righteousness, and truth is always freshly emerging. This two-way interaction is true with particular reference to the drama of enthronement, but is generally characteristic for Israel.

The enthronement liturgy of world-making, enacted regularly in the Jerusalem Temple under the supervision of the king, lives in strange tension with the root memory of the exodus event which celebrated the overthrow of tyrannical kingship. It is therefore necessary to explore the particular way in which the Exodus narrative utilizes and nuances the general categories of the ritual of enthronement. This particular utilization shifts the general pattern in the direction of social liberation. The exodus is surely a concrete historical event, but its initial castings in the tradition are already liturgical.[17] We have no preliturgic castings of the exodus memory, either poetic or narrative. Israel's first use of the enthronement liturgy is with reference to the exodus event. Israel uses this liturgic pattern in order to shape and stylize its primal experience of transformation.

Already when Miriam and her friends sang and danced, the very first utterance of the exodus occurrence, we have a liturgical event. The liturgy of enthronement thus comes to be embedded in the Exodus narrative. At the same time the Exodus narrative reshapes the enthronement pattern for a specific dramatic use. Through this initial liturgic processing, the memory of liberation is voiced as gospel for generations to come. The exodus event is made into news, which is to be told again and again among the nations. What is to be told is that Yahweh has defeated Pharaoh. The world has become a place of justice and freedom because the empire is overcome. The world has become and continues to be such a place; and each time the exodus memory is reenacted, the empire is overcome again.

The exodus memory, then, is not simply an old memory, but is news from *there* told *here*, news from *then* announced *now*. The news is of Yahweh's power and fidelity. The repeated narrative account pushes powerfully into the present. The world is remade each time the liturgy is reenacted for the sake of the ones who wait to be liberated. For them, each reenactment of Yahweh's triumph over Pharaoh is like fresh news of the present world being opened to freedom. Pharaoh the historical figure is a powerful metaphor readily identified in each new situation with each new oppressor who is, in the liturgic moment, defeated and dismissed. Each time the triumph is announced, new social possibilities are evoked. The ones waiting do not wait for an old act of remembering. The memory has no power or authority, certainly no efficacy, if it is not also a present moment of world-transformation. The mere act of remembering is a luxury that the waiting, oppressed ones cannot afford. They are interested in no old liberations, but only in the present one that sets their world and them free.

Exodus 15:21

The Song of Miriam (Exod. 15:21) is, for our purposes, the key text of the Exodus.[18] The initial assertion of the women is a doxology that has two parts:

> [A singing of new truth now proclaimed:]
>   Sing to the Lord,
> [A reason out of real life:]
>   for he has triumphed gloriously,
>   the horse and his rider he has thrown into the sea.

The women do not articulate an argument, a description, or a proof. This lyrical, imaginative speech enthrones Yahweh as the agent of decisive power. Miriam's moment of lyrical enactment asserts that the hated imperial rider (Pharaoh) is done and that Yahweh is triumphant. That is the message, the gospel. But the song not only remembers, it also dreams and waits. Each time the women sing and dance the memory, they evoke in Israel all the sensitivities and hopes belonging to slaves on the brink of liberation.[19]

The singing thus is a moment of vengeance, hate-released energy, a new beginning when we thought it was not possible. Yahweh did what we could not do and could not imagine done. The celebrators do not give explanations for the liberation. What counts is the world rendered by the text, a world wrought from the reality of Yahweh, who lives in and through the songs of the women. The world is open again and life is possible. There is no questioning, only joy and singing and dancing and timbrels.

Exodus 15:1-18

The larger explication of Exod. 15:1-18 begins with the same words of Miriam.[20] It describes the conflict and triumph in detail (vv. 4-10). It relives the journey to freedom and to land, the journey which terrorized and terrorizes the recalcitrant nations (vv. 14-16). Every retelling makes the members of the ruling junta nervous and defensive, because the world is indeed being constructed against them.[21] Psalm 96 exhorted, "Say among the nations, 'the Lord reigns'" (v. 10). Well, it has now been said. The psalm commanded, "Tremble before him, all the earth" (v. 9). Well, they tremble. The nations, "once for all" and again and again, are filled with terror and dread (Exod. 15:16), because they know the false world of domination and land monopoly has been nullified. They tremble not only because of potential loss, but because they are in danger, profoundly vulnerable. The poem culminates with a doxology of enthronement: "The Lord will reign for ever and ever" (v. 18). Yahweh's enthronement asserts Pharaoh will not reign, and if Pharaoh will not reign, his brick quotas are obsolete and his social privilege is terminated. Among the others who will not reign are the inhabitants of Philistia, the chiefs of Edom, the leaders of Moab, the inhabitants of Canaan (vv. 14–15).[22] Early on, the nations learn that Yahweh governs (cf. Ps. 96:3, 10). They find themselves displaced, their land lost, their preeminence irreversibly shattered.

As the world is made for Israel, so the nations notice that their world is being quickly unmade. The strange social power given through recognition and legitimacy is withdrawn. As we have seen with Marcos, when the myth of recognition ends, the plausibility of power crumbles immediately. Power rests on social sanction given through words. When the words are withdrawn, power vanishes. The liturgy means to nullify the myth of recognition, and nothing remains but trembling and dread, and finally defeat. It happened there in the exodus, but it is acclaimed here, and here, and here. It happened then, but it is asserted now, and now, and now. In every fresh here and every new now, the power shifts, the nations tremble, the peasant women dance, and a new world begins again.[23]

The news is borne and enacted by the women who dance with timbrels (v. 20). They dance against Pharaoh. They dance toward freedom. For a long time they had not been able to dance—too tired, too fearful, too endangered, too intimidated. In the very act of unpermitted dance, the world is transformed.[24] The control of the empire turns out to be not so tight, not so fearful, not so convincing, not so credible. New possibilities are opened through bodies which dance joyously in freedom. The women at the exodus do what the hills and trees and fields do in the psalm, because they also are about to enact their true identity in this new world that did not exist until this moment when the truth of the memory is made available in a way impossible before this liturgical articulation. The dance asserts that they are daughters of Yahweh's freedom.[25]

Exodus 14

In the derivative narrative of Exodus 14, the account of liberation is not a report on a past event, but the creation and mediation of a present event. A new world is thrust upon Israel. Israel listens to the narrative, and in the liturgy imagines the move from bondage to freedom. Israel freshly imagines the charging, enraged Egyptians. Egyptians are always enraged and always charge when they sense that free labor is about to be forfeited. The human persons they have reduced to imperial tools are now lost to them. The loss entails the crumbling of a world of privilege, monopoly, and disproportionate well-being. Israel comes to trusting stillness (Exod. 14:13–14). It sees the ruined chariots and the dead horses, the Egyptians "dead upon the seashore" (v. 30). Israel would not have thought such an inversion possible, not possible the first time, or possible any time since. But it is possible. The liturgy says it is possible and promised. We are children of this liturgy, creatures of this liturgy, created by this liturgy—as is our world. It is a world not known by the Egyptians, because they do not share the liturgy.[26] That is why they try to silence our liturgy—by laws forbidding assembly, or even laws banning Christmas carols.[27] They sense the power of the new world generated here in this season of news.

The Egyptians cannot stop the move of freedom, however, because Israel is engaged in world-making. All Egypt's crushing indignities do not stop Israel's relentless, God-given capacity for world-making. We continue to make this world that they do not want, do not permit, and cannot stop. We make a world in which the claims of Yahweh reign, in which the drama of reversal is enacted:

> I will get glory over Pharaoh and all his host. (v. 4)
>
> I will get glory over Pharaoh and all his host. (v. 17)

Yahweh did indeed get glory. The old common liturgy of enthronement had said (Ps. 29:1–2; cf. Ps. 96:7–9):

Ascribe to the Lord, O heavenly beings,
Ascribe to the Lord glory and strength.
Ascribe to the Lord the glory of his name;
worship. . . .

In this Exodus narrative, glory is indeed ascribed, because glory
emerges in the Israelite victory and the corresponding defeat of
Egypt. All the world, all creation trembles. The oppressive ones
tremble in defeat. The oppressed ones tremble in disbelief. The
liberated ones tremble in delight. The transformation enacted in
the story causes all to tremble.

Psalm 114

This psalm[28] begins in vv. 1–2 with something like a narrative
report, but it moves quickly to mocking lyric (vv. 3–4):

The sea looked and fled,
    Jordan turned back.
The mountains skipped like rams,[29]
    The hills like lambs.

Then the poem teases and taunts (vv. 5–6):

What ails you, O sea, that you flee?
    O Jordan, that you turn back,
O mountains, that you skip like rams?
    O hills, like lambs?

What are you afraid of, "scaredy, scaredy"? The ones who were in
a service resistant to Yahweh must run and hide, fly to Paris, take
their money to Switzerland, because a new regime is under
way. Tremble, earth (Ps. 114:7). Tremble before him indeed (Ps.
96:9). Tremble because Yahweh reigns (Exod. 15:15). New actions are required. New possibilities are permitted. New social
arrangements are visible. New social reality emerges where the
news is enacted, here and now.

   Israel engages in imaginative, transformative world-making, but
Israel engages in no fantasy. Israel can identify the taproot of
credibility for this unthinkable new world. It is the experience
of transformation in the exodus that legitimates the liturgy. The
experience sanctions the liturgy. Conversely, the liturgy makes
the experience available. The long period of repression since the
exodus makes the exodus itself remote and not available. The new
world was made there and then in the moment of liberation, but it

must be made and remade and made again, here and now, again and again, in the face of distortions, repressions, and betrayals. The act of remaking the world lets us see clearly in the face of distortion, permits fidelity in the midst of massive betrayal, invites liberated order in the face of repressive intimidation. If the world is not remade, it will disappear and we will settle for the world of tyranny and despair that is so much with us. Clearly Israel has taken up the enthronement pattern in these Exodus texts. It has shaped and articulated that model in a peculiar and powerful way, however, a way distinctly Israelite. That way has continued to authorize hope for a new world and evoke courage on behalf of that new world.

A NEW WORLD FOR EXILES

The memory of that new world and the means of world-making continue to be available in Israel. In most times the liturgy was so routinized that the new world did not seem urgent, and because that new world was not urgent, it was not difficult or costly. The liturgy could be routinized so that we did not notice what we were doing. We only exhibited the clichés one more time, each time in the liturgy. We went through the motions, sang the songs, said among the nations, ascribed glory, trembled, but it contained no bite of threat or gift. The world-making forms seem to go on and on without cost or notice, world without end. We made the liturgy routine because we carelessly equated the world of visible arrangement with the world of the news. The news was domesticated to fit the present world. The news is heard so familiarly that it seems simply to be an endorsement of the world we already have at hand.

The material for fresh world-making was nonetheless kept available, waiting to be used. The liturgic form was familiar to us, perhaps too familiar, but therefore available to our children. For the liturgy to be taken up with power again seems to require two things. First, it requires a situation which makes clear that the world offered through the liturgy is either in jeopardy or has nearly vanished, about to be crushed, but worth clinging to. Second, it requires a poetic tongue, a liturgic manager to bring the world-making language to powerful speech in the face of domestication. We may surmise that it is this poetic tongue which in fact evokes the situation of jeopardy, for without such a tongue, the community would not recognize its jeopardy, nor its yearning. The jeopardy requires the recovery of the world-making liturgy. A fresh effort at world-making must be made. The yearning moves the world-making language to practice in the conviction that a better world is offered through this liturgic action than is offered in the presumed, visible world which seeks to preclude this lyrical, alternative world.

Such a moment of tongue and situation, of jeopardy and yearning, is given us in the poetry of Second Isaiah.[30] Whether one follows conventional criticism of Second Isaiah, which lodges the poetry in the exile, or the more recent canonical work, which makes Isaiah 40—55 a response to 1—39, this is a poetry of newness.[31] As I have indicated, it is the poetry of the Isaiah tradition that claims the verb *basar* of Ps. 96:2 for intentional theological use. The burden of the poetry of Second Isaiah is to assert that

- homecoming is possible, and
- exile can now end, because
- Babylonian power is now nullified.

It will not do to make the poet simply a commentator on Persian foreign policy. That is not an adequate rendering of this strong poetry. Rather, this poet knows that homecoming is possible only when the powerful grip of Babylon on the imagination of Israel is overcome. To cause the nullification of such a powerful grip on imagination, a social scientific analysis is neither needed nor effective. What is needed is imaginative, liturgic world-making that enacts a world more credible than the world of the empire. To do this, the poet reenacts the old enthronement liturgy. The poet reclaims the old exodus memory. Both the liturgy and the memory, the experience and the enactment, are brought into the midst of a dangerous, imperial situation which requires exiles to decide between subservience and homecoming. That decision is of course based on a conclusion about the relative power of Babylon (based largely on military control and economic power) and Yahweh (based largely on the liberated lips of the poet).

Again, we are not dealing with description, but with an evocation that in the moment of speech enacts a world that did not exist until uttered.[32] The poet experiences the disbelief of Israelites who found his offer of a world in the poetry to be too dangerous, demanding, and scandalous. The rebuke of 45:9–13 suggests resistance:

> Woe to him who strives with his Maker,
>   an earthen vessel with the potter! . . .
> Will you question me about my children,
>   or command me concerning the work of my hands?

In 49:14, the liturgy of despair is quoted:

> Zion said,
>   "The Lord has forsaken me,
>   My lord has forgotten me."

In 50:2, the Lord responds in indignation to what must have been in doubt:

> Is my hand shortened, that it cannot redeem?
> Or have I no power to deliver?

The resistance the poet encounters is due to the military, economic power of the empire which seems more credible than the poetic scenario of an alternative world. The empire has managed Israel's perceptual field through the power of its ideology, so that the most elemental poetry by which Israel lives is largely robbed of its authority and power.

The poet counters disbelief, resistance, and despair with news that allows for life and hope (40:9):

> O Zion, herald of *good tidings;*
>   lift up your voice with strength,
> O Jerusalem, herald of *good tidings,*
>   lift it up, fear not;
> say to the cities of Judah,
>   "Behold your God!"

The poet does not argue rationally. The poet calls Israel to live in a new world. The poem depends on the double use of "good tidings," *basar*. This is not descriptive language, for the community is called to see God: "behold." This is not description, but imagination. Israel is urged to reconstrue its present experience through the old lyric of enthronement and the foundational narrative of Exodus. The poem of Second Isaiah invites Israel to pay attention to what the world does not see, to believe in a world to which Babylon has no access. The coming of God, the leadership of God, urges that Yahweh has defeated Babylon. We are not told

where or how. The "then and there" of this news happens where
Israel has no access, but that does not matter to the poet. What
matters is to bring the there here, the then now. In this here and
now, Israel has its heart set free, so that a free heart, freed from
the oppressive imperial imagination, may make new moves in a
world of political reality. What happened then and there is crucial. But what is effective for social power is the here and now of
announcement.

The other text, the most important in Second Isaiah for our
purposes, is 52:7:

> How beautiful upon the mountains
> are the feet of him who brings *good tidings*,
> who publishes peace, who brings *good tidings* of good,
> who publishes salvation,
> who says to Zion, "Your God reigns."

The verb *basar* is used twice, matched by two uses of *masmia'*.
The sequence is "brings tidings, publishes, brings tidings, publishes." It is a messenger, the one who tells there here, who tells
then now, who carries a message of "good tidings, peace, good
tidings, good, salvation," who arrives breathless. The watchmen
wait. In this poetic scenario, they watch as discerningly and ur-
gently as does David in 2 Samuel 18. They imagine they can discern the news of the battle by the way the messenger runs. They
observe that his feet are "welcome."[33] They have been waiting a
very long time. In the world of this poem, the watchmen know that
there was a battle. The assumption of such a battle is essential to
the poetic argument. They know there was a deep conflict in
which everything is at issue for them and for their city.[34] They do
not know the outcome of the battle, however; for this they are
dependent on the messenger and his message.

The watchmen see the messenger approach. They are able to
anticipate what he will say, because the messenger does not run
like a bearer of defeat. His feet are "beautiful." They glide with
buoyancy. He arrives breathless, all the way from Babylon—
breathless with news, finally blurting out the only thing that matters: "Your God reigns."

According to this poetry, the messenger came all the way from
Babylon, when all the time the news was already there in the
liturgy of the Psalms. The news that Yahweh reigns was already
present in Israel's life and faith. It was present in the liturgy, and it

was present in the heavenly arena where Yahweh fought the imperial gods of Babylon. But these previous victories mean nothing until brought to new speech in this moment of evangel out of fresh enactment. Yahweh is vindicated. He has won again. The moment of the creation of the new world is not the moment of the triumph, but the moment of the telling. The joy at the word is like the joy of liberated creation in Psalm 96 (cf. Rom. 8:18–25). The watchmen shout for joy, the way they shouted in Manila when it was announced that Marcos had left for Guam. They sing for joy. The city sings. The slaves dance. Jerusalem knows it can now get on with its proper business of being who it is to be. The news is of Yahweh, but the newness of the world follows from the newness of its sovereign. Where Yahweh rules, there is another world of human possibility. Everything depends on the rule of Yahweh now established. When Yahweh does not rule, there is no singing because there is no equity, no righteousness, no truth. But Yahweh does rule—and there is this other world.

The gospel enacted in Second Isaiah is that Babylon is defeated. It is only a liturgic, poetic event. The imperial armies still march. The imperial media still seduce. The imperial economy still discriminates. But the news breaks out of the liturgy and begins to erode the old world. The liturgy begins to subvert the empire. People begin to notice the cracks in the establishment. Some begin to sense that the truth of the gospel invites the first-time acts of civil disobedience against the empire.[35] Confidence wanes. Support is withdrawn. The observant begin to sense a difference. A new world pushes with determination against the old one. It begins in singing: "Sing to the Lord a new song" (Isa. 42:10). That invitation to song is grounded in the old liturgy of Psalm 96, but the actual singing and the new song are at the edge of exile. The community is invited to stop singing the old domesticated songs of the empire. There need be no more government slogans, no more subservience in singing of loyalties that make us choke. No more empty salutes need be given to imperial symbols that evoke only resentment, not allegiance. It is the old story of Exodus become the new song of homecoming. The liturgy moves to song.

The poetry of Second Isaiah reenacts the dangerous alternative of the exodus. This poetry carries a political verdict not unlike the one spoken over Pharaoh:

> My glory I give to no other,
>   nor my praise to graven images. (Isa. 42:8)[36]

My glory I will not give to another. (48:11)

The assertions of Second Isaiah were all anticipated in the enthronement liturgy: "Say among the nations, 'Your God reigns.'"
The gods of the nations are idols now dismissed by Second Isaiah.
Yahweh has triumphed in glory over Pharaoh, and now in this poetry, over Nebuchadnezzar (cf. Jeremiah 50—51; Isaiah 47), and
also over Bel and Nebo and the gods of the empire (Isa. 46:1). The
glory is attained in a fair fight. The Babylonian gods lost and will
not share in the new governance. They are excluded from the new
government. Yahweh need form no coalition. There is a monopoly
of glory, of the claim to sovereign celebration. Ascribe glory. Tell
among the nations that Yahweh has achieved glory. The rights of the
other gods are terminated. Do not serve them.

From the theological assertion come political, economic deci-
sions that entail the transformation of the world. It is remarkable
that the theological transfer of power raises issues about work and
bread and wine and milk and money (Isa. 55:1–2a):

> Ho, every one who thirsts,
>   come to the waters;
> and he who has no money,
>   come, buy and eat!
> Come, buy wine and milk
>   without money and without price.
> Why do you spend your money for that which is not bread,
>   and your labor for that which does not satisfy?

It is an act of civil disobedience to cease laboring for that which
does not satisfy. The old oppressive economy is undermined. That
economy seems to operate still, but news changes worlds. Israel
can now act differently. Homecoming is, to be sure, geographical;
but it is also more than that. It concerns the geography of imagination.[37] Homecoming is the imaginative appropriation of a new
world which can be embraced in the liturgy and can be practiced
concretely here and now. Even when contained in the liturgy,
homecoming is risky, for the imperial police dogs are vigilant and
can sniff out a dangerous poem. These dogs are trained not to look
for drugs, but for poems, because poems of alternative worlds
constitute the greatest threat to the empire, especially poems that
speak of milk without money and bread without cost. The risk

that is the liturgy must be run, however, because without the liturgy a humane alternative to the empire by Israel is not even possible. Without the liturgy, this other world of possibility is simply not available. The news invites those who are beaten, broken, and despairing to a world where life is not lived in vain. It is a dangerous world founded on dramatic news.

The dangerous world is based on the liturgy, an awesome invitation on which everything depends. The new world which this poem offers is so dangerous, it is no wonder they "all alike began to make excuses" (Luke 14:18). The poet is relentless and insists on that world anyway, even in the face of hardened excuses. Some trusted the poem enough to depart the empire for home.[38] Some believed the world offered by the liturgy enough to act freely against the presumed world of Nebuchadnezzar. Excuses will not silence the poet who sings of new life and new worlds. The book of Scripture and the people of Scripture attest that the world of these dangerous poets is more powerful, more humane, and finally more real than the world of the empire where Yahweh does not rule. That is why the singing will not be stopped.[39]

CONCLUSION

Two conclusions may be drawn about Israel's liturgic action which makes a particular world in which Israel may live. First, Israel's doxological activity which celebrates Yahweh also makes available a world over which Yahweh rules. Because Israel's doxological practice of world-making includes both the grand claim of legitimacy (in the enthronement psalms) and the concrete story of hurt and transformation (in the Exodus narratives and the exilic lyric), the doxology is both promise and threat. The world of Yahweh's righteousness both is legitimated and makes demands.

The world-making doxology of Israel is indeed promissory, because it bespeaks a world of compassion, mercy, justice, righteousness, truth, and equity. That is a promise against all other worlds characteristically imperial. The other worlds of Pharaoh and Babylon—and even Solomon—negate all these dimensions of human possibility. In these acts of dangerous praise, Israel sings this true world against all the pretenders which will destroy, enslave, and brutalize. The doxological act in Israel is at the same time political, eschatological, and cultic. It is political because it mediates a polity for Israel. It summons Israel, and especially the human king (who is Yahweh's agent and regent), to embody in polity, law, and institutions the great theme of the new sovereignty. It is eschatological because it promises something not yet visible, but the hope is certain and settled. It is cultic in that it is an imaginative act which runs out beyond visible reality.[40] Thus the doxology is an act of hope. It promises and anticipates a hoped-for world that is beyond present reality. Whenever Israelites sing this doxology, they commit themselves again to that hoped-for world that is sketched in the liturgy before their very eyes.

The world-making doxology of Israel is a threat precisely because it is a formidable act of legitimation. It asserts "this world and no other," "this God and no other." The jealousy of Yahweh means Israel is permitted no world but this one (cf. Isa. 42:8; 48:11). The First Commandment on exclusiveness destines Israel only for this world. No other god, no other world. Israel sings that the world of justice, mercy, equity, righteousness, peace is the real world, even if not yet available in a polity. It is the "no other" that is a threat to all pretended worlds. The capacity to legitimate is inevitably also the capacity to delegitimate, to declare some arrangements dysfunctional, lacking in authority, effectively nonexistent. The world-making of the liturgy is also world-breaking and world-nullifying. The God who "plants and builds" is the one who "plucks up and tears down" (Jer. 1:10; cf. Deut. 32:39; Isa. 45:7). The liturgy which brings life to certain worlds can also bring death to others. When Israel finishes its doxology, not only is a God enthroned and a world available, but other gods and other worlds are excluded from Israel's social horizon and possibility.

Second, we have spoken of world-making and have been informed by Mowinckel's programmatic statement that the cult does create worlds. Now we are in a position to assess that claim. If we mean by world-making creation *ex nihilo* of the physical world, then obviously the cult does not do so. We are realistic enough to know that words and acts in cult do not form rocks and rivers and minerals. But Israel rarely speaks of creation in that sense. Israel's sense of creation characteristically is not *ex nihilo*, but refers to the organizing act of imposing order, shape, sequence, pattern, and meaning on already existing elements which are disordered and chaotic until acted upon. This action of creation of course is what Israel does in liturgy. Creation is the forming of a social world which makes human life possible, legitimating arrangements of power and value, and authorizing certain modes of personal existence.

Yahweh's peculiar version of power and meaning is newly established among the gods through the liturgy. Life under this sovereignty is shaped as equity, righteousness, and truth. That is the real world, and any world other than this is a false world ordered by false gods. Derivatively, the liturgy sets a pattern of power and meaning upon social relations which reflects Yahweh's sovereignty. A world of justice, mercy, peace, and compassion is created in the imaginative act of liturgy. This is the real world, created in the moment of liturgy, which asserts that every rival claimant and candidate for the real world is false and destructive. Thus the doxology is polemical because it means to "uncreate"—disestablish other worlds and affirm this as a better world.[41] Departure from this liturgy leaves Israel imaginatively prepared for and mobilized against other patterns of meaning and power which embody other worlds. The praise of Israel evokes the power of Yahweh. It also evokes the possibility of Israel. The empire tries to silence the doxology, because where praise is stopped, Yahweh is not so formidable and Israel is not so open to a different future. Israel's testimony, however, is that the doxology cannot for long be silenced. The song breaks out in newness because Yahweh's power for life will not be contained. Israel sings freely because Yahweh acts freely.

Doxology at the Edge of Ideology: The King of Majesty and Mercy

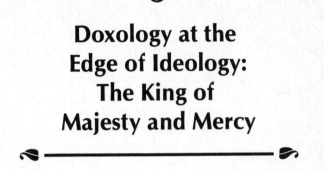

I have considered thus far the enduring liturgic enactment of news found in the Psalms. I have considered the way the enthronement liturgy was utilized concretely and mobilized toward liberation, first, to liberate Israel from Pharaoh; second, to invite Israel home from Babylonian exile. The liturgy continues to be available and one never knows when the news will take on new, concrete, unexpected power. One has the impression that now, in many unsettled and unsettling places in the world, this old liturgy, with its narratives of freedom and vision, of justice and righteousness, is creating worlds, authorizing actions, and nullifying other worlds. People are dipping into the liturgy and finding the news that permits a new world of equity, righteousness, and truth. They are finding power and legitimacy there to act and live in new ways, with a legitimacy long denied them.

REALITY GIVEN, REALITY IMPOSED

In these uses of the enthronement liturgy in the practice of ancient Israel, there is a deep tension between the *slave memory*, which is so concrete and peculiarly Israelite, and the *grand claims* of the Jerusalem liturgy (largely shared in the Near East), which is reflected in the enthronement psalms. There is an unresolved tension between the abrasive realities rooted in experiences of oppression and liberation, and the great assertions of the liturgy,

which over time take on imperial tones. The tension persists because the old narratives continue to reflect the pain and articulate
the hope of the ancient world of slaves in Egypt, while in the
Psalms the rule of Yahweh in the Jerusalem Temple is so sure, so
settled, so here-and-now, and so abiding. Despite his acute discernment, Sigmund Mowinckel does not seem to have noticed that
the entire enterprise of the enthronement liturgy reflects the royal
establishment and so serves Israel's own status quo.

In this chapter I will deal with the reality of social interest which
operates in the liturgy of ancient Israel, as indeed it does in every
liturgy, and therefore in every act of world-making. According to
Mowinckel, Israel borrowed from the great imperial liturgies that
served to arrange vast holdings of royal power which imposed order. But Israel transformed these liturgic borrowings for its own
purposes, its own experiences, its own God, its own world. Israel
pressed what is borrowed into the service of its own memories of
hurt, oppression, and liberation, of yearning for emancipation and
homecoming. This combination of *appropriation* and *transformation* is a powerful and unresolved tension in Israel's world-making.
There is something odd and incongruous about appropriating great
state strategies as vehicles for memories of hurt and hope, of yearning for well-being among the marginal. There is something odd and
incongruous, for the great state strategies do not seem very well
suited to serve as vehicles for Israel's hurt and hope.[1] But it is precisely in the midst of that oddness and incongruity that Israel
shaped its world.

There is a second way we may think about the tension in Israel's
world-making. On the one hand, these liturgies are gifts of God
that well up in experience to express the new truth of the gospel,
the news of what happened then and there. That is their theological character that we gladly affirm. They are revelatory—in some
sense, inspired—articulations of God's new reality out beyond
our horizon.[2] On the other hand, however, realism compels us to
recognize that such liturgies do not fall from heaven. They must
be designed, planned, and implemented. That is, as many will
attest, hard work. In the ancient world, the design and implementation are done by a guild; in the modern world, by a committee.
Either way, liturgic performance is hard work, done by those designated on behalf of the community. In the ancient world of
Jerusalem, the one who designated, at whose behest the guild or

committee functioned, was the king. The liturgy belongs in, profound ways to the king.

This tension discloses an important reality. The liturgy may be an inspired disclosure from heaven, but it also is a managed, administered, designed human process. The ones designated for this function of management and administration never forget who designated them. The liturgy, even in the Jerusalem Temple, is never cleanly from heaven, never disinterested. It reflects the will and purpose of its sponsor, which means it serves an interest in Jerusalem, not unlike the interest it served more generally in the Near East, from whence it was appropriated. That powerful interest, while related to the memory of liberation and the yearning for homecoming, is not easily or readily compatible with such memory and yearning. It is more concerned for the maintenance and legitimation of a certain social arrangement in the present which must necessarily co-opt the memory and administer the yearning. The world-making that results is not characteristically the world of Yahweh's peculiar interest we have explicated earlier (concerning justice and equity), but more likely is the intensely interested world of the king. Characteristically the interests of the king in Jerusalem did not readily cohere with the celebrated interests of Yahweh.

The problem of relating administered liturgy to experiences of transformation may be commented on in three ways.

1. This issue of concrete memory and appropriated myth stands at the center of Old Testament scholarship, lodged in debates over the extent to which Israel borrowed the mythic tradition of the Near East and the extent to which its faith grows out of its peculiar experience.[3] There is clearly truth in both borrowing and peculiarity, and scholars vary on the relative power of the two. On the one hand, the grand myth came to comprehend the experience. Thus, even the Exodus narrative is cast in patterned categories reminiscent of the great state liturgies of the Near East. On the other hand, the concrete Israelite experience powerfully impinges upon the grand claim of the liturgy for order. No doubt the formation of the biblical text (which reflects the liturgy) includes both such comprehending and impinging upon.[4]

2. It is possible and necessary to do a social analysis of this tension between remembered experience and established liturgy. The experience of Israel is rooted in the irreducible memory of

oppression which becomes slavery, of human pain only resolved by
heavenly power. This experience of oppression and liberation stays
very close to the slave huts in which people live in the midst of
social pain, where kings and great priests neither want to go nor
have access. But the established liturgy is not placed in the slave
huts. It is lodged in the temple with its great columns, splendid
choirs, majestic dress and style, and all the accouterments of dig-
nity, order, pomp, success, and symmetry.[5] While the shaping,
normative experience of Israel *emerges from below*, the liturgy to
some extent is *imposed from above*, done by those who are skilled
in and claim authorization to impose from above.

Without offering a developmental scheme, one may imagine
three distinct social contexts for the gospel announcement,
"Yahweh reigns." The balance between experience and establishment shifts as the social context shifts. The first context is a dangerous whisper at night in the slave huts, in which people are kept
marginal and never free. This moment of the whisper is a terribly
subversive moment, for it is a dark fantasy and hint that Pharaoh's
presumed world is not real and will not last. The very whisper of
the phrase "Yahweh reigns" is a destabilizing assertion. It is that
dangerous whisper of an alternative governance that powers Israel's faith.[6] In that first whisper, it is only a daring yearning, as
yet without worldly embodiment.

Second, we may imagine that in the days of Samuel and the
Judges, the community of Israel was free, but still marginal. In
that context the enthronement formula of the gospel (as reflected
in the "ark narrative" of 1 Samuel 4—6) is an invitation to a sectarian consensus which asserts that we Israelites are not like the
Philistines or like anyone else. In the "ark narrative," it is not
claimed that Israel, through Yahweh, has power to govern other
peoples.[7] It is only asserted that Yahweh is free. In that assertion
that Yahweh is not subject to Dagon or any other power, Israel
establishes a zone of freedom for itself that it may believe in this
free God, and so think and act freely. That zone of freedom is still
circumscribed by the hard reality that other peoples are powerful
and not to be challenged beyond occasional forays, but the assertion "Yahweh reigns" begins to change the calculus of power.
Israel has embraced a different definitive loyalty. Israel was resolved to continue to trust the rule of Yahweh, even in the face of
the powerful Philistine and Canaanite threats.[8]

3

Third, in the high days of monarchy under Solomon, this same formula, "Yahweh reigns," has been situated statically in the temple and is sponsored by the king. Now the rule of Yahweh has come to be equated with the rule of the dominant order. There is now a sociopolitical economic realm on earth which corresponds to Yahweh's claim among the gods. The king can claim to be the heir of this powerful tradition of Yahweh's governance. The doxology of enthronement through all of these uses (in the slave huts, in the time of Samuel, and in the temple of Solomon) prevails, but the old energizing experience that Yahweh overturns royal power is increasingly an embarrassment to the royal agents who manage the liturgy. The establishment liturgy has largely co-opted the experience of liberation and transformation and has reduced its terrible rawness to conform to a legitimate order. The God who liberated is now celebrated as the one who sanctions this entrenched system of order in the name of liberation.[9] This royal order prefers to allude to the transformative memory of the exodus, but to enact the borrowed liturgy of royal adherence.

The liturgic formula "the Lord reigns" thus may have several different functions and intentions in various social contexts. I suggest at least three different functions in three contexts: first, among the marginal and powerless in the slave huts where the formula may destabilize; second, in the free but marginal community of early Israel where there is free religious imagination but not commensurate social freedom; and third, in the settled rule of Solomon where the formula serves to legitimate a settled, visible social reality. The formula varies in social power and significance, depending on where and by whom it is sung, heard, and believed.

3. A third general way in which we may ask about the tension between slave memory and royal liturgic claim, between experience from below (reflected in Exodus and Second Isaiah) and the liturgy from above (reflected in the enthronement psalms), is to examine the parallel tension faced by pastors. Most pastors I know are troubled by the duty of reasserting the old memory of hurt in a context of affluence where the symmetrical liturgy of Yahweh's sovereignty seems settled and resistant to such an awkward memory.[10] Indeed this is the material out of which great church quarrels may be wrought. The tension between experiences of hurt and rescue and liturgies of order and legitimacy is enormously problematic, but also enormously illuminating. Here I intend to deal

with that problematic as it is present in Israel's memory, Israel's text, and contemporary pastoral life.

Clearly, experience *wells up*, unextrapolated and underived. That is how the liberating sovereignty of Yahweh is portrayed by the exodus event. That is the narrative mode for the experience of the burning bush (Exod. 3:1–6). The initial assertion of Yahweh's alternative rule is given abruptly, unexpectedly, directly in the midst of suffering and oppression.[11] By contrast the great liturgy in Jerusalem, which stages the great hymns of enthronement, is *sponsored*, and therefore programmed and managed. That is, it does not spontaneously well up. The enactment of the royal liturgy is dependent upon its careful administration. I want to approach this tension in Israel's life between what *wells up inexplicably* and what is *intentionally sponsored* by focusing on the liturgy of order and legitimacy.[12]

The liturgy of enthronement, as it was sung and enacted in the Jerusalem Temple, is closely tied to the politics of the city of Jerusalem, the Temple establishment, and finally to the Davidic dynasty.[13] It could not be otherwise. It is that connection to political reality that is most important and most problematic. The Temple and its liturgy exist in connection with and for the sake of that political enterprise. We do well to study this matter so that we may discern how our own use of these royal texts is situated in the same problematic between what is inexplicably given and what is intentionally contrived. The liturgy which holds together the inexplicably given and the intentionally contrived is both powerful and seductive.

THE GOSPEL UNDER ROYAL SUPERVISION

Because the enactment of the liturgy is situated in the Jerusalem Temple over which the king presides, the role of the king takes on crucial importance for our understanding of the social process of world-making. In Jerusalem, as in every royal temple, the king is the high priest, from whose office all other priests and priestly orders are derivative. The presence of the king in the midst of the liturgy decisively and inevitably changes the character of the liturgy, its intent, and its effect. Special attention therefore must be given to the cruciality of the king in the worship in the Jerusalem Temple.

The Davidic monarchy was linked to and involved with the liturgy of Yahweh's enthronement and kingship in important ways. I suggest four ways in which the king was related to the liturgic enthronement of Yahweh. The first three of these arise out of the predictable conventions of state-sponsored liturgy, and should therefore be treated critically. The fourth is quite unlike the other three and reflects what is most central to Israel's faith. I shall argue that it is the fourth of these that provides a clue for the character of Israel's faithful praise.

1. The king was a *participant* in the drama. It could be, as Aubrey Johnson and J. H. Eaton have suggested, that the king played the role of Yahweh, or if that is too much, that the king is the dramatic recipient of the new world now enacted.[14] One way or the other, the king participated dramatically in the ritual of emptying and enthronement, the humiliation and exaltation.[15] Either in the role of Yahweh or in visible alliance with Yahweh, the king receives his kingship through liturgic legitimacy.

2. Even if the notion of participation claims too much (because it cannot be demonstrated with certitude), there can be no doubt that the king (and his priests) were *sponsors* who staged the festival. Much effort is required in the implementation of such a dramatic liturgy. Someone must attend to it, answer for it, and especially, pay for it. In Jerusalem the Davidic house becomes the inevitable and predictable sponsor of the liturgy. In so doing, the Davidic monarchy exercises a role characteristic in every society in the Near East. Such a role confirms this truism: kings sponsor state liturgies. But that truism requires more critical attention than it has received, because some in the slave huts must have noticed that this magisterial liturgy is not disinterested.[16]

3. In his position as participant and/or sponsor, it takes no great imagination to see that the king is the *principal benefactor* of the liturgy, and that the benefit of others is derivative from and mediated through the benefit of the king.[17]

The world being made in Jerusalem liturgy is not a fantasy for heaven or a pretend world on earth. The world made in this world-making is a real world which requires and receives concrete political, economic, and social implementation. If one asks about the world made in this liturgy through which Yahweh rules, one concludes it is the world of Jerusalem over which the Davidic king presides as Yahweh's agent and regent. If one asks where the new rule of Yahweh is evident, it is in the authority of the Davidic king. If one asks how and where the new rule of equity, righteousness, and truth is evident, the answer is that the new rule of Yahweh is embodied in the politics and policies of the Davidic monarchy. If one asks why the creation should rejoice, the answer is that Davidic policy is to sponsor and enact equity, righteousness, and truth which will touch all of creation. The king is indeed the Adam of Genesis 1—2, who is to subdue the earth so that it is fruitful and multiplies (Gen. 1:28), who is to tend and care for the earth (Gen. 2:15).[18]

Israel's memory had been rooted in a notion of governance that, in contrast to Pharaoh, was not exploitative. In the slave huts, the initial news of Yahweh's rule was, first of all, negative in its function. It served to dethrone and delegitimate Pharaoh, to assert that Israel need no longer submit to the power of Pharaoh and his empire. In the dramatic moment of Exod. 8:18 (Heb. 8:14), Israel learned that Pharaoh "could not," that Pharaoh's claimed power was a fraud that did not need to be honored.[19] But as Israel became stable and prosperous, the formula of enthronement came to have positive, practical, concrete embodiment. It was not only a negative assertion, but an enduring social force with which to be reckoned. That practical embodiment of Yahweh's rule was precisely and explicitly entrusted to the Davidic monarchy, which guarded Israel's recently acquired monopoly of wealth and presided over the legitimating liturgy.[20] The world of Yahweh's rule created in the liturgy is the world over which David is to govern with equity, righteousness, and truth. The well-being of that world depends on the effectiveness, fidelity, and power of the dynasty. Israel depends for its life on the legitimacy of and adherence to this particular social arrangement.

4. The king, however, is not only participant, sponsor, and benefactor. These three functions position the king as the shaper of liturgy who is the agent who holds the initiative. But in Israel's normative tradition the king is not free to shape the liturgy. Rather the king is to present himself to be shaped by the liturgy. That shaping does not happen by royal prerogative but by the deep and abiding claims of the community concerning pain, amazement, and transformation. The king is not free in the face of these claims to do as he pleases. Thus the fourth dimension of the king's involvement in the liturgy is very different from the first three and in fact stands

as a critique of them. Israel's central tradition, I propose, intends that the king should not be the powerful shaper of liturgy but should be powerfully shaped by it, submissive, and obedient to its central vision.[21] Obviously such an expectation powerfully critiques conventional notions of royal power and privilege.

The liturgy intends that the king shall be *creature, child, and heir* of the liturgy, shaped by it and submissive to it. As the liturgy characterizes the rule that Yahweh practices, so it also articulates the rule authorized by Yahweh that it is to be done on earth. As the king is authorized in the liturgy for rule on earth, so the king is mandated in the liturgy for a certain kind of rule on earth. The king is not intended to be only the sponsor and benefactor of the liturgy without also being decisively instructed by its claim. That is, the king is expected to "listen" to the liturgy and be shaped by it. The notion that the king "participates" does not mean simply that the king "plays a role," but that he actually submits to the world acted out before him in the drama, a world marked by justice and righteousness. The king is to believe in and embrace this world and no other.

An Israelite king in Jerusalem was inevitably placed in a tension between memories of hurt and transformation, and grand dreams of royal power. As benefactor and sponsor of the liturgy, the king was drawn to royal power and legitimacy. As a creature, child, and heir of the old memory, the king was committed to the memories of hurt and transformation. That deep tension may be articulated in three aspects.

First, the liturgy (and its resultant world) shows God moving between majesty and mercy.[22] Yahweh as *a God of majesty* governs in royal splendor befitting the best-established imperial power. Yahweh as *a God of mercy* is peculiarly attentive to the cries of pain and wretchedness among slaves, peasants, and all those who are marginal in society. This deep polarity in the person of God must not be reduced in either direction, to the neglect of either affirmation. It is my argument that the polarity of majesty and mercy is pertinent not only for the character of God but also for the intent of the liturgy and for the office of the king.

Second, the king is cast in a dual and ambiguous, if not contradictory, role in the liturgy. The king is sponsor and benefactor, so that the liturgy of God's majesty inevitably serves to enhance the majesty of the king. But the king is child, creature, and heir of the liturgy, so that the king is to enter into the mercy and compassion of God that belongs to this liturgical memory of hurt and healing. The king is inescapably both sponsor and benefactor, heir and creature, and so must live and function in this tension. As both aspects are crucial for the character of God, so both aspects are essential for the practice of the king.

3. Third, the control of the liturgy is entrusted to the king who inevitably presides over the process in his own interest, which predictably is in the direction of absolute earthly power. Yet the real authorization is in the holiness of God who lives beyond the king and the royal apparatus and in whose holiness the authority of the king is made provisional and penultimate. It is so important and so difficult for the king, in the face of God's offer of majesty and authority, to remember that the holiness of God keeps royal power always in some way provisional.

Thus the tension concerns the earthly arrangement of the king's power on earth as much as it concerns the rule of God in heaven. The grand dream of power and order articulates in a stunning way the claim of legitimacy for both God and king. The tension presents both alternative vocation and absolute legitimacy, the former peculiarly Israelite, the latter more generally shared. In the midst of the liturgy, the king has choices to make and options to exercise concerning the significance of Yahweh's rule for his own reign in Jerusalem. The liturgy of Yahweh's rule enacted in Jerusalem has Yahweh moving back and forth between Israel's memory of hurt and the grand claim of the Temple. Attraction to God's majesty and embrace of God's mercy both have decisive spin-offs for royal power in Jerusalem.

We may thus suggest a correlation of three factors which are involved in our analysis:

The role of the king:	participant, sponsor, and benefactor	creature, child, and heir
The basis of the liturgy:	grand imperial dream	experience of hurt
Mode of God's presence:	majesty	mercy

These elements together go far toward determining the intent and outcome of the liturgy. One characterization of these factors is for the king as participant, sponsor, and benefactor to be rooted in the grand imperial dream and committed to God's majesty. The other is for the king to be present as creature, child, and heir of Israel's experience and memory of hurt and therefore attentive to the mercy of God.

The reality of the king in Jerusalem is that the tension cannot finally be resolved or escaped. It belongs to the very character of the institution as Israelite (and therefore covenantal) and as Jerusalemite (and therefore royal). Both sets of factors come together and the king must take both seriously. But the relative importance of the two sets of factors and the attention given to each can be nuanced and arranged in very different patterns, so that the grand claims can crowd out the painful memories, or the painful memories can be stressed and celebrated at the expense of the grand claims. The king has considerable freedom in how the two are to be set vis-à-vis each other. It is clear that very much is at stake for Israel, for its faith, and for its social policy, in shaping the liturgy in one direction or the other.

The tension between God's majesty and mercy is not limited to the experience of the king, however. It is operative throughout the life of Israel. We see the tensive balance between majesty and mercy in the enthronement psalms which are tied most closely to the Jerusalem king, but we can also observe this interface in the Exodus narrative and Second Isaiah. In the enthronement psalms, the memory of hurt and freedom concerns Israel in peculiar ways:

> The princes of the peoples gather
>   as the people of the God of Abraham. (Ps. 47:9a)

> The Lord loves those who hate evil;
>   he preserves the lives of his saints;
>   he delivers them from the hand of the wicked. (Ps. 97:10)

> Moses and Aaron were among his priests,
>   Samuel also was among those who called on his name.
>   They cried to the Lord, and he answered them. (Ps. 99:6)

On the one hand, the enthronement psalms concern this particular people in this particular place with this particular history of liberation (mercy). On the other hand, the psalms express the grand claim of majesty, which concerns world sovereignty, smashing the idols, elimination of other gods, subjugation of other peoples. Taken together, the two themes of the psalms express the dialectic of majesty and mercy.

The Exodus narrative (see chap. 2) takes up these two themes of the liturgy in a particular way. The majesty of Yahweh and Yahweh's absolute legitimacy are expressed as "getting glory over Pharaoh."[23]

> And I will harden Pharaoh's heart, and he will pursue them and I will get glory over Pharaoh and all his host; and the Egyptians shall know that I am the Lord. (Exod. 14:4)

> And I will harden the hearts of the Egyptians so that they shall go in after them, and I will get glory over Pharaoh and all his host, his chariots, and his horsemen. And the Egyptians shall know that I am the Lord, when I have gotten glory over Pharaoh, his chariots, and his horsemen. (Exod. 14:17–18)

The mercy of Yahweh, on the other hand, is reflected in the Israelite memory of rescue, which concerns the historical future of the slaves:[24]

> And Moses said to the people, "Fear not, stand firm, and see the salvation of the Lord, which he will work for you today; for the Egyptians whom you see today, you shall never see again. The Lord will fight for you, and you have only to be still." (Exod. 14:13–14)

> . . . and the Egyptians said, "Let us flee from before Israel; for the Lord fights for them against the Egyptians." (Exod. 14:25)

> Thus the Lord saved Israel that day from the hand of the Egyptians; and Israel saw the Egyptians dead upon the seashore. (Exod. 14:30)

The same God who claims ultimate authority by "getting glory over Pharaoh" is the God who intervenes on behalf of suffering slaves.

In Second Isaiah, which has again taken up the enthronement liturgy in a specific way, the two motifs are articulated respectively in salvation oracles[25] and lawsuit speeches.[26] In the salvation oracles, we learn of Yahweh's gentle attentiveness to needful Israel. The other gods are not mentioned in such reassurance. In the lawsuit speeches, however, the other gods are ridiculed and dismissed as weak and worthless. In these, Israel is an innocent bystander who is not mentioned.

The majesty and mercy of Yahweh are nicely held together in Isa. 40:10–11, which follows directly the words of 40:9 which uses the term "gospel." The poet characterizes the God who is announced:

> Behold, the Lord God comes with might,
>   and his arm rules for him;

behold, his reward is with him,
    and his recompense before him.
He will feed his flock like a shepherd,
    he will gather the lambs in his arms,
he will carry them in his bosom,
    and gently lead those that are with young.

The same God comes like a warrior with bared arm and like a
nursing mother. The warrior enacts the sovereignty of Yahweh
(and his royal regent), the nursing mother reminds participants in
the liturgy of the experiential basis in Exodus.

This tension of majesty and mercy, of "getting glory" and
"fighting for," of lawsuits of ridicule and salvation oracles of assurance, is not a new tension. It has long been recognized. But
the point I wish to insist upon is that in the very function of the
liturgy, this tension between grand claim and concrete memory is
enormously important. It matters decisively how the two factors
are juxtaposed and which is given emphasis. How the two are
juxtaposed is important for the God evidenced in worship, and
the social system legitimated by worship. It matters enormously
that the king (and the derivative managers of liturgy) recognizes
the large zone of freedom and discretion, so that choices can be
made and must be made. On balance, the king is tempted by
interest and placement always to opt for the royal side of the
equation. But Israel's memory always insists on a hearing, even in
the royal precincts where the hymns are sung. And because of the
hearing, the assertion of God's cosmic sovereignty is qualified
and redefined by Yahweh's characteristic attentiveness to the
lowly. In all three cases we have considered, the enthronement
psalms (and the derivative royal psalms),[27] the Exodus narrative,
and the poetry of Second Isaiah, the grand royal claim is corrected and adjusted in important ways by the power of the old
memory. As a result, the old memory becomes, in this singing, a
powerful subversive hope.

When this dialectic is brought to the social realities of earth,
the mandate of the Jerusalem king is to shape, administer, maintain—indeed, to embody—that same majesty and mercy. The
liturgy is to imagine and evoke a world of utter majesty and
transformative mercy. The king is to form that world. The liturgy
moves into life. It is through the power arrangements of the monarchy that the world "made" in the liturgy is to be concretized in

social transactions. What is first of all imagined is then, as the king is faithful and effective, embodied in policy.

Liturgy requires the practice of the new world evoked by Israel's faith. The king is to be an intervener for equity, righteousness, and truth, exactly as is Yahweh, exactly as the liturgy articulates. The king is to do on earth what Yahweh does among the gods. Indeed, Israel could imagine no other kind of king, because it could believe in no other kind of God. The liturgy intends to *make a world* of justice and righteousness. That is what the liturgy is all about. And the king is to *live that world* and make it concretely available for those in the liturgy. The praise of Israel is not done in a social vacuum. It is not an idle verbal act, but a resolve to honor in life the God sung in worship. Praise is the beginning of political practice.

THE INTERPLAY OF RESILIENCE
AND DISTORTION

We may explicate this deep tension by reference to three texts.

Psalm 72

First, Psalm 72 is perhaps the best articulation of the way in which the king is to be shaped by the royal liturgy and the Davidic dynasty is to embody the rule of Yahweh.[28] One can see that this psalm is closely linked to the memory of hurt. It focuses on the poor, needy, and marginal (vv. 1–4, 12–14). It is also deeply informed by the grand dream of the royal vision, which is not particularly Israelite and not closely linked to the memory of hurt and liberation (vv. 5–11, 15–17). Thus the psalm again reflects the same tension between the experience of hurt and the grand dream.

The mercy, availability, and attentiveness of the king are closely associated with the marginal, who are variously slaves, peasants, and exiles (Ps. 72:2–4, 12–14):

> May he judge thy people with righteousness,
>   and thy poor with justice! . . .
> May he defend the cause of the poor of the people,
>   give deliverance to the needy,
>   and crush the oppressor! . . .
> For he delivers the needy when he calls,
>   the poor and him who has no helper.

> He has pity on the weak and the needy,
>   and saves the lives of the needy.
> From oppression and violence he redeems their life;
>   and precious is their blood in his sight.

Psalm 72 also knows that such a king, in order to have sway among the world of the nations, must have glory, glory as of the only regent of Yahweh. As glory is ascribed to Yahweh (already in heaven according to Psalm 29, well before the liturgy on earth),[29] so the liturgy ascribes glory to the king (Ps. 72:5–6, 8–9, 11):

> May he live while the sun endures,
>   and as long as the moon, throughout all generations!
> May he be like rain that falls on the mown grass,
>   like showers that water the earth! . . .
> May he have dominion from sea to sea,
>   and from the River to the ends of the earth!
> May his foes bow down before him,
>   and his enemies lick the dust! . . .
> May all kings fall down before him,
>   all nations serve him!

The king departs from the liturgy filled with possibility and destiny for his governance. If the other kings lick the dust, bow down, bring gifts, fall down, serve him, it means that the order of compassion is secure and powerful. The royal order of the Davidic king is secure in Jerusalem. That order will bring well-being to Jerusalem, but also blessing to all the families of the earth.[30] The liturgy does not flinch from legitimating a king who will practice such a social embodiment.

The king in Jerusalem, and every manager of doxology, are cast in various roles. The roles of participant and sponsor may be formally neutral and permit various postures. It is to the roles of benefactor and creature of the liturgy that we may pay special attention. As the principal benefactor of the liturgy, it is predictable that one's inclination would be toward the matter of majesty, because majesty generates authority, power, prestige, and security. On the other hand, to be a creature, child, and heir who is to submit and be shaped by the liturgy is to be pulled toward the matter of mercy, to understand that the world now constructed is a world in which the marginal are cared for. The liturgy is about both majesty and mercy. The king is both the benefactor who enjoys the majesty and the child of liturgy who is summoned to mercy. When these two are kept in balance and tension, the liturgy does its proper work.

As the king sponsors the liturgy, however, it does not surprise us that the king is characteristically more interested in the legitimacy of his majesty supplied by the liturgy than in the summons to mercy issued through the liturgy. It does not surprise us that the king turns out to be more attracted to majesty, which enhances, than to mercy, which costs. It follows that the grand claim shared everywhere in royal liturgies is more powerful than the painful memory indigenous to Israel. That painful memory is never completely lost in Israel's royal liturgy, but it is often made peripheral and reduced to a minor voice. The Jerusalem liturgy, at the outset, seeks to make a world appropriate to Yahweh, the God of equity, righteousness, and truth. But over time, the functionaries of the king use the liturgy to construct the world preferred by their patron who sponsors the liturgy.

When such preferential and partisan world-construction occurs, we may expect various measures of distortion as the liturgy moves from the kingship of Yahweh to the realities of Israel's social life. Doxology then becomes, I suggest, not only unencumbered praise of God, not only world-making that is derived from and responsive to the will and purpose of God, but also tendentious and distorting in the service of those who sponsor the world-making enterprise and who benefit from it. The king as sponsor and benefactor finds the liturgy useful for purposes of legitimacy. The king can indeed refuse to be shaped by the liturgy and only use it to his own ends. Then the world made by the liturgy is a false world, a betrayal of the very memories that the liturgy claims to enact. The resilient substance of equity, righteousness, and truth (which is deeply rooted in the memory of Israel) is nonetheless persistently present. The world practiced by the king is not and cannot be a complete denial of the content of that powerful memory.[31] What we discover in the enactment of the liturgy, then, is the interplay of distortion and resilience.

I wish to illustrate this operation of resilience and distortion in Israel's world-making to two texts, one a *critical disclosure* and the other a *responsive alternative*. We shall not find texts, I believe, that show the liturgy as distorted. It is more subtle than that. What we do find are royal texts that reflect the legitimacy of majesty without the embrace of mercy. We may imagine that the liturgy functioned as a legitimating program and as a cover-up for a regime that forsook the memory of hurt and the vocation of compassion.

1 Kings 4:20–28

A *critical disclosure* of the world of the monarchy occurs in 1 Kings 4:20–28.[32] The verses that precede this text (vv. 1–19) are a statement about the royal bureaucracy that is mostly devoted to the collection of taxes. Such a program for tax collection may put us on notice about the departure of the regime from the memory of hurt. The text is followed in vv. 29–34 by a statement of Solomon's wisdom, which suggests he was imitating the intellectual pursuits and rationality of the great empires.[33] Both bureaucracy and sapiential rationality suggest that the monarchy has moved some distance from the experiences of hurt and transformation that give rise to the liturgy in Israel.

Verses 20–28 show Solomon's regime marked by unmitigated well-being from which all hurt has been removed. This is "realized eschatology" with a vengeance. Everything is already given. Israel and Judah are many. They eat and drink and are happy. Solomon rules over the land bridge from the Euphrates to Egypt. The royal supplies are enormous, indicating prosperity; also indicating a considerable royal appetite. All dwell in safety. There are 40,000 horses, 12,000 horsemen, and a vast collection agency to keep it all operating.[34] Everything works. Everybody is well fed. Everyone is happy. Solomon has peace on all sides (v. 24). The narrative of 1 Kings 4:20–28 seems to echo Ps. 72:7–8:

> In his days may righteousness flourish,
> and peace abound, till the moon be no more!
> May he have dominion from sea to sea,
> and from the River to the ends of the earth!

Solomon has peace and dominion, well-being at home, control abroad. The system is indeed Solomon's solution. All of the promises have come to fruition for Solomon (cf. Josh. 21:43–45). The majesty of God has "worked" and Solomon has unqualified legitimacy. One may imagine that in such a context, no ground for serious criticism of the regime would be tolerated.

We cannot determine for certain how Israel's historians intend us to take this narrative. Perhaps it is mere description. Or perhaps it is propaganda, wanting us to believe the regime at its best. Or it could be a more subtle narrative, intended as critical irony about a regime that believes its own press notices. There are no problems for such a regime. None are acknowledged, nothing seems to trouble anyone.

We may ask two questions about this characterization. First: Was Solomon's world like this, marked by unmitigated prosperity and joy? There is no doubt that there was enormous prosperity. But there also is no doubt that there was oppression under Solomon. There was forced labor (1 Kings 11:28), which is said to be a "heavy yoke" (12:4). In the end, the people refused to pledge continued loyalty to the crown on the basis of such exploitation. Such refusal does not surprise us. We are able, out of our experience, to conceive of a regime which claims to be adequate and comprehensive, only to discover it is a fraud held together by repression, propaganda, and hutzpah. The outcome in 1 Kings 11—12 suggests that 1 Kings 4 offers either more or less than meets the eye. There was prosperity and order, but we conclude that it was a prosperity and order enhancing the crown, disregarding the human, social reality of needful people. Or if we may put it so, there was majesty and not mercy. The grand claim triumphed over the practice of the hurtful memory. The king was glad to be sponsor and benefactor of the liturgy, but was not shaped by nor submissive to the liturgy.

The second question we may ask is: What is the liturgy that operated to legitimate the practices that seem to be embraced by Solomon? The answer, I submit, is that Solomon fully embraced and appropriated the great claim for Yahweh's majesty and glory, glory over earthly kings and over other gods. Solomon sought to embody in his court the majesty and glory on earth which corresponded to the claims of Yahweh. Solomon clearly opted for the majesty offered by the liturgy to the neglect of the mercy. If indeed Solomon had had a lectionary committee, we may imagine that in the use of Psalm 72, that committee, like some present-day committees, might have utilized only vv. 5–11 and 15–20 to the exclusion of vv. 1–4 and 12–14.

We have seen that the concrete memories of Israel characteristically impinged upon the liturgy, upon the rule of Yahweh, and upon the character of Yahweh. Derivatively, that same concrete memory of pain and transformation was to impinge upon the earthly rule of the king. That part of the doxology, however, is absent from Solomonic practice. The king apparently practiced the legitimacy of the liturgy, but not the memory of social hurt and social possibility. I shall argue in the next chapter that when the act of praise attends to legitimacy and drops out the themes of hurt and possibility, it has become a practice of ideology. The world made in such a liturgy is a skewed world, essentially alien to the character of Yahweh. In 1 Kings 4:20–28 the king takes only part of the world made in the liturgy and uses a distorted liturgy to legitimate that self-serving world.

Ezekiel 34

Our third text on the royal embodiment of doxology is Ezekiel 34, which I shall treat as a text concerning a *responsive alternative* out of the memory of hurt to the failed monarchy. The monarchy was preoccupied with its own majesty, prosperity, and security. Such one-sided preoccupation with royal majesty had failed and led to disastrous results (vv. 1–10). Now, in a new assertion made by the prophet in exile, the God of mercy takes a fresh historical initiative which will lead to a new social practice and, indeed, a new kingship (vv. 11–16).

The text begins with a forceful critique of the kings (shepherds) of Israel and their harsh dismissal. What interests us, however, is the offer of a new world in which Yahweh will rule as king. Israel has long said in the liturgy, "Yahweh has become king." Ezekiel 34:15–16 characterizes how this new king will act:

> . . . I will make them lie down . . .
> I will seek the lost, and
> I will bring back the strayed, and
> I will bind up the crippled, and
> I will strengthen the weak . . .
> I will feed them in justice.

Yahweh will do what Jerusalem's kings are intended to do (Psalm 72), and mostly do not do.

There is a remarkable turn in Ezekiel 34. After this long assertion of what Yahweh will do directly, in vv. 23–24 it is asserted that the Davidic king will do all these things. What is first claimed for Yahweh now is tersely assigned to the human king. The evidence is not at all clear on the view the Ezekiel tradition has of the monarchy.[35] At least in this unit, the text anticipates a recovered monarchy which will indeed do what kings must do, that is, care for the weak and vulnerable and give them a place in the community. The king is to continue to operate with mercy and to participate in the reality of hurt and healing, precisely the reality which is nullified by excessive attention to majesty.

In the world of Israel's royal experience, kings do not characteristically attend to these matters.[36] But the liturgy is relentless
against that sorry historical reality. The liturgy will not yield to
the failure of history. The liturgic tradition of Israel continues
to make such a world of royal caring, a world in which Yahweh as
king and David as shepherd are focused on the reality of pain
and hurt and need. The kings or the projected kings of the world
of Ezekiel are invited to be formed by this liturgy, to be heir,
child, and creature, and not exclusively participant, sponsor, and
benefactor.

The memory of Israel is not romantic about its kings. The memory
knows that Yahweh summons the king to care (Psalm 72). The tradition knows all about kings who work only for self-aggrandizement
(1 Kings 4).[37] The liturgy is not enslaved to that present reality,
however. The liturgy waits and hopes and evokes a king who will
come to embody the mercy and passion of Yahweh (Ezekiel 34).
The liturgy persists in its mediation of Yahweh's rule and in its resilient hope for a humane role on earth. The liturgy enacts the
conviction that the summons of Psalm 72 and the prospect of
Ezekiel 34 are more powerful in the end than the present practice
of 1 Kings 4.

WORLD-MAKING AND ROYAL
LEGITIMACY

We have now established the central tension and dialectic
through which we may make a critical analysis of Israel's praise in
the Jerusalem Temple. Our premise is that praise is in fact world-
making. What kind of praise is practiced goes far to determine
what kind of world Israel will make and live in. We have seen that
Israel's primal act of praise and therefore Israel's proper world are
marked by a revolutionary impetus toward justice, equity, and
righteousness. Israel engages in praise of the God who acts for
justice, equity, and righteousness, and Israel commits itself to the
ordering and maintenance of just such a world. The narrative
recital in the liturgy is for the sake of the social world to which
Yahweh and Israel are committed.

But this world-making praise rarely happens in such purity. It is
almost always and everywhere drawn into a tension which tones
down its radical intent. That tension emerges because:

1. The God of radical mercy intervenes for the slaves and promises justice for them. This God, however, is increasingly presented as a God of majesty not unlike the other imperial gods of the Near East. The dangerous mercy of God lives in tension with the reassuring majesty of God.

2. The king who is to be shaped by this radical liturgy so that he is creature, child, and heir of the memory is not politically disinterested. The liturgy which carries the dream and the vision of Israel, however, also turns out to be a source of legitimacy for the regime. Thus the king is not only child and heir formed by the liturgy, but also benefactor and sponsor who shapes Israel's praise to enhance the royal apparatus. When this happens, Israel's praise is already diverted from its shaping intent.

3. As God is drawn into the tension and as the king lives in the tension, so the liturgy begins to take on an ambiguous function. The liturgy shows that the core claim of Israel is enormously resilient and keeps powerfully reappearing, even though we thought it might be lost.[38] But at the same time, this resilient liturgy is also subject to distortion, in the interest of the benign majesty of God and in the interest of royal legitimacy. Israel's praise is always enacted midst this tension of resilience and distortion. Thus in all these dimensions the liturgical articulation of Israel's memory and Israel's world can be an act of resilience or an act of distortion.

Thus far I have proposed a sociological perspective on the liturgic utilization of the Psalms. While we cannot be precise about such matters, there can be no doubt that something enormously important and problematic for Israel's old liberation memory was lodged·in and taken up by the royal worship. That shift from slave memory to royal stability preserved the Psalms which turned out to be remarkably resilient in their claims, but also open to both subtle and crass distortion.

On the basis of that generally plausible social analysis, I wish now to consider that same movement from slave memory to royal legitimation by way of literary analysis. The literary analysis I will offer is, I believe, congruent with the sociological proposal I have made. I will seek to show that the social transition in the monarchy is matched by important literary adjustments which characteristically tone down the transformative affront of the memory, and give added accent to the stable claims of the hymnic conclusions. The

royal "adjustments" prefer the settled conclusions of the Psalms to
the dangerous remembered route to those conclusions.

The most characteristic way of praise in Israel is the imperative
hymn which lives close to the transformative memory and experience. The imperative hymn characteristically has two parts: a
summons to praise in an imperative, and a *motivation* or *reason*,
introduced by *ki*, which gives the ground for praise. Sometimes the
summons develops into a verdict, summary, or conclusion about
the rule and character of God, but that element is not as predictably present. The imperative hymn is characteristically "sung
down" *from* summons *to* reason, but Israel experiences its life and
faith "up" from reason to praise.

The simplest, cleanest example of "singing down" we may cite is
Psalm 117, which is unencumbered and uncomplicated:[39]

> SUMMONS:
>   Praise the Lord, all nations!
>   extol him, all peoples!
> REASON:
>   *For* great is his steadfast love toward us;
>   and the faithfulness of the Lord endures for ever.
>   Praise the Lord!

The summons consists in two characteristic imperatives: "praise,
extol." The reason is also twofold: his steadfast love is great, his
faithfulness is forever. The nations and the peoples are to praise
and extol Yahweh because God's faithfulness and steadfast love are
constant and reliable. The hymn is completed by a reiteration of
the summons as the last line. Clearly the summons to praise is
because of *hesed* and *'emeth*, "grace and truth." The two parts are
further distinguished by the vocative in the summons and the pronouns in the reason. The vocatives invite "all nations" and "all
peoples" to praise. The praise of Yahweh should be universal and
all peoples should join. The reason, however, is *hesed*, "for us" —
presumably Israel. The nations are invited to praise because of
what Israel knows and has experienced about *hesed* and *'emeth*.
The "world" for all the nations is grounded only in the experience
of Israel. The world for all arises from the experience of some. The
world arising out of Israel's experience is dramatically imposed on
the nations.

This world of Yahweh's sovereign rule and the ready obedience
of the nations is rooted in, grows out of, and relies upon Israel's

assertion of *ḥesed* and *'emeth*. The Yahweh acknowledged by the nations is a Yahweh characterized by *ḥesed* and *'emeth*. That is the only God celebrated in this liturgy. The nations are to live in the world known and confessed by Israel, presumably on the basis of Israel's testimony about God's *ḥesed* and *'emeth*. Insofar as this or any doxology is an act of enthroning, acknowledging as sovereign, the nations are to join the hymn which in fact "makes" Yahweh sovereign.[40] The allegiance of the nations subscribes to (and enhances) the reliability, dominance, and legitimacy of this particular world which is known primarily, or even exclusively in Israel's experience of *ḥesed* and *'emeth*. And as this particular world is legitimated, other worlds are implicitly nullified, and that by the very action of the nations.

In each of the three literatures of praise we examined in the second chapter, we can see Israel "singing down" from summons to reason. This dynamic is definitional and constitutive for Israel's way of praise. In the Song of Miriam (Exod. 15:21), the song moves down from summons to reason:

> Sing to the Lord,
> for he has triumphed gloriously.

The ones summoned to sing must accept the testimony given in the reason, even if they were not present for the "glorious triumph." In Psalm 96 the summons is passionate:

> Sing to the Lord . . .
> sing to the Lord, all the earth!
> sing to the Lord,
> bless his name;
> tell of his salvation . . .
> declare his glory.

But the reason is weak and nearly muted:

> For great is the Lord, and greatly to be praised . . .
> for all the gods of the peoples are idols.

All the earth is summoned to join this world of Yahweh's sovereignty, but the reasons are not very powerful or explicit. And in Isa. 42:1–12 all creation is summoned to this world of Yahweh's sovereignty. But the reason in v. 13 is an appeal to the language and metaphors of the Exodus. Again the sweeping invitation to a new world is based in a more exclusively Israelite grounding.

"SINGING DOWN" AND "SINGING UP"

As noted, the Psalms are "sung down" from summons to reason. But they are "experienced up" from reason to summons. It is this relation between "singing down" and "experiencing up" that is at the center of our argument about doxology and its ideological uses. I suggest a correlation between the way Israel forms the world and the way Israel understands its psalms. At the beginning of this chapter I contrasted liturgy which wells up and liturgy which is imposed. I suggest that liturgy which "wells up" out of experience is matched by psalms that are "sung up." Conversely, liturgy which is imposed corresponds to psalms that are "read down." Liturgies and psalms which well up are "from below," whereas liturgies which are imposed and psalms which are sung down are "from above."

The summons "sing to Yahweh" states the large liturgic claim that Yahweh is to be praised and thereby enthroned. The reason, however, gives the specificity of experience and memory upon which everything rests and which gives credibility to the summons. *The credibility of the summons depends on the authenticity of the reason.* If one says to the nations, "Praise Yahweh," and the nations ask "Why should we praise Yahweh? Why should we act in allegiance to Yahweh? Why should we accept the sovereign rule of Yahweh?" Israel must be prepared to answer concretely out of its experience and memory: "because (*kî*) . . ." Israel must give a reason out of its direct experience. Everything depends on this.

When Miriam was seeking recruits for Yahweh's freedom movement and the fearful slaves asked "why?" Miriam answered, "Because Yahweh has thrown the horse and the rider into the sea." When Second Isaiah was seeking volunteers for homecoming, and some yearned to go but feared the empire more, they asked, "Why should we risk freedom against the empire?" The poet answered, "Because Yahweh goes forth like a mighty man of war." The two reasons of Miriam and Second Isaiah are closely paralleled. One can identify some stylization resulting from poetic constraints. But the picture of a warrior holding Pharaoh under water until dead cannot be any more concrete. Or the claim that Yahweh is coming boisterously and shouting against the empire cannot be expressed any more vividly or concretely. The powerful, disruptive coming of Yahweh is the reason for the summons. That is why the nations should praise, why the slaves should leave, why the exiles should head home. The summons by itself does not compel. It is the reason that compels. If the reason is persuasive, others will join the song and subscribe to the new world of order, justice, truth, equity, righteousness, freedom, and homecoming.

The reason, however, must be specific, growing out of what is seen, heard, known, experienced. In Psalm 117 (which we have taken as the simplest case of Israel's hymnic praise) the reason given, that Yahweh's *hesed* is great and his *'emeth* is reliable, lacks specificity. That formulation is already a stylized summary, whose link to concrete experience is difficult to locate. It is not as specific as the statement of Miriam or Second Isaiah. We do not know how to "experience this psalm up" from reason to summons because we are given no specific clues to its experiential foundation.

In order to grasp fully the claim of Psalm 117, we must move below the stylized formulation of *hesed* and *'emeth* to find out about the actual experiences out of which this conviction of *hesed* and *'emeth* derives. We must move below what is "sponsored" to what experience "wells up." What is the concrete experience that permits Israel to affirm that Yahweh's *hesed* is great and Yahweh's *'emeth* endures? In order to create and sustain the world in which Israel is called to live, the reasons for praise must move below the grand claims to Israel's transformative memory. In order to ground a summons convincingly, the reasons, whether as vivid as that of Miriam or as programmatic as in Psalm 117, must be quite specific and bear witness to God's transformative power in the midst of human need, pain, deficiency, or vulnerability.

If we ask about the specificity of *hesed* and *'emeth* out of which the summons is issued and the world is made, we may look in two directions in Israel's literature. First, Frank Crüsemann suggests that the imperative hymn revolves around a recital of the saving deeds.[41] The ground for the world of the imperatives is found in the credo recital of mighty deeds.[42] Psalm 136 provides the fullest evidence for the concrete, specific, nameable content of *hesed* and *'emeth*. That psalm is a recital of Yahweh's faithful actions, including Israel's normative transformative memory as well as a lyrical confession about creation (vv. 4–9), in which

each specific line states a transformation wrought by Yahweh.[43]
After each such memory, Israel summarizes and stylizes and
theologizes,

>   for *(kî)* his *ḥesed* endures forever.

We read *kî* not as "because," but as "surely." The specifics of
Yahweh's actions lead to the conclusion and conviction that God is
surely faithful and loyal. But that conclusion of loyalty and fidelity
depends on Israel knowing, naming, and embracing the concrete
occasions and the specific ways in which that faithfulness has been
present in Israel. Crüsemann is surely correct in saying that
the psalm form is based in recital. Behind the stylized recital is the
experience of transformation which is discerned to be a victory
wrought by God over the power of chaos, injustice, death. Concrete experiences become concrete memories.

It is the process whereby experiences-become-memories that
warrants the praise and summons the nations to subscribe to this
world. This world is based in the *ḥesed* and *ʾemeth* of Yahweh, but
the claim of *ḥesed* and *ʾemeth* is rooted deeper in daily, nameable
transformations. The great victories of which Mowinckel writes,
of which the temple ritual is built, which the gods in heaven
celebrate at New Year, are in fact concrete, nameable transformations known in this community as the breaking in of the new
world.

The second area in which to look for such "reasons" is in the
personal songs of thanksgiving, which reflect the concrete experiences of individual persons.[44] To my mind, these cut theologically
underneath even the great public recitals and are religiously and
experientially more elemental. Several generations of scholars, under the impetus of von Rad and G. E. Wright, have reflected on
the mighty deeds of Yahweh in the life of Israel.[45] The enormous
gain of that scholarship is not to be minimized. One can see the
power of such public recitals of public events as they are continued in the great creeds of the church, which retell the history of
the Trinitarian God.

Every pastor knows, however, that the most powerful, shaping,
and credible "mighty deeds" are those in the spheres of intimacy
in the domestic household, where we do our birthing and dying,
our loving and hating, our fearing and hoping.[46] To these intimate
transformations the great temple liturgies of the king scarcely

have access. These more immediate recitals tell of concrete complaints made to God,[47] the praises of needy, unnamed citizens who have no recourse but to "take it to the Lord in prayer." These are those who have no access to the temple, to the priest, to the king, to the doctor, to the hospital, to the courts. The story of the person in family, in tribe, in village is not to be romanticized as rustic or idyllic, but more likely as a scene of social marginality and a deep sense of helplessness. The calendar runs not from great victories or coronations, but in "the year the twins were born," or "the time grandmother died," or "the day the well ran dry," or "the moment the cancer became unavoidable." There has been a series of good gifts we cannot explain but for which we are grateful. There has been a series of hurts and fears in which we cried out, and we, strangely, were answered.[48]

The religious dimension of these experiences is voiced this way (Ps. 73:25):

> Whom have I in heaven but thee?
> And there is nothing upon earth that I desire besides thee.

The powerful transformative experience in the midst of hurt permits the claim that Yahweh is faithful, that God's *hesed* is great, that God's *'emeth* is enduring. Confidence in God's *hesed* and *'emeth* comes in powerful attestations that laments are answered, that hurts are healed, and that life emerges in the midst of death.[49] For those to whom such transformations have happened, the experience is overpowering in its authority. The transformation compels Israel to receive a new world. The experience itself is utterly convincing for those to whom it has happened. This is the power of the *reason* in a hymn. But in the *summons*, Israel invites others to accept the truth of this new world of Yahweh's governance where the same transformations can be trusted in and are wrought by Yahweh. The nations are invited to share in a world credited by Israel's daily experience.

That new world of Yahweh's sovereignty worked through *hesed* and *'emeth* is rendered in song derived from the experience. Psalm 30 is an example which is a summons to join in the new world of praise and trust:

Ps 30

> I will extol thee.

Then the song moves to the long and convincing reason (vv. 1–3):

for thou hast drawn me up,
    thou hast not let my foes rejoice over me,
    thou hast healed me,
    thou hast brought up my life from Sheol,
    thou hast restored me to life from among those gone down to
       the Pit.

The psalm ends with praise and thanks (v.11):

Thou hast turned for me my mourning into dancing;
    thou hast loosed my sackcloth,
    thou hast girded me with gladness.

The verbs are specific, the address is direct. The speaker claims the transformation for his or her own immediate experience. The transformation cannot be doubted or disputed. Nor can the agent of transformation be doubted. That worker of newness must be trusted, obeyed, and praised.

Psalm 40 also sings of the concrete transformation wrought by Yahweh out of the midst of intimate despair. The psalm begins abruptly with no formula of introduction (vv. 1–3):

I waited patiently for the Lord;
    he inclined to me
    and heard my cry.
He drew me up from the desolate pit,
    out of the miry bog,
and set my feet upon a rock . . .
He put a new song in my mouth . . .

In vv. 9–10, we are given a jubilant, reflective response to this action of Yahweh:

I have told the glad news (*basar*) of deliverance
    in the great congregation;
lo, I have not restrained my lips . . .
I have not hid thy saving help (*ṣidqôth*) within my heart,
I have spoken of thy faithfulness (*'amûnah*)
    and thy salvation;
I have not concealed thy steadfast love (*ḥesed*)
    and thy faithfulness (*'emeth*) from the great congregation.

Notice that the psalm begins in a recital of the most elemental actions of Yahweh in transforming life. The verbs are not unlike those of the great recital of the events of the exodus—God inclined, heard, drew up.

Psalm 40 is of peculiar interest because it contains our focal word *basar* ("gospel," v. 9). The gospel is the news that life has been transformed in the most immediate way. Psalm 40 also contains the key term "saving help" (*ṣidqôth,* v. 10) which has the substance of *ḥesed* and *'emeth.* The most elemental form of the gospel is to tell the concrete story of the time when distress was resolved. That is news. That indeed is the only news that counts. The substance of the news is precisely "saving help," the making right of that which has been distorted. That making right is the substance of "faithfulness (*'emeth*) and steadfastness (*ḥesed*)." Saving help is God's powerful response to a situation of voiced need. God's specific transformative act is the most elemental substance of biblical faith. The recital of such concreteness is the main clue to evangelism. The celebrative announcement of God's new, visible rule is the normative valid ground for praise. This recital, first of all in individual songs of thanksgiving and then in the public credos of Israel, is the narrative of God's powerful transformation which happens concretely if it happens at all. This concreteness characterizes all primal praise and legitimates all convincing worlds.

The summary reason of Psalm 117,

> Great is his steadfast love toward us;
> and the faithfulness of the Lord endures for ever,

is based in the specificity of Psalms 30 and 40 and their kind. Without such specificity, Psalm 117 becomes an empty formula for a litany that has no vitality. The powerful *reason* drives Israel to issue the *summons* to others, to the nations, and the summons has credibility among the nations only because of the reason. The poem of faith is formed in our experience up from specificity. We move from (a) "He drew me up from the desolate pit" (Ps. 40:2), to (b) "Great is his steadfast love toward us" (Ps. 117:2), to (c) "Praise the Lord" (Ps. 117:1), to (d) "The Lord reigns" (Ps. 97:1). Or to collapse the sequence and streamline it, we move from "He drew me up" to "Yahweh is king." That Yahweh is king is based only on the validity of the affirmation that "he drew me up."

The world of Yahweh's *ḥesed* and *'emeth* to which the nations are invited is made up of little news items which cannot be doubted because they are identifiable experiences before they become stylized memories. Spoken by firsthand witnesses, these unexpected transformations could not be invented because they violate reason and because, if invented, no one would trust them enough to repeat them. They are the inexplicable turns, gifts, and newnesses that cannot be argued about, but only narrated. This whole evangelical world depends on them and on nothing other than these passionately narrated news items.

My argument is that in the "reasons" the hymn lives closest to the real ground and substance of praise. Everything placed on top of that, such as summons or verdict, is a move away from that ground and substance. Israel's most powerful praise lives closest to the reality of God's inbreaking actions.

But hymns have as their social function the making of worlds. Therefore the hymn of praise must always move from the reason to the summons which is the call to a new world. The king who is creature, child, and heir of this transformative memory begins to think about legitimation and so becomes participant, sponsor, and benefactor. When the king begins to think in that new way, the reasons begin to thin out and the summons to the royal world grows stronger. Israel's tenacity for the memory of God is displaced by a notion of majesty that is somewhat removed from Israel's hurt and hope. The concrete memory becomes something of an embarrassment and the praise is tilted toward the grand imperial vision. The memory is to yield a new world, but the world of royal liturgy wants to be at a distance from the memory. And when the distance is great enough and maintained long enough, a fully ordered world emerges, but one without passion, without possibility, and without humaneness.

For those of us who are baptized into a Christian history of praise, we know that the singing of Israel leads finally to Jesus and to the specificity of his ministry.[50] When we move from ancient Israel to Jesus, we still struggle to honor the specificity which is so embarrassing. John, asking for the entire community, wanted to know if Jesus is the one who is to come (Luke 7:18–23). John seems to want a general, certain messianic assurance. But the answer Jesus gives is characteristically a recital of concrete transformations given in narrative specificity (v. 22):

> Go and tell John what you have seen and heard:
>   the blind receive their sight,
>   the lame walk,
>   lepers are cleansed, . . .

the deaf hear,
the dead are raised up,
the poor have good news preached to them.

Jesus' response keeps Christology very close to concrete transformation. Out of that concreteness comes the world over which Jesus is king. Out of such a reason, the nations are called to praise and trust!

A WORLD SUNG AS RAW, PRIMITIVE, REVOLUTIONARY

We cannot overstress the primal character of the foundation of Israel's faith and doxology. The experience of transformation in its earliest, most primitive articulation is not a reasoned description, but a doxological affirmation driven by amazement and gratitude. Israel did not think twice, first about the experience and then about the articulation; Israel only thought once, and its thought is primarily doxological.

This mode of thought, speech, and faith is raw in its power, primitive in its epistemology, revolutionary in its world-making. It is raw in its power because it dares to discern the power of eternal holiness in the moment of hurt needing to be healed. The naiveté of such faith did not reflect on transcendence and imminence, on *homoousia* ("of like substance"). It knew intuitively and trustingly that the One who heals is the One who reigns over all.

It is primitive in its epistemology because it seeks no secondary causes. It does not believe in miracle as violation of natural law. It is not so fixed on conventional order that it finds the gift of life to be an aberration. It is not so educated that it must explain or justify. It is as innocent and credulous as the boy in John 9:25 who can say, "One thing I know, that though I was blind, now I see." Or the father in the story which is equally primitive in its epistemology, "This my son was dead, and is alive again; he was lost, and is found" (Luke 15:24). The experience of transformation is not cause for argument or proof, but for making news, for making worlds, for making praise.

This mode of faith is revolutionary in its world-making because it names and tells of this God who is no respecter of persons or forms or structures or institutions or traditions. It is a tale of unexpected transformation. The move upstairs from reason to summons is a proposal to make and embrace a world that is filled with raw power that we cannot administer. This world is unembarrassed that its governance lies out beyond our knowledge, our certitude, our morality, our social power. Its attraction is that we have discovered that our knowledge, certitude, morality, and social power cannot generate life. Its danger is that we are not sure we want the power of life turned loose when we cannot administer it.

This raw faith is not disordered and structureless. It does propose an order. It is an order of transformation and transfiguration. The summons of this doxology is an invitation to inversion, to abandon the world where these transformations do not happen. We sing and make worlds of the former dead who now live, of the former blind who now see, of the former poor who now rejoice. The nations are invited to this new world knowing that these strange transformations will continue to happen. We shall all discover that we are among the "former ones" but we shall not be "former" any longer, because the *ḥesed* and *ʾemeth* endure forever and will finally prevail. The nations are invited to a new world with a public ethic rooted in and normed by the tales of nameless peasants, widows, and orphans. It is enough to make trees sing and fields clap and floods rejoice and barren women laugh and liberated slaves dance and angels sing. The new tales based in the credibility of concreteness lead to a different world.

There are places among the nations where this raw power of life is not spoken of, where this epistemology is too embarrassing, where the revolutionary world of Yahweh is too dangerous. In that world, such stories are not permitted, such turns are not experienced, such news is not entertained. It is a world in which this kind of doxology is neither possible (because no one feels like it) or permitted (because the authorities prohibit). That world is a world of second thought, of distance between experience and articulation, a world of explanation and order which permits, notices, or acknowledges no transformative breaks. The yearnings are not voiced, because the possibilities are not trusted in.[51]

Nations and kings and empires are asked to take the word of peasants that there is another world of powerful, life-giving transformations now available. The nations are invited to join the new world wrought out of these tales of transformative experience. It takes no great insight to see that some can keep the present world tame by stopping the tales. The question for Israel's own kings, for those who sponsor the liturgy is this: Will the king be open to the resilience and power of this new, raw world, or will the king suppress its revolutionary power and invite the people instead to tame but distorted lives? Will Yahweh reign, authentically and freely, or will Yahweh reign, administered and controlled? These are Israel's questions, these are our questions.

4

Doxology without Reason: The Loss of Israel's World of Hope

❧ ———————————— ❧

The liturgy moves. In the memory of Israel, the liturgy first happened in Miriam's dance on the edge of the waters of freedom (Exod. 15:21). It occurred by the waters of the Babylonian canals (Isa. 40:9–11; 52:7). It occurs where the hopeless ones are re-created to new life. It happens in nameless places and cases. Those who are re-created will characteristically sing. Because the liturgy of this "news" is so powerful and compelling, the liturgy is moved into the temple and enacted with a fresh authority. The song first sung at the edge of freedom and new life is now sung in the capital city. Now the song is taken over from the women and sung by the king's choristers (who surely are not women).[1] This move from the edge of freedom to the temple is a necessary move, for it permits the tales of transformation to become visible and solidified as "world"—royal world, visible world, ordered world, safe world, new world. This move guarantees continuity for the news of Israel's memory. The move ensures that the liturgy will not be lost. The liturgy and the temple in which it is enacted are now a liturgy and a house befitting an abiding king, an abiding God, an abiding life-world.[2]

As we have seen, when the peasant tales move into the temple to provide continuity, they also move into the hands of the king. The king is participant, sponsor, benefactor, as well as creature of the liturgy. The king either participates in the liturgy or observes it approvingly. Either way, it is now a liturgy that is confiscated for

royal uses. The king notices and celebrates the power of Yahweh
for which he is regent. The king is glad for the powerful sanctions
given by the liturgy. The king also notices, however, that this
power in the liturgy is marked by rawness, abrasive epistemology,
and revolutionary implications for an order characterized by con-
tinual transformation.

When the liturgy moves from the experience of the peasants to
the sponsorship of the king, a new dimension is added. The king
also has to translate this *tale-become-liturgy* into *public policy*.
That translation of tale into policy is both difficult and dangerous,
for the tale will scarcely sit still long enough to become policy.
Whatever policy the king devises, the tale keeps coming up "from
below" through the liturgy to probe, shatter, and delegitimate.
The tale is so open, free, and unrestrained in its surging, subversive power that it will scarcely allow a policy, at least not the kind
the king prefers. The song stays so close to pain, so in touch with
death, so poignant on the tongues of the transformed, so con-
vinced of impossibilities now become possibilities, that it is un-
bearably impatient. The tale-become-liturgy insists on translation
into policy, but at the same time it continually jeopardizes the
established public policy of the king "from below." The liturgy
cannot be locked away in the temple, the key held by the king, for
there is an inalienable restlessness to this memory. Israel's transformative liturgy must dance and cry.[3] The king wants to take the
tale-become-liturgy seriously, but he is faced with a deep
dilemma. Will he allow the liturgy its full voice, thus perhaps
jeopardizing his very empire, or will he allow the empire its full
voice, thus perhaps jeopardizing the very "world" mediated in the
liturgy? Clearly the king cannot have it both ways, but either
choice is exceedingly costly.

WHEN SUMMONS PREEMPTS REASON

My thesis here is this: the claims of royal theology want to have
the "world" of Yahweh's kingship, but without the transformative
tales that are at the same time energizing and troublesome. The
world of Yahweh can be administered as an orderly world of humanness, but the tales and their concreteness are troublesome because they characteristically call into question every administered
arrangement. There is always a new voice below in the liturgy that

wants to question, challenge, and transform what has been settled. Therefore there is a tendency in the royal utilization of the doxology to tone down the raw power, the primitive epistemology, and the revolutionary impetus of the voice from below. This is done by shifting the weight away from the *reason* to the *summons,* or away from the *authenticating experience* to the *authenticated world.* It is as though the king convenes the temple guilds and choirmasters and issues a general mandate to recast the move up from "reason" to "summons" in ways that will permit the tale to become reliable policy.[4] The end result is a legitimate world, but without the validating experience or the concrete memory of why *this* world is legitimate rather than some other, or why *this* king is authorized rather than some other. The reasons for this authorized world tend not to be given, or the reasons given are not as passionate as the primal ones. Eventually we arrive at a "world" which does not emerge out of concrete transformation, but as an absolute. It must be accepted now not because of passionate witnesses, but on the basis of self-proclaimed legitimacy. In the end, the royal world is an absolute arrangement, out of touch with its evoking memory. Those who hold power are disposed to thrive on the conclusions without the narrative underpinning that gives the conclusions credibility.

Here I want to consider the social function of praise in the liturgy of the Jerusalem Temple. That liturgy must be understood in its social function, if it is to be understood at all. I have already considered the general act of world-making (chap. 1) and the specific world-making of Israel's characteristic and primal faith (chap. 2). But now I want to ask, What were the needs, interests, and hopes (and therefore world-proposal) of those who gathered regularly in the Jerusalem Temple? While they obviously employed and appealed to Israel's old memory, they clearly had very different needs, interests, and hopes from those who formed the old memory. In their liturgy, therefore, they proposed a very different world. I shall argue that their different needs, interests, and hopes caused an important recharacterization of God and an important redescription of the world as a social system. I shall contend that the God and the social system of this proposed royal world stand a considerable and unfortunate distance from Israel's primal memory.

In my analysis I will be working primarily with the Psalms as the central residue from that liturgy, and more specifically with the hymnic structure of summons and reason. When the "summons" grows more powerful as a summons of the king to his world, and when reason is reduced or made weaker because it is an embarrassment or a threat, we do not actively participate in world-making as did Miriam and her sisters, but only receive a world always made. We no longer have access to the process of pain and rescue from whence the new world comes. The royal world is just there, always there, "world without end." And if it is always there, it is the only one that could possibly be there, and one has no option but to embrace it.

Psalm 150

We can identify three ways in which such a shift from experience to world, from reason to summons, is accomplished. The first way is to minimize the extent of the "reason" and to extend the words of the "summons." Psalm 150 is an extreme example of this move. This psalm is all summons and no reason. It may be, as Patrick D. Miller asserts, that this lack of reason is because Psalm 150 is the last psalm in the hymnal and the reasons have all been given heretofore.[5] My more suspicious reading, however, suggests that this psalm has pushed the emphasis upstairs. The world offered is absolute, presided over by an absolute God who has no history, no past, no future, no history of transformation.

No reason is given for praise. No reason is given for the world over which Yahweh rules and in which Yahweh is to be praised:

> Praise the Lord!
> Praise God in his sanctuary;
>   praise him in his mighty firmament!
> Praise him for his mighty deeds;
>   praise him according to his exceeding greatness!
> Praise him with trumpet sound;
>   praise him with lute and harp!
> Praise him with timbrel and dance;
>   praise him with strings and pipe!
> Praise him with sounding cymbals;
>   praise him with loud clashing cymbals!
> Let everything that breathes praise the Lord!
> Praise the Lord!

This psalm assumes that everybody will praise, and no one will ask why. And if one asks why praise, the imperatives are recited again with nonnegotiable authority and without reason. The God

offered here with the accompanying "world" is absolute, without
memory, without experience, without cause, simply a given that
must be received and enacted. The world of doxology is solidly in
place, but the odd, embarrassing, revolutionary grounding for
such a world has been eliminated.

Psalm 146   *B wordbrook*

Psalm 150 may be contrasted with Psalm 146 that is dominated
by reason with only a lean summons. Verse 1 offers a simple paral-
lelism inviting to praise which is seconded in v. 2 by the responsive assertion, "I will praise the Lord as long as I live." Then, after
a negative sapiential warning in vv. 3–4, the reasons are given in
vv. 5–7a concerning the God

> who made heaven and earth,
>   the sea, and all that is in them;
> who keeps faith for ever;
>   who executes justice for the oppressed;
>   who gives food to the hungry.

In vv. 7b–9, the rhetoric changes slightly to name Yahweh repeatedly, but the continued poetry offers even more reason for praise:

> The Lord sets the prisoners free;
>   the Lord opens the eyes of the blind.
> The Lord lifts up those who are bowed down;
>   the Lord loves the righteous.
> The Lord watches over the sojourners,
>   he upholds the widow and the fatherless.

The basis for praise of Yahweh is clear and unarguable. Anybody
who knows this story will no doubt join the praise.

When we compare Psalms 146 and 150, we see that the more
powerful doxologies are those which "overflow" with telling and
telling, and telling again the concrete ways in which Yahweh has
transformed life.[6] These concrete ways, when "read up," lead to
the simple invitation to praise, an invitation which need only be
issued, because the specific evidence is itself so compelling. No
great rhetoric of persuasion is needed when the memory itself
persuades. Such a raw, embarrassing, revolutionary statement
lives happily and trustfully in the still-available memory and experience of transformation. The summons may be very lean because
it knows and is confident that the listener will want to join "the

world of doxology" because the memory and experience are so compelling.

Psalm 148

Psalm 146 is filled with the vitality of reason.[7] Psalm 150 lacks all such vitality. On the way typologically from 146 to 150 we may observe Psalm 148 which is largely summons, though the reason has not been fully eliminated. It contains much more reason than Psalm 150, but the reason is much more subdued than in Psalm 146. The reason is still present in vv. 5b–6 and in 13b–14:

> For he commanded and they were created.
> And he established them for ever and ever;
> > he fixed their bounds which cannot be passed . . .
> > for his name alone is exalted;
> > his glory is above the earth and heaven.
> He has raised up a horn for his people . . .
> > for the people of Israel who are near to him.

The psalm is basically a set of imperatives mobilizing all of creation to affirm, praise, and legitimate. The reasons are compelling, but they are nearly smothered beneath the succession of imperatives.

The loss of reason and the preoccupation with summons reflect a shift in theological sensitivity that begins to cut off the worshiping community from its own experience. Israel's song becomes generalized. The doxology begins to get free of the awkwardness of imagining there is a God who causes concrete transformations in the real world of hurt, pain, and unrighteousness. In Psalm 146, there are still powerful and vivid memories of oppressed, hungry, prisoners, blind, bowed down, sojourners, widows, fatherless. They are still a recognized part of social reality. The very mention of them is an act of social realism and social criticism. Marginal people really do exist. Moreover, the psalm offers a substantive, critical portrayal of God. In this psalm God is not a bland cipher who takes no sides and makes no difference. That might be the God preferred in the royal liturgy. But Yahweh is here one who attends to, notices, and intervenes on behalf of the powerless and marginal. This is a God who acts decisively against the status quo in order to create new social possibility. Every singing of these "reasons" is a reenactment of the reality of this world which includes marginality. And it is a reassertion of this God with a particular inclination toward them. Every singing reasserts this special, dangerous world and its particular, passionate ruler.

Psalm 146 has the intent and effect of bringing Israel very close to the reality of painful social experience and of keeping God committed to the same social experience, so that new social possibilities are imaginable. Indeed, it is this connection of God to the reality of hurt that is the ground of doxological experience. Israel is to praise Yahweh because the reality of human hurt and the reality of Yahweh's attentiveness converge in the faith and life of Israel. Insofar as the summons enacts a "world," the world made by this doxology is a world of social hurt, social possibility, and social transformation. Each named transformation creates hope and possibility for those in parallel circumstance, and each bespeaks a criticism of the established world which had generated the oppressed, hungry, prisoners, and blind.[8] Insofar as the world has marginal, hurting people in it, it is clear in this psalm that Yahweh does not disregard them.

In Psalm 148, the weight has shifted from ground to summons. Now the singing congregation is not revisiting the world of memory and experience as much, a world we have seen occupied by the marginal. The singing serves instead to order a world by summons, so that all gather around the glorious throne. All—heights, angel host, sun, moon, stars, heaven, waters, earth, sea monsters, fire and hail, snow, frost, wind, mountains, hills, trees, cedars, beasts, cattle, creeping things, birds, kings, princes, rulers, young men, maidens, old men, children—join the happy song. Everybody!

Why? Because God has created, established, fixed the boundaries (vv. 5b–6). Because God has raised up a horn for his people (v. 14).[9] That is all. There is nothing here of oppressed people, of the hungry, blind, bowed down, widows, or orphans. One can of course claim that these people are all effectively cared for by "the horn" whose business it is to right such wrongs (cf. Psalm 72). That is what a king is to do. But I submit that reading is too easy. The very language of the doxology directs Israel's attention (and we may believe the attention of the king) away from the human world of hurt, need, and injustice to the safe, ordered world of happy royal well-being. The community that sings this doxology has no memory of another time, but only a focus on the way the world seems always to have been. A community which sings only such songs will after a while not remember its own former pain, will not notice the reality of pain in the world around, and will not connect God with such pain. Such a community will end without hope or expectation, but only with complacency. The praise of God has been emptied of its passion. The majesty of God has been cut off from the power of mercy. The world of God has been clearly separated from the world of serious concrete human experience and observation. The hymn makes it possible not to notice. Over time, the hymn shapes the horizon and purview of those who sing.

WHEN CONCRETENESS IS GENERALIZED

A second way in which *vitality* of the psalm is traded for *solidity* is to move from *declarative* to *descriptive* language, a move observed with great sensitivity by Claus Westermann.[10] By "declarative" Westermann refers to a recital with a finite verb of what God does, of a specific time and place when God acted to change the world. By "descriptive," Westermann means a recital with a participle in which God's characteristic actions are recited, but without meaning a particular time and place, or even suggesting there might have been a time and place.

The declarative statements are more immediately linked to a concrete memory and experience. As I have indicated, such concrete memories and experiences will be located in Israel's great recitals of mighty deeds and in the intimate retelling of thanksgiving songs. For the former, we may mention Psalm 136, a recital built of finite verbs concerning creation ("made, spread, made," vv. 5–7), and exodus ("smite, brought out, divided, made to pass, overthrow, led, slew, gave," vv. 10–22). These verbs are not, in the first instance, paradigmatic. They are not archetypes, but they are locatable, identifiable moments in the life-experience of Israel, the raw data out of which Israel is prepared to construct and live in a world where such transformations have happened and will happen. To be sure, these events become paradigmatic, but they are not authoritative and energizing models unless they have experiential rootage and Israel can say when and where and to whom these great deeds were done.

In parallel fashion and more intimately, the songs of thanksgiving sing of concrete rescue.[11] Psalm 138 is an example. There is a generalized reference to steadfast love and faithfulness (as in Psalm 136), but it is rooted quite concretely (vv. 3, 7):

> On the day I called, thou didst answer me,
>   my strength of soul thou didst increase . . .
> thou dost preserve my life;
>   thou dost stretch out thy hand . . .

The speaker knows when and where, on which day.

In Psalm 107, we can see a tendency to generalize from concrete experience to less specificity.[12] The subject is "some" (vv. 4, 17, 23),[13] but at the center of each unit is the confession, "they cried . . . Yahweh delivered" (vv. 6, 13, 19, 28). These verbs are finite. Reference is made to an actual crying and an actual delivery. One has the impression that the congregation can still name the ones who cried and the time in which they have been delivered.

But such a memory is so awkward. It is awkward in a temple liturgy to deal with such specificity which seems increasingly remote. The temple is where we enact the claims of state and the reasons of state. It is so awkward to bother with specificity of certain people in crisis. It is not only awkward, but such references in fact detract from the main point. If the main point is the national cause, the reliability of the monarchy, the national budget, the imperial program, to stop to make references to such specificity simply defuses the energy and weakens the focus. President Ronald Reagan, for example, in a gesture characteristic of those who preside over great national liturgies, dared to assert in response to questions about the national budget that the real news (*basar?*) is state policy. Conversely, it is not news when one person from South Succotash is unemployed.[14] Such specificity rubs abrasively against the grand claims of the generalized liturgy. The declarative hymns continued to assert that the need and deliverance of one such needful person was news, but for reasons of state, such local, concrete news was dropped out of the great doxologies. As such detailed news dropped out of the royal liturgy, it also dropped out of the royal world of those who sing the doxologies. The loss of such specificity enhanced the royal-temple monopoly on "news."

It is an intellectual embarrassment midst the grand claims of the state to use finite verbs of specificity in dealing with God's transformations. The urban liturgy of Jerusalem does not mind speaking of God's transformative deeds in a general way. But it would be presumptuous and embarrassing to bring the grand claim down to the concreteness of this or that action. The "unenlightened" tend

to speak in such primitive ways about God's transformative inter-
ventions. They dare to make the assertive claim: "Thou didst answer, thou didst increase strength, thou dost preserve my life,
thou dost stretch out thy hand." But from the perspective of the
Jerusalem Enlightenment, such talk is primitive and excessively
anthropomorphic. With the coming of a new rationality that celebrated human wisdom and human capacity, the claims of holiness
needed to be more subdued.[15] As human capacity and reasonableness displaced the threat and possibility of holy intervention, the
liturgy had to change. It backed away from the concreteness.

Because such primitive, concrete praise is politically awkward,
liturgically offensive, and intellectually embarrassing the praises
of Israel have been generalized and move to description. It is not
that we do not believe the primal claims, but they ought to be
better expressed, "better" as in participles, not specific but general, not concrete but stereotyped. This is what God always and
everywhere does, always and everywhere so that this world of
praise is to be received as the real one (Ps. 145:13b–19):

> The Lord is faithful in all his words,
>   and gracious in all his deeds.
> The Lord upholds all who are falling,
>   and raises up all who are bowed down.
> The eyes of all look to thee,
>   and thou givest them their food in due season.
> Thou openest thy hand,
>   thou satisfiest the desire of every living thing.
> The Lord is just in all his ways,
>   and kind in all his doings.
> The Lord is near to all who call upon him,
>   to all who call upon him in truth.
> He fulfils the desire of all who fear him,
>   he also hears their cry, and saves them.

The psalm is powerful and makes sweeping claims. But notice
that it lacks all specificity, every reference to a time, a place, an
identifiable subject. It is my judgment that all such sweeping
claims lack the power of one named, specific transformation.

It may be that we are too hard on Israel's hymnic rhetoric. Perhaps Westermann has made too much of this particular distinction
of finite verb and participle. The change to descriptive language
may be only a convenience and a convention. It may be only a way of
speaking. But since words make worlds, since language leads to

reality, the trade-off is not inconsequential, however it may have been intended. Or perhaps we must say of our own situation that the concrete language is too primitive, because we know about secondary causes and we know God does not uphold widows or deliver shipwrecked people. Such elemental language will not work liturgically and we must use language that is not so unsophisticated, language which does not ask us to violate our philosophical presuppositions and our scientific discernments. That, I assume, is the same argument made by the intellectually sophisticated in ancient Israel.[16] The shift from declarative to descriptive, however, is not so much a comment on the problem of language as it is a comment on us. We find concrete declarative language too costly for our epistemology, our economics, and our sense of having shaped and defined the world in our terms, which are terms of control.

Participial liturgy may be more congenial to us, but it is not likely to rescue us from the deceptive myth of self-sufficiency. Thus perhaps our proper critical work is to see what happens to us intellectually, emotionally, economically, if we make faithful use of finite verbs, either to discover that there really are concrete transformative references we can trust in our experience and memories, or to discover that we mouth the generalities but doubt the actual claims. We would either find new language to lead us to new faith, or we would have fresh awareness of our loss of language and commensurate loss of faith. The propensity for distanced participles is not a new practice in the late twentieth century. There no doubt were those in the Jerusalem Temple in the tenth century B.C.E. who had the same preference, and there are those in twentieth-century Richmond who do not fear finite, confessing verbs. The participles are not a fate of our late, technological state, but are a function of our self-serving sense of sufficiency and control that acts linguistically to eliminate this One who transforms and who makes things new, we know not how. The problematic of such language is not tied to modernity, but to intellectual and economic self-sufficiency in any context.

Perhaps it is the attraction of participial generalities that leads to loss of concrete reasons in the hymns. If the reason is only vague and general, lacking in concreteness, it may as well be dropped. Psalm 149 is a most telling example of what happens in this awkwardness. Verses 1–3 are an elaborate summons which is continued in vv. 5–6a. The only reason is given in v. 4, expressed with a participle:[17]

> For the Lord takes pleasure in his people,
> he adorns the humble with victory.

To be sure, this is a reference to the humble or afflicted, but mainly the language celebrates Israel's special role. Then in a surprise move, vv. 6b–9 are a summons not to praise, but to action:

> . . . to wreak vengeance on the nations,
> and chastisement on the peoples,
> to bind their kings in chains,
> and their nobles with fetters of iron,
> to execute on them the judgment written!

The summons and the conventional reason are used as motivation for human action.[18] I find this to be a remarkable move made by the psalm. The proposed human actions of vengeance, chastisement, and judgment are actions we might elsewhere have expected Yahweh to perform. In this psalm, however, Yahweh does not act, so that Israel must. Indeed Israel in this psalm does not even expect Yahweh to act. The psalm appears to affirm that Israel must do what Yahweh used to do, as though "God has no hands but ours." The doxology which ostensibly turns life over to God is instead a hymnic exercise of claiming transcended authority for human activity in God's name. That God delights in his people and gives victory (v. 4) is now warrant for vigorous action of vengeance and judgment as public policy.

Moreover the action proposed is against nations and peoples, against kings and nobles, the ones over whom Yahweh's kingship is asserted in Psalm 96. Only now the assertion of sovereignty is not wrought by Yahweh, but by Yahweh's subjects, that is, by the Jerusalem king and his establishment. This, I suggest, is a case in which the loss of real concrete "reason" (which is absent in this psalm) permits doxology to become a tool to justify royal policy for the sponsor and benefactor of the liturgy. The warrant for such royal policy is that something must be done, but since God no longer has any real verbs of action, power, or authority assigned, the verbs are preempted by human agents, specifically by the king. The shift from declarative to descriptive has the effect liturgically of slowly shifting power away *from* the God who never does anything concrete *to* the king who is perfectly capable of enacting God's sovereignty and doing what the king knows God wants done.

WHEN TRANSFORMATION BECOMES
ABIDING ORDER

A third way in which the world-making process of praise is "kicked upstairs" is the move from liberation to creation themes. I incline to take a more critical view of creation theology in ancient Israel than do many of my colleagues.[19] I understand that creation theology may indeed express a bold claim for the sovereignty of Yahweh against idols and false orderings of the world. The social function of creation theology, however, is characteristically to establish, legitimate, and advocate order at the cost of transformation. It is of course reassuring to claim that God's good order of creation is a sure decree against chaos. The problem is that regularly (I believe inevitably), creation theology is allied with the king, with the royal liturgy, and therefore with reasons of state. The outcome is to coalesce the royal ordering of economic distribution and political power with the goodness and reliability of God's intended order, thereby absolutizing the present order as the very structure God has decreed in and for creation.[20] In more recent times one can observe a parallel practice in the justification of many social relations by an appeal to "natural law," when in fact "natural law" is nothing more than simply the dominant values held by the dominant class.[21]

The Jerusalem liturgy makes the move from liberation to creation in giving reasons for the world offered in doxology. We are able to see creation and liberation themes treated together in Psalm 146. In vv. 7b–9, the recital concerns liberation themes. In vv. 6–7, the themes of creation and liberation are nicely intertwined:

> . . . who made heaven and earth,
>   the sea, and all that is in them;
> who keeps faith for ever;
>   who executes justice for the oppressed;
> who gives food to the hungry.

The God who made (participle) heaven and earth is the God who keeps faith forever. The term 'emeth in this context could mean guaranteed fertility or reliable world-ordering.[22] In v. 7, the liberation theme of justice for the oppressed is linked to food for the hungry which could be a statement of liberation (as in 1 Sam. 2:5), or a part of reliable creation as in Pss. 104:27–28; 145:15–16.

In Psalm 147 the liberation themes are minimal (vv. 2–3):

> . . . he gathers the outcasts of Israel.
> He heals the brokenhearted,
>   and binds up their wounds.

This motif is echoed in v. 6:

> The Lord lifts up the downtrodden,
> He casts the wicked to the ground.

But in the midst of vv. 2a–3, 6, comes God's creation activity (vv. 4–5):

> He determines the number of the stars,
>   he gives to all of them their names,
> Great is our Lord, and abundant in power,
>   his understanding is beyond measure.

This theme is enlarged upon in vv. 8–9, 14–18. It is known and acknowledged that Yahweh does transforming actions, but the preponderance of words is focused on the reliability, generosity, and prosperity of the created order.

In such a recital, critical awareness about social reality disappears. It is very difficult to engage liturgically in celebrations of God's extravagance and yet to remember and affirm that in the midst of such extravagance there are hungry people who need food, prisoners who need release, and blind who need sight. I submit that the very accumulation of words about abundance diminishes the likelihood that the social reality of need and scarcity will remain visible to Israel. Such a psalm reflects a singing community which continues to hold on to the old recital of transformation, but which is increasingly preoccupied with the goodness of the present order, a goodness experienced with benign gratitude, without context, without memory, without critical awareness. In the end, the massive rhetoric of present well-being overrides the memory of another needful time. And when one's own memory of a needful time is nullified, one is not likely to notice a present needfulness that contradicts one's own present abundance. God becomes the guarantor of this wonderful world which is now uncritically legitimated, and as God is transformed, the world changes to become an absolute beyond question or criticism.

In Psalm 148, we have seen that there were only two reasons

given, vv. 5b–6 and 13b–14. The first of these concerns the governance of creation:

> For he commanded and they were created,
> and he established them for ever and ever;
> He fixed their bounds which cannot be passed.

The second reason of vv. 13b–14 ostensibly concerns Israel, but even here it is royal Israel, "a horn for his people," that hints only of power, abundance, and security. Moreover this psalm is dominated by the summons which mobilizes all of creation. The dominant picture which is sketched is a perfectly ordered world, everything in glad harmony in praise of the Creator. In this glad doxology of creation, there are no abrasive scandals, no dissonant voices, no disobedient choir members in the great cosmic choir, no problems, no wrongs, no evil, no injustice. All is "very good" (Gen. 1:31), which I submit is an uncritical cover-up of the real world in which Israel's awkward, identity-giving history has happened.

The evidence of the significance of the shift from transformation to creation is not clear, neat, and simple. Nor do I intend to impose any developmental explanation on the psalms of praise. Nor do I credit the king per se with these liturgic changes. I rather refer to the king as a symbol of the shift in Israel's economics and epistemology that requires these remarkable shifts in liturgical phrasing.[23]

I have identified three rather different ways in which the shift is made in the hymns of praise, from authenticating experience to legitimated world:

- A shift in the balance between the rhetoric of reason and summons. Israel loses its concrete memory and experience, and ends with no reasons for the praise that is compelled with an imperative. The summons to praise becomes absolute and unjustified.
- A shift from specificity to generalization. Israel loses its specificity and recites generalizations which have a bite of neither affront nor energy.[24]
- A shift from the motif of liberation to the motif of creation. This shift softens the memory of displacing transformation which is both threat and gift, and evokes a happy, organic world of harmony and well-being.

These three shifts, I submit, reflect Israel's move away from a radical world of disciplined obedience and imaginative commitment to a new community of humane possibility, to a world of complacency, triumph, prosperity, and self-sufficiency. In this world obedience is not as urgent, human possibility is not as cherished, hope is not as defiant or dangerous.

In addition to these three changes in rhetoric, I should mention a fourth dimension of such an adjustment which I shall not pursue. There is, I believe, a reduction of language so that the great narrative accounts of God's activity are reduced to barren adjectives and finally to comforting nouns. In Psalm 136, the *hesed* of Yahweh is given fleshly content, because its formulary use in each verse is paralleled and supported with specific transformative content. In that psalm one could not recite the claim, "Yahweh's *hesed* endures forever," without knowing exactly what the *hesed* is. In Ps. 145:8–9, the same marvelous words of the covenant tradition no longer have such specific content, but are now reduced to refer in participles to God's governance of the world. The words articulating Yahweh's faithfulness have lost their concreteness.[25] While the concrete memory may linger in Israel, as no doubt it did, it is not present in the words of the psalm. Further movement away from specificity is evident in Psalm 117 (already cited) in which the characteristic words to portray Yahweh are used without any substance and so have become a conventional slogan.

It may be argued that the context of these words is so clear and well known in Israel that the specific content never needed to be reiterated. But given the other liturgic adjustments we have identified, we may surmise that the great words recalling concrete transformation became flat and empty, devoid of their dangerous promise and weighty possibility.[26] The kings of Jerusalem and their established urbane constituency with their tendentious ideology likely preferred to keep the treasured words as useful appeals to the support of the tradition, but emptied of their rawness, embarrassment, and revolutionary potential.

A MUTE GOD, A STATIC WORLD

When these moves away from Israel's primal, transformative memory are accomplished in the royal liturgy, we are a long way from the social world envisioned in the Exodus and offered in the

Sinai covenant. Indeed, the managers of the Jerusalem liturgy found that envisioned world too dangerous, too embarrassing, too subversive. The changes wrought in the praise of Israel which I have exposited, changes made wittingly or unwittingly, make a very different world available to Israel. I wish now to turn from the Psalms and from the actual practice of praise to suggest the royal world that was intended by and mediated through the royal liturgy. That world is in marked contrast to the world of liberation and covenant, and it was made possible, at least in large part, by the recasting of Israel's praise. As the praise now minimized rawness, embarrassment, and revolutionary potential, so the world wrought in this changed praise was more benign and palatable, a world of stability, equilibrium, and predictability. The praise administered by the king helped to generate the kind of world needed and wanted by the king and his constituents.[27] In making this argument, I will move outside the Psalms and consider other texts that reflect the new world generated by the royal construction.

1. *The royal liturgy articulates a God who does nothing concrete or specific.* The loss of specific, transformative "reasons" in hymns of praise takes away from Israel the memory of the deeds of deliverance, and therefore any present hope or expectation that God would transform in concrete ways. In the place of reasons of concrete transformation, the hymns now articulate a God who is there, who abides, who sustains order, who characteristically does deeds of faithfulness and loyalty. But those deeds are not locatable for Israel anywhere in memory or in experience. And because they are not specifically locatable, they generate no specific hope or obligation. In the most extreme expressions of this articulation of God (as in Psalm 150), Israel is left with a God who does nothing, but who is blandly trustworthy, conventionally predictable, and marvelously legitimating. Such praise robs Yahweh of Yahweh's characteristic way in the world and offers instead a weak substitute who is at most a bearer of conventional slogans. Doxology which robs Israel of its concrete memory yields a god who does not do anything and who is therefore an idol. Summons to praise a god who has no transformative reasons to support the summons is an act of idolatry. The act of praise that should be most vital in Israel's life in actuality robs Israel of vitality. Doxology thus *results in idolatry*, in the portrayal and construction of a god who is a pale replica of Israel's God.

An idol in Israel is not a nonexistent god, but a god who has no power, has done nothing, has no story, no recital of transformative acts.[28]

> Our God is in the heavens;
>   he does whatever he pleases.
> Their idols are silver and gold,
>   the work of men's hands.
> They have mouths, but do not speak;
>   eyes, but do not see.
> They have ears, but do not hear;
>   noses, but do not smell.
> They have hands, but do not feel;
>   feet, but do not walk;
>   and they do not make a sound in their throat.
> Those who make them are like them;
>   so are all who trust in them. (Ps. 115:3–8)

Second Isaiah, who draws on the hymnic tradition, assaults the idols who legitimate Babylonian imperial power (46:1–2):

> . . . their idols are on beasts and cattle;
> these things you carry are loaded
>   as burdens on weary beasts.
> They stoop, they bow down together,
>   and they cannot save the burden,
>   but themselves go into captivity.

These failed gods are then countered by and contrasted with the magisterial claim of Yahweh (Isa. 46:4):

> I am He . . .
> I will carry you.
>   I have made and I will bear,
>   I will carry and will save.

The contrast is precisely between gods who can do nothing, that is, whose hymns have no concrete transformative reasons because nothing has been done, and Yahweh who is praised as the God who carries, bears, delivers, saves. The contrast in praise is derived from a concrete memory.[29] The idols, in contrast to Yahweh, are dismissed by Second Isaiah:

> Behold, you are nothing,
>   and your work is nought;
>   an abomination is he who chooses you. (Isa. 41:24)

> Behold, they are all a delusion;
>   their works are nothing;
>   their molten images are empty wind. (Isa. 41:29)

Or in a different, more pregnant mode, the Assyrians (as presented
and mocked in Israel) misperceive Yahweh as though Yahweh were
just like all the other gods who cannot save:

> Beware lest Hezekiah mislead you by saying, "The Lord will deliver
> us." Has any of the gods of the nations delivered his land out of the
> hand of the king of Assyria? Where are the gods of Hamath and
> Arpad? Where are the gods of Sepharvaim? Have they delivered
> Samaria out of my hand? Who among all the gods of these countries
> have delivered their countries out of my hand, that the Lord should
> deliver Jerusalem out of my hand? (Isa. 36:18–20) Thus you shall
> speak to Hezekiah king of Judah: "Do not let your God on whom you
> rely deceive you by promising that Jerusalem will not be given into
> the hand of the king of Assyria. Behold, you have heard what the
> kings of Assyria have done to all lands, destroying them utterly. And
> shall you be delivered? Have the gods of the nations delivered them,
> the nations which my fathers destroyed, Gozan, Haran, Rezeph,
> and the people of Eden who were in Tel-assar?" (Isa. 37:10–12)[30]

Second Isaiah subsequently contrasts this God who has power to
act with idols who cannot act. The Assyrians have treated Yahweh
like the other gods, and have failed to recognize that Yahweh is
unlike them. Yahweh alone among all the gods has a history of
transformation. The other gods have no recorded glory about any
saving deed.

But when the hymn is adjusted so that there is no "reason," then
it is a "summons" to praise a god who has no story of transformation. The loss of reason in Israel's praise is tantamount to the
reduction of Yahweh to an idol who is like the other gods who do
not act, will not intrude, cannot transform. The loss of reason
means the dismissal of the memory. So Jeremiah can critique Israel
for its loss of memory which is a loss of reason which is a misper-
ception of Yahweh:

> They did not say, "Where is the Lord
>   who brought us up from the land of Egypt,
>   who led us in the wilderness,
>   in a land of deserts and pits,
>   in a land of drought and deep darkness,
>   in a land that none passes through,
>   where no man dwells?"

And I brought you into a plentiful land
to enjoy its fruits and its good things . . .
The priests did not say, "Where is the Lord?" (Jer. 2:6–8)

In the Psalter, Psalm 150 articulates a god without reason, a community without memory, a faith without concrete transformation:

Praise the Lord!
Praise God in his sanctuary;
Praise him in his mighty firmament!
Praise him for his mighty deeds;
  praise him according to his exceeding greatness!
Praise him with trumpet sound;
  praise him with lute and harp!
Praise him with timbrel and dance;
  praise him with strings and pipe!
Praise him with sounding cymbals;
  praise him with loud clashing cymbals!
Let everything that breathes praise the Lord!
Praise the Lord!

Of course it is too much to suggest that Psalm 150 is an act of idolatry. My point is that the tendency in that direction is unmistakable. This god does nothing and has done nothing and will do nothing. Of course one can imagine simply that it is a communal act of utter release and ecstasy. But for what? It takes no great imagination to think the psalm reflects a community of self-sufficient people who are engaged in absolutizing the present because it is so good, and the god needed for that absolutizing is one with an eternal present, no past and no future. It is not imaginable that a community recently released from slavery, a person recently rescued from death, a people recently in touch with a concrete transformation could sing so long without reference to the inversion. Nothing is expected of this god and nothing is given.

A god without a story of transformation is an idol, an object of worship and not a subject, who has not saved and who cannot save, who cannot shatter, cannot make new, cannot raise from the dead, cannot begin again. I submit that it is the reduced, uncritical doxology of the temple liturgy that finds reason an embarrassment and so leads Israel to idolatry, to the praise of a god who cannot save. With such a god, Israel ends in despair.

2. *The royal liturgy legitimates a social order that cannot be criticized or changed, even if it is unjust.* Such uncritical praise in fact functions as an ideological legitimation of the status quo. The

primal function of Yahweh in the Exodus narrative is to criticize and change the imperial order that has become enslaving. It was the sovereign power that intervened in scathing passion that let the gospel be announced, "Your God reigns." It was the reign of this God that permitted the departure, the withdrawal, the home-coming, the keeping of promises.[31] It is the telling of this story and dozens of others like it that has always evoked and authorized criticism of the established social order, that has caused the notice of pain, dysfunction, and brutality, that has been the standing ground from which to discern that this present order is in fact a disorder.[32] It is Israel's repertoire of transformative stories that gives a basis for making a critique of present social arrangements and that offers energy for the transformation of such arrange-ments. Transcendent rule, either of God or of king, without access to social pain is never a catalyst for transformative action.[33] It is precisely these stories which provide a lens for seeing what is not acceptable in the present, and a ground of authority for its change. ⟶ *N B* Transcendent rule by itself will never lead to change. But pain by itself will not either. Pain without narrative access will not permit change but only despair. It is only these old narratives of transfor-mation that give weight in Israel to present pain that generates courage and energy for present change. That is why the old narra-tives are so potentially subversive for Israel in the present.

The king of Jerusalem had made the easy move of saying that the present order is the order willed by God. It is an easy move from

> Thou openest thy hand,
>   thou satisfiest the desire of every living thing (Ps. 145:16)

to the claim that

> Judah and Israel were as many as the sand by the sea;
> they ate and drank and were happy. (1 Kings 4:20)

The general affirmation of God's providential care was easily co-opted for support of the regime. The king's policies and arrange-ments were simply an earthly embodiment of the good governance of God known in heaven.[34] The king asserted an identification between royal power and the transcendent will of God which would tolerate no criticism (cf. Amos 7:13). And the people who had access to royal power and a disproportionate share of the goods celebrated the identification.[35] They wanted to thank God

for their good fortune. They wanted words with long vowels that
assured them that all creation was eating as well as they were.
They preferred acrostic poems in which everything is ordered and
in place. Psalms 111, 112, and 145 express such serene, acrostic,
comprehensive confidence in a well-ordered world, in which God
rules and we benefit. So, for example, in Ps. 112:2-3, 7-8:

> His descendants will be mighty in the land;
>   the generation of the upright will be blessed.
> Wealth and riches are in his house;
>   and his righteousness endures for ever. . . .
> He is not afraid of evil tidings;
>   his heart is firm, trusting in the Lord.
> His heart is steady, he will not be afraid,
>   until he sees his desire on his adversaries.

I do not suggest that this is necessarily bad theology, but it is on its
way to an absolutizing of the present order in which there are no
harsh tales of intrusion or transformation.

Israelites who were well off and shared in this liturgy agilely
viewed life through a double glance. They knew very well that
power was in the hands of the king. But they blinked and looked
again and it was God's rule, right before their eyes, "world without end." They were able to celebrate the present social arrangement under the king as the ultimate rule of God. So they sang
(Ps. 46:1-7):

> God is our refuge and strength,
>   a very present help in trouble.
> Therefore we will not fear
>   though the earth should change,
>   though the mountains shake in the heart of the sea;
>   though its waters roar and foam,
>   though the mountains tremble with its tumult.
> There is a river whose streams make glad the city of God,
>   the holy habitation of the Most High.
> God is in the midst of her, she shall not be moved;
>   God will help her right early.
> The nations rage, the kingdoms totter;
>   he utters his voice, the earth melts.
> The Lord of hosts is with us;
>   The God of Jacob is our refuge.

The psalm celebrating king and Zion had now silenced the hard
tales of hurt, bondage, and injustice. All of that sordid reality
deep in Israel's memory now was gone, overcome, ruled out of

court, and the world was now whole, good, lovely, ordered, under control.[36]

Such self-assured doxology as was featured in Jerusalem surely leads to social ideology.[37] Israel now has, according to its praise, a God who does not do anything. Israel, according to its praise, also has a social order that is absolute and cannot be changed or criticized. To change it is to tamper with God's created order. To criticize it is to attack God's will and to appear ungrateful. Doxology as social ideology happens when the transformative story is lost from below the summons. I use the term "ideology" to refer to

- vested interest which is passed off as truth,
- partial truth which counterfeits as whole truth,
- theological claim functioning as a mode of social control.[38]

The alliance of temple and king, church and state, creed and flag, is a tempting business. And it is dangerous when translated in legitimating liturgies of praise. Liturgy becomes domesticated and praise of God becomes endorsement of the way the world is presently arranged. In such psalms, Israel no longer remembers the old stories of hurt and amazement. The old stories contain too much dangerous potential. They have been silenced.[39]

The prophets are the ones in ancient Israel who understood the problem of liturgy as ideology. They articulate their strictures against the cult, not because they are nineteenth-century rational Protestants who have no sensitivity toward liturgy, but because they saw the powerful distortion when the claims of a class and institution are identified with the truth of God. Their critique of cult is in fact a critique of ideology, an attempt to make visible the destructive vested interest that was a charade, and to assert the whole truth of God's rule.

> I hate, I despise your feasts,
>   and I take no delight in your solemn assemblies.
> Even though you offer me your burnt offerings
>   and cereal offerings,
> I will not accept them,
> and the peace offerings of your fatted beasts
>   I will not look upon.
> Take away from me the noise of your songs;
>   to the melody of your harps I will not listen.
> But let justice roll down like waters
>   and righteousness like an ever-flowing stream. (Amos 5:21–24)

What to me is the multitude of your sacrifices?
  says the Lord;
I have had enough of burnt offerings of rams
  and the fat of fed beasts;
I do not delight in the blood of bulls,
  or of lambs, or of he-goats. . . .
Your new moons and your appointed feasts
  my soul hates;
they have become a burden to me,
  I am weary of bearing them. . . .
Even though you make many prayers,
  I will not listen . . . (Isa. 1:11–15)

Because you have uttered delusions and seen lies, therefore behold, I
am against you, says the Lord God. My hand will be against the
prophets who see delusive visions and who give lying divina-
tions; . . . Because they have misled my people, saying, "Peace,"
when there is no peace; and because, when the people build a wall,
these prophets daub it with whitewash; say to those who daub it with
whitewash that it shall fall! (Ezek. 13:8–11)

It remained for Jeremiah to make the critique of ideology in the
clearest, most trenchant way. He critiqued the governmental practice and policy which announced "peace and prosperity" when
social reality was the very opposite (6:14; 8:11). Jeremiah assaulted the liturgy which repeated reassuring slogans (7:4). He
denounced their temple worship which had become a device for
deception that hid the reality of social life (7:9–11).
  In place of the ideological deception entrenched in Jerusalem,
Jeremiah does not simply offer judgment for which he is so famous.
The only antidote to the current trouble in royal Jerusalem is *recovery of the story* (cf. 2:6–8; 5:24) and *public notice of pain* (4:19;
6:15; 8:22—9:1). Jeremiah knew that his people were in the grip of
ideology which kept them from either seeing clearly or acting faithfully. And he understood that by the use of self-deceiving doxology
Judah was denied a future on the only terms that it could be given,
that is, on terms of the justice and righteousness that are rooted in
the old memories of transformation. Jeremiah understood that release from doxology was necessary both for faithfulness and for
survival. And he understood that only a recovery of the old "reasons" found in Israel's primal memory could effect a release from
ideology.
  The world of Jerusalem and of the royal liturgy was not by definition a bad world. It was indeed a theologically legitimated

world. But it went awry when it was cut off from its generating story. It became a legitimated world without legitimating grounding. The "reasons" kept the world of Jerusalem open and responsive. When it lost these reasons, it became absolute, self-satisfied, beyond criticism. A dreamed-of Israelite community became one more Canaanite city-state.[40] Such a city with all its attendant oppression and injustice finally will end in death. The loss in praise finally in Israel resulted in the loss of city, temple, and life.

3. Derivatively, from the *idolatry* of a god who will do nothing and has no story, and the *ideology* of a social order that cannot be critiqued or changed, Israel loses the narratives out of which it continues its world-making. *The royal liturgy then evokes persons who become loyal conformists without capacity to judge, discern, critique, or risk.*[41] How could it be otherwise? The idolatry of a god who will not act and the ideology of a system that will not change and does not need to change lead to a religious-political conclusion that the present arrangement is abidingly true, and the way to live life is to conform. It is the old story that reminds us that God has acted and will act so that the system can and must change. It is the old story that asserts that the system will be changed, social power will be reassigned, disproportions will be corrected, and justice will be given. But in the royal liturgy, that old story has been muted if not dismissed. No reasons are given for praise. There is no memory of such transformation. Without the story, the system is experienced as absolute. Something crucial happens to persons who commit themselves to such an absolutism which Robert Jay Lifton calls totalism.[42]

The Case of Job. In the Old Testament, Job's friends embody this temptation and this outcome. They have come to embrace fully the settled liturgy and the predictable world of that liturgy. They believe that the world is well and fully governed. There are no ungoverned parts, no unexplained edges, no surprises yet to be given. Their faith is reduced to a practice of legitimation and justification of what has always been in this well-ordered system. Andre Neher characterizes their sorry practice as loyal conformists:

> As soon as they first hear Job cry out, they counter-balance it with the word and engage him in an exhausting dialogue. Can Job resist the extortion of this grave, insidious, and harassing form which the word assumes in the mouth of his friends and which the Greeks call rhetoric? . . . they hold the floor sufficiently long to leave

something of their venom in the reader's mind. It is in the substitutional structure of the rhetoric that its offensiveness lies. Job's friends speak as though they were God's deputies. They arrogate the right to speak at a time and a place where God is silent. Their human word supplements the deficiency of the divine Word and replaces it.[43]

In the end a system of human control is substituted for the free rule of God. Job's friends cannot entertain a God who is in fact free. They can therefore permit themselves no risk and no unthinkable awareness. In the end they cannot muster compassion outside their tidy system of control.

I am helped in this connection by object-relations theory of personality study and particularly the work of D. W. Winnicott.[44] I do not reduce theology to psychological theory, but Winnicott's understanding of how a person is formed is illuminating for how a person is formed in liturgy. It is Winnicott's thesis that a small baby grows to have a strong personal identity center because of the mother's attentiveness. The very small baby must have an experience of omnipotence, of having a sense that the mother is responsive to and available for the will and wish of the baby, and will intervene at any need of the baby. The baby must have certitude that the mother intervenes as needed to transform life for the well-being of the baby. This early experience does not lead to selfishness, but to health, strength, and freedom to relate honestly to the mother and then to others.

Conversely, if the mother does not yield to the baby in ready and transformative ways, if the mother is always in charge, always determinative, always the one who decides, the baby learns quickly that the way to get along in the world is to please mother, to comply, conform, obey, flatter, be docile. The outcome is a "false self" that must live a life of pretense and fake, engaged in denial of the true self.[45]

This insight of object-relations theory is useful to us in understanding the character of praise. I propose that if God is experienced in doxology as always unqualifiedly good, fixed, sovereign, in charge, never acting, never impinged upon, it leads to worshipers who are docile, passive, and who finally act in bad faith to please God, whatever they may in fact feel. Some unqualified praise is inevitably an act of denial.

We may identify three evidences of the "false self" which

engages in praise and finally in denial. First, insofar as the wisdom tradition reflects the perception of the well-off, such denial consists in an inability or refusal to notice the failure of the system.[46] Psalm 37 is a clear example of a perception of the world that is skewed by supreme and uncritical confidence in the system (vv. 25, 28b–29):

> I have been young, and now am old;
>   yet I have not seen the righteous forsaken
>   or his children begging bread. . . .
> The righteous shall be preserved for ever,
>   but the children of the wicked shall be cut off.
> The righteous shall possess the land,
>   and dwell upon it for ever.

This voice is untroubled by the problems of the real world.

Second, the friends of Job are congenial to the voice of Psalm 37, but go further in assigning all problems to guilt and sin, thus protecting and maintaining the governance of God and the legitimacy of the system:

> As for me, I would seek God,
>   and to God would I commit my cause . . .
> Behold, happy is the man whom God reproves;
>   therefore despise not the chastening of the Almighty.
>   (Job 5:8, 17)

> Behold, God will not reject a blameless man,
>   nor take the hand of evildoers. (Job 8:20)

> If you will set your heart aright,
>   you will stretch out your hands toward him.
> If your iniquity is in your hand, put it far away,
>   and let not wickedness dwell in your tents.
> Surely then you will lift up your face without blemish;
>   you will be secure, and will not fear. (Job 11:13–15)

They cannot entertain a critical thought outside the moral, social system to which they are committed.

Third, at the other extreme from Psalm 37 and Job's friends, Psalms 10 and 14 articulate the ultimate foolishness which says, "There is no God."[47] These psalms then characterize persons who no longer believe in the sovereignty of God, no longer trust in the equity of God, no longer submit to the command of God:

> For the wicked boasts of the desires of his heart,
>   and the man greedy for gain curses and renounces the Lord.

> In the pride of his countenance
>   the wicked does not seek him;
>   all his thoughts are, "There is no God." . . .
> He thinks in his heart, "I shall not be moved;
>   throughout all generations I shall not meet adversity."
>   (Ps. 10:3-4, 6)[48]

> The fool says in his heart,
>   "There is no God."
> They are corrupt, they do abominable deeds,
>   there is none that does good. . . .
> They have all gone astray, they are all alike corrupt;
>   there is none that does good, no, not one. (Ps. 14:1, 3)

It is not a far move from *excessive submissiveness* to *utter autonomy*. In both extremes (as in Job's friends and the fool in Psalms 10 and 14), serious interaction with a live God is impossible, and serious engagement with a world in transformation is inaccessible. When God is not engaged and when the world is not under change, the most available alternatives are either blind submission or self-sufficient autonomy. Both are forms of "false self."[49]

The "false self" is the counterpart to idolatry. A false god who cannot act requires a false worshiper who defers—never asks, insists, doubts, or finally cares. As doxology can mediate an idolatrous god, so doxology can evoke false selves who only offer flat, uncritical, absolute praise, who have no stories to tell of pain resolved, of guilt forgiven, of death overcome, of life changed. Everything for God and for humankind is put in an eternal holding pattern because as Joseph Heller asserts, "Nothing Happens."[50]

The Case of Jonah. This kind of person expects nothing to happen and wants nothing to happen. Along with Job's friends, we may cite the figure of Jonah as a false self who is committed to an idolatrous God. Jonah's mission, according to the narrative, is the repentance and rescue of Nineveh. Jonah does not want the mission, nor does he want Nineveh to be saved. He regards hated Nineveh as worthy of judgment and death and wants nothing beyond the full settlement of just punishment. The problematic of the narrative is that Yahweh is a free God who wants otherwise because of compassion. Jonah resists this freedom and compassion on the part of God:

> I knew that thou art a gracious God and merciful, slow to anger, and abounding in steadfast love, and repentest of evil. (Jonah 4:2)

Jonah recites the creed of Exod. 34:6–7. He knows the creed and knows that it is true of God. But he resists it and ends in a withdrawing depression because the reality of God is incongruent with his ideological view of the world. Because God is free and compassionate, something is about to happen, something saving. Jonah wants nothing to happen, certainly not freedom that violates his preconceived world, certainly not compassion that will break the rigid calculus of his life.

A liturgy of praise without reason is a counterpart to relation with mother which permits no self to emerge. I find the work of Lifton on "symbol gap" illuminating for this crisis. In a recent work, he writes of *The Broken Connection*.[51] His argument is that the brokenness of death can be handled through symbolization when there are significant and live relations in the human community. When there are no serious relations, however, the symbols wither. And where the symbols are inadequate, there emerges an uncaring, despairing commitment to death which is, in our society, expressed as worship of "the bomb."[52] I am suggesting then that we need to consider the contribution that idolatrous, ideological doxology plays in the production of false selves that in turn results in deathly public policy.

4. A God who will not act, a system which cannot be critiqued or changed, persons who are despairingly submissive even to dishonest denial or cynically resistant to God—all of that produces a situation in which pathological social relations are generated through the liturgy. The liturgy trains and disciplines one not to notice or to speak about any noticed dysfunction. *In such a doxological system as the royal liturgy, the justice questions disappear from one's moral religious horizon.*

The justice questions are foundational to Israel's initial world.[53] It was affirmed in the enthronement liturgy of Ps. 99:4 that Yahweh is a "lover of justice" (cf. Pss. 96:10–13; 19:9; Isa. 61:8). That is, Yahweh is the one who notices injustice and acts to right it. Indeed the entire "news" (*basar*) is that Yahweh has won a decisive victory over the forces of injustice, for example, Pharaoh, Babylon. I have already shown (chap. 2) how the defeat of the systems of injustice constitutes the central substance of the "news" of Israel's narrative and Israel's liturgy.

Corollary to that, Israel is a community of people which emerges in history precisely because it cried out against injustice, cried out for justice, evoked God to act. Israel and Yahweh are movers and actors in the historical process who care passionately and in powerful ways about justice. As we have seen, passionate powerful care about justice determines the tone and content of Israel's characteristic "reasons" in the Psalms. The reasons that ground the summons are first of all matters of justice. Yahweh is to be praised because Yahweh has done justice. Yahweh has fed the hungry, set the prisoners free, given righteousness to the oppressed, cared for widows and orphans (Ps. 146:7–9). That transformative justice is the foundation of the new world, wrought precisely in such concrete acts. Those concrete acts are the models of interaction between the king who governs and the people who submit in praise.

Many of the psalms we have looked at, however, become top-heavy. That is, Israel is summoned to praise the King of heaven and earth and the king in Jerusalem, but the king in Jerusalem prefers to give no reasons for praise. The King is to be praised simply because the king is there. Israel celebrates the world, but forgets the distinctive ways in which Yahweh has shaped the world. There are no reasons, no memories, no hopes or expectations, no basis out of which to rejoice, no ground out of which to address new issues of justice. The disregard of the reason for the sake of the summons dramatically cuts Yahweh off from Yahweh's central passion for justice. Psalm 68 is an example of a hymn of Yahweh's enthronement which must surely have been "useful" to the legitimacy of the Jerusalem king.

The outcome of top-heavy psalms which are summons without reason (of which Psalm 150 is the extreme example) is that singing, praising Israel does not acknowledge that this God cares about justice. The king in Jerusalem does not want Israel to know or remember. It is enough to celebrate the cosmic symphony, the harmonious voices in which all sound unified, reconciled, and the abrasive issues of justice become invisible and uncouth.[54]

Perhaps the extreme case visibly connected to the royal liturgy is the temple dedication liturgy of 1 Kings 8. In vv. 12–13, the choirs sing about God's eternal presence in the temple. The prayer and speech which follow are an assertion of God's unconditional commitment to the temple establishment. The words are those we would expect on such an occasion. But it is nonetheless worth noting that there is no mention of the social criticism and social possibility which has been definitional for Israel. That is, there is no mention unless one pays particular attention to the odd note of v. 9: "There was nothing in the ark except the two tables of stone which Moses put there at Horeb, where the Lord made a covenant with the people of Israel, when they came out of the land of Egypt." Somehow, some voice managed in the midst of the pageantry to sound the old memory one more time. It is striking that this odd voice of memory appeals directly to Moses, Exodus, and Sinai, all otherwise forgotten on the king's great day of legitimacy. Clearly that sounding of the memory does not fit the flow of the liturgy.

When the cosmic claims of God's eternal presence and munificence are the dominant voices of the liturgy, both the rule of Yahweh and the rule of the Davidic king have their way unquestioned. No Jeremiah (12:1) or Job (21:7) is permitted in the liturgy to raise hard questions. Unmitigated praise assures that God is, by definition, in the right. Indeed the way things are is right. And if someone is not fed, not healthy, does not prosper, it is only because they have departed the norm, violated the code, failed to produce, sinned. No question may be asked whether the norm, code, or production schedule is skewed or wrong. There is only condemnation from those for whom the system works so well and so reliably. Those for whom the system works are content with the summons and are relieved not to have to practice the reason. The summons is enough. "Praise the Lord, Praise God in his sanctuary, Praise him" . . . "where never is heard a discouraging word," or a harsh, abrasive word, or a questioning, protesting word. Theodicy as a crisis is banished and theodicy, the justice of God, exists only as an unquestioned settlement to which all who belong readily subscribe. Those who praise either affirm in joy because it works, or they affirm in guilt because they have failed. There is no third alternative, no questioning of either God or the system God has legitimated, no expectation that God will do a new thing.

A WORLD ORDERED AGAINST HOPE

The idolatry of a god who does not act, the ideology of a system beyond critique, the evocation of false selves who conform in self-renunciation, the eradication of justice questions—all of this finally leads to a satiated, conformist community without energy, a

people without a vocation, an assembly without hope, who can
only treasure and defend the status quo as the best available
arrangement beyond which nothing better is imaginable.[55] The
outcome of such idolatrous ideological doxology is a loss of moral
sensitivity (cf. Jer. 5:1–5, 22–28) because nothing seems amiss.
But underneath the loss of moral sensitivity is a desperate,
despairing complacency, incapable of hope, expecting nothing
from God. This is not wickedness or disobedience but theological
satiation:

> At that time I will search Jerusalem with lamps,
>   and I will punish the men
> who are thickening upon their lees,
>   those who say in their hearts,
> "The Lord will not do good,
>   nor will he do ill." (Zeph. 1:12)

In the company of the god who will do nothing, Israel will expect
nothing from god, Israel will do nothing in response to god or in
initiative toward god. The outcome is a despairing, administered,
contained people who mouth praise to a god who can do nothing,
who live in a system which cannot be changed, and who grow more
brutal where the memories of transformation fade.[56]

In royal liturgies of praise removed from the elemental "news"
of God's transformative action
  • God is banished as a serious agent of history,
  • the historical process of transformation is nullified,
  • memory of saving deeds, public or personal, is eradicated,
  • hope is destroyed.

The world has become fully legitimated. The old hurts are no
longer permitted voice and the memory withers. Present hurts are
not noticed because they are of only marginal significance in an
enterprise that goes from strength to strength, from certitude to
certitude, from legitimacy to legitimacy. Life grows very quiet,
because the generative speech from below is terminated. Things
grow very quiet because Israel is no longer engaged in the hard,
joyous, hopeful work of world-making. Now Israel is fatigued,
satiated, very near a complacent despair. Israel now has no energy
for world-making, no passion for new possibility. Israel is now
content to accept the world that has already been given, seemingly
forever. Israel's satisfaction with that given world appears to be an

act of obedient trust. But it may be only a weary cynicism too exhausted to care, to protest, or to act.

When a liturgy keeps giving us a fixed world from an immovable god, the best we can muster may sound like this:

> All streams run to the sea,
>   but the sea is not full;
> to the place where the streams flow,
>   there they flow again.
> All things are full of weariness;
>   a man cannot utter it;
> the eye is not satisfied with seeing,
>   nor the ear filled with hearing.
> What has been is what will be,
>   and what was done is what will be done;
>   and there is nothing new under the sun. (Eccles. 1:7–9)

There is an endless, passionless "waiting" for a new God and a new world which cannot come.[57] We are left as it "was in the beginning, is now and ever shall be, world without end," without memory, without hope, without passion, without a reason.

5

Doxology inside
the "Claims of
Time and Sorrow"

In the preceding chapters, we have examined the inescapability
and possibility of world-making, particularly as it is evident in
Israel's life of praise (chap. 1). World-making is a constitutive
human activity. In Israel, faithful world-making is designed to
form and sustain a world of celebrative liberation, hopeful homecoming, and glad obedience (chap. 2). Israel's world-making was
not always faithful, however. At times Israel distorted the world
entrusted to it through its life of praise, and perverted the process
of world-making to which it was summoned. This distortion of
Israel's world is present in the vested interest of the king who is
more attached to order than to transformation, more responsive to
majesty than to mercy, more concerned to maintain present power
arrangements than to critique and alter those arrangements (chap.
3). Then we noted the ways in which Israel's hymns of praise
shifted in order to reflect the "made" world of the king and his
social interests. In particular, the emerging hymnic structure contains less and less remembered reason and more and more unjustified summons in order to comply with the seemingly preferred
world of Yahweh now known to be embodied in the Jerusalem
establishment (chap. 4).

In this final chapter I want to reflect on the significance of this
analysis for the praise of the contemporary church and on the
opportunity and responsibility for pastoral leadership as world-
making.[1] We have seen that doxology, when made a vehicle for

established power, functions in the service of a safe idolatry and
an uncriticized ideology. Such praise "makes" a world for a god
who does nothing. It offers a social system that cannot be critiqued
or changed. With that kind of world-making, the odd, embarrassing, revolutionary possibility of a new world is denied us. Such
praise becomes top-heavy, offering summons without reason, system without story, world without memory, power arrangements
without justification, claims uninformed by hurt or healing.

As pastors, we are charged to face the reality of such idolatry
and ideology and the death-dealing impact they have on the world
in which we live and the people whom we serve. We are called to
look below the "summons" to a world that still has "reasons,"
reasons that announce pain and injustice confronted and transformed, surprising newness where we thought there was only
death. The call of our vocation is to be "world-makers," makers of
an alternative, evangelical world, a world of news (*basar*), a world
in which the sovereign of truth, equity, and righteousness has just
come to power (cf. Psalm 96). Out of these reflections on the
Psalms, I suggest that the critical work of the pastor in his or her
world-making is to help the community move back down

- *from* the buoyant summons *to* the concrete reason,
- *from* the settled world *to* the shattering experience,
- *from* the system *to* the story.

A WORLD TOO CERTAIN

In Israel's life, there were pastors who did that very work of
offering a concrete world of transformation. They were neither
fooled nor seduced by the grand claims of the liturgy, but they
knew instead that Israel's hope for life rested in concrete and
nameable acts of pain and grace.

1. *Jeremiah.* The world of idolatry and ideology, wrought
through royal doxology, was well advanced in the years approaching
587 B.C.E. Such a world of idolatry and ideology is the world in
which Jeremiah had to speak his word, live his hurt, and pay his
price. It is the power and reality of this false world that evoked
his pathos. The ideology he had to counter in Jerusalem was a royal-
political-economic system which said "peace, peace" when there
was no peace (6:14; 8:11). The idolatry he had to meet was the
self-deceiving worship of an indifferent god who provided cover,

security, and rationalization for covenant breakers (7:8–11). The worshipers of this god felt that they could cynically presume on liturgic assurances, come to the liturgy after covenant violations, hug the altar and say, "We are delivered" (7:10). When not delivered, they could say in confident, demanding, and ingratiating voices:

> Is the Lord not in Zion?
> Is her King not in her? (8:19)

In the face of such numbed deception about heaven where God is tolerated and used, and earth which pretends peace, Jeremiah speaks his hurt (4:19), the hurt of God (9:1–2), the hurt of mother Rachel who refuses to be comforted (31:15). Jeremiah seeks to penetrate the façade of doxology by the reality of broken experience in the midst of which healing may come. He knows that if healing may come, it will come nowhere but in the midst of hurt.[2]

2. *Second Isaiah.* In a very different context, Second Isaiah faces the same deception in the claims of the Babylonian establishment. The idolatry tempting Israel in exile concerns the Babylonian gods, the great gods of imperial legitimacy and rationalization. The poet mocks them to nothingness, declares them to be big bubbles of empty air (41:24, 26–29; 45:20), and reduces them in liturgic nullification until they do not exist. In a powerful song of mockery, he humiliates the gods of the empire and dismisses them as burdens of passivity.

> They set it in its place, and it stands there;
>   it cannot move from its place.
> If one cries to it, it does not answer
>   or save him from his trouble. (46:7; cf. Jer. 10:1–16)

As the gods are dismissed and dismantled by this powerful poetry, so the powerful ideological pretensions of the state are overcome. The poet knows that state pretensions and high-handed gods are linked to each other. The poet likens the pretentious empire to an arrogant woman who imagines to herself,

> I shall be mistress for ever. (47:7)

> I am, and there is no one besides me. (47:8)

> No one sees me. (47:10)

The poet enacts a lamentation over the death of Babylon (47:1–4). That poetic act is the negative counterpart to the enthronement of Yahweh who has defeated the Babylonian gods and who dismisses imperial Babylonian power even as the grass withers and fades (40:6–8). The lamentation is flung in the face of imperial arrogance. The poem, and the world-making of the poet, run ahead of reality. The poet dares to enact a funeral while the empire still imagines it is in full strength and vitality. The combination of idolatry and ideology prevents the empire from noticing the reality of death that the poet sees so clearly.

In different but not dissimilar situations, Jeremiah and Second Isaiah do the world-making entrusted to pastors and poets. In different ways, they both expose and dismantle the false world which leads to death. For Jeremiah, the false world is the beguiling world of the royal-Temple establishment of Jerusalem. For Second Isaiah, it is the formidable, seductive world of the empire. In both cases the poets critique and dismantle. More remarkably, in both cases they offer another imagined world which faith may embrace. The new world offered by Jeremiah is a world of deep grief and relinquishment which runs counter to royal buoyancy. For Second Isaiah the new world is one of joyous homecoming, based on a departure from the claims and benefits of the empire. Both Jeremiah and Second Isaiah by their poetry invite Israel *to depart* the false world of royal-imperial construction and *to enter* the world of Yahweh, a world of grief embraced and new possibility enacted.

3. *Their World/Our World.* The practice of world-construction by these ancient pastors and poets provides an invitation for us in our pastoral activity in the contemporary church. Indeed, the parallels between the dying world of Jeremiah and the hopeful world of Second Isaiah on the one hand, and our Euro-American situation on the other hand, are worth our attention.[3] In a way not unlike the numbed world of Jerusalem and the displaced world of exile, we also have arrived at a religion without compelling power and at a social world that is organized against our own humanity. In our situation, beset as we are with alien propaganda and hostile social values, we have lost touch with the daily concreteness of human reality. The hard-won day-to-day healings and the regular costs of human hurt and hope are screened out as irrelevant to the great policy questions of security and economics. As a society, we have lost our "reasons," our concrete memories which liberate, energize, and legitimate. We find ourselves enmeshed in, indebted to, and committed to world-arrangements for which we can give no "reason," and beyond which we can entertain no serious hope. The

drive of consumerism and the momentum of the arms race cause us to ride roughshod over the immediacy and wonder of human transactions that could inform our public life.

In our contemporary society we have arrived at a manufactured religion, worshiping a god from whom we dare expect no serious transformation. Indeed we prefer a god who has become a guarantor of the way things are. We absolutize the present and imagine it has always been the way it is. Because we have no memory, we articulate a god who has no history. Because we treasure no past, we cannot recall God's past with us.[4] The erosion of our language about god is rooted in

- our failure of nerve about our memory,
- our loss of authority about tradition,
- our embarrassment about our concrete and therefore scandalous experience.

The outcome, surely, is an idol, an immobilizing transcendence, a god so secure, so established, so allied with the American dream that there is no space left for anguish, ambiguity, uncertainty, hurt beyond guilt.[5]

The stridency of this religious idolatry is of course present in the religious right allied, as it tends to be, with American militarism and participating in all of the fears that justify such militarism. But that idolatry has its counterpart in the excessive self-confidence of religious liberalism which is so sure of its problem-solving capacity that doxology is crowded out by the claims and perspectives of the social sciences. Our contemporary religious situation of idolatry is also evidenced in a political-economic situation in which established legitimacy is beyond question, in which incumbents always win, and in which it is treasonable to question present arrangements and assumptions. I submit that our pastoral situation is precisely one of idolatry—of a god who has everything settled, has sanctioned the proper positions, and has sorted everyone out.

There is little doubt that religious idolatry is matched by social ideology in which the American dream is the goal of life, has its own "daily diary," until even our own children are consumed by their consuming.[6] This social ideology has so much the appearance of the good life that one is caught very short with criticism, because none of us can conjure moves out of it that will not cost too much and disrupt too deeply.

We find ourselves "summoned" by massive propaganda to this world of consumerism, even as the psalms of imperial praise issue summons to Israel to join the urban monopoly. We have our cynical version of "praise the lord," which is translated into celebration of the American ideology. We find ourselves summoned to a world in which god benignly guarantees, in which the system comes very close to being the solution. Talk outside the scheme runs the risk of being dismissed as unreasonable, if not absurd.

This powerful combination of idolatry (of a god who has no history and will not act) and ideology (of a social arrangement that will not change and cannot be criticized) is conveyed well in the doxologies of civil religion in which the living God becomes the patron of the status quo, and the present system feels very much like the kingdom. The religious seduction of civil religion is found not only in the powerful propaganda of consumer advertising but is also present in much of the church which is simply an echo of and guarantor for the controlling ideology. So we join the praise. In our praise, we are forced to make denials about the powerful truth of God in heaven and the transforming truth of hurt and hope on earth.

At first such ideological denials pain us because we know they are cover-ups; but eventually they soothe. This unmitigated praise of buoyant cultural religion forces upon us a falseness about which we still know better. The praise is sponsored by our engines of affluence, but it is echoed in the church. Such uncritical praise forces on us a pretense of everything being all right. The pretense is an economic one in which we imagine that everyone is well-off, at least everyone who wants to be. The economic pretense becomes a moral pretense in which we imagine God gives well-being and security to those whom God values. We sing praise because everything works. There is moral and economic coherence. Such unmitigated praise forces on us a disregard of the power of evil in the world, of the terror of injustice, even while the parade of victims streams before us, some very close to home. This necessary seductive doxology nurtures us not to notice—not to notice neighbor, not to notice self, not to notice hurt, not to notice healing or its costs—not to notice (cf. Lam. 1:12).

When we do not notice for long enough, we lose our capacity to remember how it was. We become unable to reenter the gift of newness previously given. We lose our capacity to hope for how it is promised and how it will surely be. We lose our chance for embarrassment and we fail in our capacity to blush at what is incongruous among us.[7] After a while, we no longer notice that our dominant modes of life are incongruous with our yearning for humanity. Our public policies and our domestic practices contradict our deepest desire for humanness. In our not noticing, the ones who were our neighbors in the memory become aliens in a world that cannot be critiqued or changed, before a god who does nothing.

The truth of our faith, however, does not rest in the grand claims of idolatry and ideology that numb us to hurt and hope. The truth of our faith rests in the daily treasuring of human reality which is known and discerned in places where hurt is guarded and hope is enacted. There is need in the face of idolatry and ideology to fashion a world of *hesed* and *'emeth*, of loyalty and reliability. That world will be fashioned only one act at a time, however, in acts which have transforming power, which open up human possibility, which break the deathliness with stunning compassion and humaneness.

PAIN AS THE LOCUS OF POSSIBILITY

Dorothee Soelle has written, concerning feminist theology, that all true theology begins in pain.[8] Surely that is true for all evangelical theology, for feminists or for anyone else. It is the reality of concrete pain known in the specificity of a person or a community which is the locus of serious faith. It is there that death is to be faced in anguish and there that life is strangely given. W. B. Yeats has caught the truth present in pain this way:

> But Love has pitched his mansion in
> The place of excrement;
> For nothing can be sole or whole
> That has not been rent.[9]

Making whole (or sole) will happen, as Israel's songs of thanksgiving said so well, precisely where life is rent. And where life is not rent, there will be no sole or whole. Indeed, where life is not rent, the God of Israel is not inclined to be present. Yeats has it exactly right. It is the rending that makes life possible. It is the raw, terrible tearing that opens up healing and makes new. And it is this concrete rending, greatly feared by us, that the grand liturgy masks. The grand liturgy wants us to imagine that new life is possible without the rending. But we know better. We know better in our own experience. And we know better in our tradition of liberation, of being dead and being raised.

Wendell Berry is one who observes the power of transformation which comes in the brokenness. He is a Kentucky subsistence farmer who watches while the royal ideology destroys the land and the people with it. For him, agribusiness is the embodiment of royal consciousness that disregards concrete human reality. In his quiet polemic Berry urges that there is another way for land and for people. Berry writes always about the land and the care of the earth, and the ways in which agribusiness has destroyed land, the farm economy, and farm families.[10]

In his novel *A Place on Earth,* Berry portrays the daily, slow life of a farming community in which folks are deeply enmeshed in each other's hurt.[11] Berry intends to characterize a human community in which people still have time for each other, and the very process of interaction among them is itself a healing. In this novel, there is regular allusion to the importance of finding a place in the land, in the earth, in the fabric of human community and human experience. Berry is not romantic. In the story, there is a father who goes berserk as he watches his daughter swept away by a flood. There is a handicapped, lonely carpenter who commits suicide over the wife of another man whom he cannot have. The destructive reality of human life is available in the novel. The power of Berry's novel is that it is an act of hope in the face of a harsh, brutalizing world that no longer has any reason.

The central family of *A Place on Earth* are the Feltners. Their only son is "missing in action" in the war. He has been missing so long that the father grimly declares that Virgil is dead. In a pregnant scene, when the town has known of Virgil's "death" long enough and mumbled its genuine caring, the pastor must make his inevitable visit to the torn family. The pastor is a caring man, but the visit does not work. The conversation is stiff and irrelevant. The grieving parents who grieve too deeply for words must finally minister to the minister who is of little help to them. All parties are relieved when his duty is done and the visit ends.

The failed visit requires considerable reflection. First, the pastor, Brother Preston, knowing he has failed, goes to the sanctuary to reflect:

> He came away from the Feltner house grieved by the imperfection of his visit. It was not, as he had hoped it would be, a conversation. It was a sermon. This is the history of his life in Port William. The Word, in his speaking it, fails to be made flesh. It is a failure particularized for him in the palm of every work-stiffened hand held out to him at the church door every Sunday morning—the hard dark hand taking his pale unworn one in a gesture of politeness without understanding. He belongs to the governance of those he ministers to without belonging to their knowledge, the bringer of the Word preserved from flesh.[12]

It is in fact faith that is upstairs (like the summons of the psalms which have lost their concrete reason). The minister articulates a world without reason, mandates without memory, truth without experience. Such an articulation has no compelling power. It fails to transform.

When the preacher is gone, Mat, the father, without mocking the ineffectiveness of the pastor, observes that the pastor does not help because he offers the hope of heaven while "I can only be comforted by the hope of earth." Berry means to say, I believe, that healing hope, prospect of transformation, comes only in the transactions of daily life where pain is surfaced and healing is articulated close at hand. Human truth of a transformative kind happens not by a grand scheme, not by a floating archetype, but by the dailyness of being present in the hurt, by waiting in the hurt with honest speech and open grief, waiting and waiting, until the turn that is strangely given, but never forced. Mat concludes:

> In the preacher's words the Heavenly City has risen up, surmounting their lives, the house, the town—the final hope, in which all the riddles and ends of the world are gathered, illuminated, and bound. This is the preacher's hope, and he has moved to it alone, outside the claims of time and sorrow, by the motion of desire which he calls faith. In it, having invoked it and raised it up, he is free of the world.[13]

This faith of the preacher is contrasted with that of the silent, hurting, reflective Mat, father of the missing Virgil:

> Mat realizes that he is not free, and never has been. He is doomed to hope in the world, in the bonds of his own love. He is doomed to take every chance and desperate hope of hope between him and death,[14] Virgil's, Margaret's, his. His hope of Heaven must be the hope of a man bound to the world that his life is not ultimately futile or ultimately meaningless, a hope more burdening than despair.[15]

Not only do the pastor and the father reflect on this failed conversation, on the failure of the Word. A third character, Burley, helps the reader interpret what has gone on. Burley is a close friend of the Feltners. He knows the family's struggle with Virgil's "death" and he has witnessed the failure of the pastor. His voice is Berry's voice of commentary. In a letter to his nephew Nathan, who is also in the service, Burley writes:

> The difference between people is what has got to be taken notice of. There's the preacher who has what I reckon you would call a knack for the Hereafter. He's not much mixed with this world. As far as he's concerned there is no difference, or not much, between Tom Coulter and Virgil Feltner. Their names fit into the riddle he thinks he knows the answer to. I wouldn't try to say he ain't right. I do say that some people's knack is for the Here. Anyhow, that's the talent I'm stuck with. For us it's important to keep in mind who Tom was. And for Mat and them I judge it's important to know who is meant when they speak of Virgil. We don't forget them after somebody who never knew them has said, "Dead in the service of his country" and "rest in peace." That's not the way these accounts are kept. We don't rest in peace. The life of a good man who has died belongs to the people who cared about him, and ought to, and maybe itself is as much comfort as ought to be asked or offered. And surely the talk of a reunion in Heaven is thin comfort to people who need each other here as much as we do.[16]

Burley's voice recalls us to the concrete, transformative reasons of the Psalms. Much of the praise that has moved up from reason to summons has only "a knack for the Hereafter." But genuine praise appropriate to the rescuing God of Israel is praise which has "a knack for the Here." It will be a recovery of "the Here" in praise that will let our praise be faithful as well as transformative.

I have given this much attention to Berry's novel because the portrayal of the pastor articulates the temptation of religion that has moved upstairs away from the realities of life. The pastor practices a faith that is removed from the daily concreteness of life which is a day-to-day hurt and an hourly hoping for healing. In contrast to the pastor, the family to whom he ministers lives in touch with the pain, regulated as it is not by the present void but by the world of concrete memories which give reason for the present hurt and present possibility. The power of the Psalms is based in such a focus on the concrete realities. The royal apparatus, like this well-meaning but out-of-touch pastor, always wants to escape such concreteness for the sake of better truth. But Israel knows, as Berry has seen, that

such a better truth is no truth at all. The truth which heals must emerge in the midst of the reality of specific pain.

Thus I propose that *access into life is mostly through the resistant door of pain.* That door is a world kept closed by idolatry (of a god who does not suffer) and closed by ideology (of a system that never fails). That door of access is so resistant because our idolatry has turned pain to guilt,[17] and our ideology has turned pain to denial. Because God can never do wrong, if something is wrong it must be our fault. And if the system contains all truth, what hurts must be denied. In the closed world of idolatry and ideology, our praise is permeated by guilt and denial. The pain is there right in the midst of praise, but it must be kept hidden, either by accepting fault for all that is wrong, or by pretending nothing is wrong. Pain is there powerfully, compellingly, persistently. Its "thereness," or in the language of Berry, its "Hereness" is the first fact in a faithful doxology. Praise always happens midst the irreducible reality of pain. If a world of *ḥesed* and *'emeth*, of faithfulness and reliability, is to be fashioned in American society, it will be fashioned only in the presence of and through the process of pain. Any other offer of *ḥesed* and *'emeth* is a charade that lacks conviction or power. Any "world" that is "made" in liturgy which does not include honest elements of pain is a false world that leads to death.

False selves generated by idolatry and ideology live in conformity, and denial of pain ultimately disregards issues of injustice. The transformation of such falseness happens only by the acknowledging speech of pain, and the "hope of earth" that is present in such speech. The hurting characters in Berry's novel are not hopeless. But their hope lives in and becomes operative only in the hurt. They sense, in contrast to Brother Preston, that serious hope cannot live "outside the claims of time and sorrow." They will receive no hope "free of the world."

To engage in evangelical world-making, our proper vocation, to lead the congregation *back down* from summons to reason is not to lead them back to the slogans and formulae of ancient Israel, but to lead them back to their own hurtful experience for which ancient Israel offers useful forms of articulation. The *pain at the center of praise* has theological warrant in Israel in the cries of hurt, rage, doubt, vengeance, and isolation. Most importantly, they are cries, not buried, not stifled, but cries passionately addressed out of the reality of life.

The liturgy, and the pastor, have access to many dimensions of such concrete pain. When it is brought to speech, the odd gift of hope and healing is given.

1. The most immediate pain consists in relations violated, in intimacy fractured, in alienations, in parents that have lived too long, in children who have stayed too long or left too soon.

2. There is pain below that, the pain of lives of quiet desperation, of having achieved all the promises of our society and discovering failure and emptiness, of having become the false self required by idolatry, of having been docile, conformist, and passive for so long that one is either immobilized or one is a raging volcano without knowing where to dump the lava. Where honest processing of such rage and humiliation is blocked, people live at the edge of violence, and often fall over that edge. The violence of self-hatred will break out, against spouse, against child, against anyone available. But while the violence builds and grows, there is still conformist success, competence, dutiful obedience, and proper praise—to keep the lid on through one more song—while the violence grows.

3. The pain is also present in our public life, although we are not so apt to name and identify it. The violence cannot finally be contained in our more intimate contexts. There are not enough people there to receive it all. Beyond normal informal social outlets, the violence finally turns to policy, to public values and public conduct which foster and legitimate violence. We would not countenance the violence were it rightly named, but we deceive about the violence by giving it other names. Indeed, we invent an entire "counter-vocabulary" so that we intentionally do not rightly identify.[18] We call the violence that we cannot manage deterrence, balance of terror, preemptive strike, maintenance of spheres of influence, military advisors, death sentence, law and order, swift justice. As every Calvinist knows, there are legitimate functions for the state. But in a society marked by idolatrous, ideological doxology, the unrelieved, unreceived, unhonored pain turns to destructive energy, and it is worked against all those who do not "obey God's laws" and cooperate with the system.[19]

The undifferentiated object of such violence becomes a brutalized "it": victims of AIDS, welfare cheats, communists, peasants, indigent mothers, and so forth. When we can no longer acknowledge our pain which is translated into self-hatred, then it is certain that we will no longer take seriously the pain of another. We will redefine their pain as guilt and failure, and we will no longer attend to, discern, or expect the transformations which make humanness possible. We only want to strike out in the service of a god who cannot act, for the sake of the system which cannot be changed. American Christians who are liturgically self-conscious characterize this closed world with the phrase "world without end, Amen." Other Christians who are not as intentional about liturgy simply say, "Praise the Lord." In whichever wording and with whatever level of liturgical awareness, the two formulae come to the same thing. A lid is put on all the present reality! Everything is focused on a generalized "Hereafter," and "the knack for the Here" is forfeited. The shared ache for social transformation is reduced to resentment, hate, rage, and so on. Serious justice questions disappear from the conversation, because everything must conform to the norm which has no history; no frail emergence at the beginning, no exhausted finish at the end, only is, has been, and will be. Everything must yield to the norm. Everything must be done to sustain that world, even at the shameless cost of denial of our hurt and the hurt of our neighbor.

4. The pain is finally unavailable in our relentless hopelessness. After so much guilt and denial, we do not believe in an alternative future. We do not believe there is a God who makes things new, who cares so about truth, equity, and righteousness that the present must give way to the force of God's promise. That is, we do not believe the gospel that "The Lord reigns." We arrive at a beaten numbness with a sense of "no exit."[20] We cannot see how the race to death with nuclear arms and in nuclear families can ever be halted or disrupted. We cannot imagine a different future for the world, nor for those closest, most precious, most troubled around us. The only available alternative is thus to live as fully and self-centeredly as is required of us and permitted for us. We end in despair. We can see no more prospect of a transformed world than we can of a transformed marriage, or a transformed self, or a transformed job. We manufacture a world whose reasons are hate, hurt, and fear, not any longer *hesed* and *'emeth*. The alienation grows. And with it grows the brutality—untamed.

All the while we engage in the hymns required of us to keep the royal world intact. We sing songs serving the ideology, even though it requires denial. We engage in these acts of praise which in fact are acts of guilt, acts of denial. But the pain lingers, unattended, unhonored. Our devout singing is all in praise of some unapproached, inaccessible Hereafter, without a knack for the Here so pained. We either sing lustily, still believing the ideology and trusting in idolatry. Or we sing tepidly, knowing better. But tepidly or lustily, we lack the singing which engages us in the claims of time and sorrow.

PAIN AS THE MATRIX OF PRAISE

The biblical community knows about the pain which needs no theoretical justification. It knows it is simply there. It lingers there relentlessly, silently, heavily. Moreover the biblical community knows the pain cannot be handled alone. In isolation, the power of pain grows more ominous and more hurtful. The pain must be handled in community, even if a community of only a few who will attend. It knows that finally pain must be submitted to the power of the holy God

> who forgives all your iniquity,
> who heals all your diseases,
> who redeems your life from the Pit,
> who crowns you with steadfast love and mercy,
> who satisfies you with good . . .
> [who] works vindication . . . for all who are oppressed.
>   (Ps. 103:3–6)

The biblical community of faith knows in its deepest truth and deepest honesty that the God of this community transforms.

Israel holds the conviction about God's transforming power quite concretely. It knows of the transformations because it tells concrete stories, employs concrete metaphors, cherishes concrete memories. Israel enacted and trusted liturgical practices that made the transformation of pain vivid, powerful, and credible. It did its singing and praying and praising in ways that shaped pain into hope, and grief into possibility. The biblical community of faith always returned to its memories, for there it found subversive models of speech for how pain in this community has been turned to praise-filled energy. I will mention three such models of subversive speech, each of which begins in pain, and each of which ends in praise.

Canonical Memory

Gerhard von Rad[21] and G. E. Wright[22] correctly focused on the credo as the core and center of Israel's memory and Israel's faith. That hypothesis has now become hackneyed and is the subject of weighty scholarly dispute.[23] But in highly stylized form, the credo formulations (Deut. 6:20–24; 26:5–9; Josh. 24:2–13) did indeed assert the main affirmations about Israel's faith out of its memory. Israel regularly remembered that "we groaned and cried out" and Israel also remembered that the Lord "saw and heard and remembered and knows."[24] The recovery of the canonical memory of Israel bears witness to the way Israel publicly submitted its pain to the high purpose and holy power of God. The pain of Israel is brought to speech in community before God. In that act God is summoned relentlessly into the now.

The connection between *canonical memory of credo* and *concrete pain* is articulated in Psalm 77.[25] The first ten verses of that psalm are a personal complaint of a speaker who cannot sleep and cannot speak. It is focused completely on personal hurt. There is deep doubt about God.

> I think of God, and I moan,
>   I meditate, and my spirit faints.
> Thou dost hold my eyelids from closing;
>   I am so troubled that I cannot speak. . . .
> "Will the Lord spurn for ever,
>   and never again be favorable?
> Has his steadfast love for ever ceased?
>   Are his promises at an end for all time?
> Has God forgotten to be gracious?
>   Has he in anger shut up his compassion?" (vv. 3–4, 7–9)

These are serious questions about God's faithfulness. Israel conducts honest probes about God for which the answer is not given beforehand. Israel asks whether God is indeed gracious and faithful. Israel is willing to entertain the notion that the answer is yes. After the questioning of God, there is a startling turn in v. 11 which abruptly changes the subject, away *from* self-doubt *to* an affirmation about God. That change of subject opens the psalm to a powerful memory that leads the speaker back to the credo (vv. 11–15).

> I will call to mind the deeds of the Lord;
>   yea, I will remember thy wonders of old.

> I will meditate on all thy work,
>   and muse on thy mighty deeds.
> Thy way, O God, is holy.
>   What god is great like our God?
> Thou art the God who workest wonders,
>   who hast manifested thy might among the peoples.
> Thou didst with thy arm redeem thy people,
>   the sons of Jacob and Joseph.

Two things have happened in the speech of this desperate person. First, there is a shift from "I" to "Thou." Now God becomes the center of the rhetoric, as the speaker turns to Israel's normative memory. Second, the psalm engages in concrete remembering which takes the mind off the hopelessness of self. The memory of hurt resolved contextualizes present hurt, as yet unresolved. The remembering is so concrete that it is stated in finite verbs recalling quite specific actions of transformation.[26] The speaker of Psalm 77 now moves to speak in detail (in credo) about the liberation of the exodus:

> When the waters saw thee, O God,
>   when the waters saw thee, they were afraid,
>   yea, the deep trembled.
> The clouds poured out water;
>   the skies gave forth thunder;
>   thy arrows flashed on every side.
> The crash of thy thunder was in the whirlwind;
>   thy lightnings lighted up the world;
>   the earth trembled and shook.
> Thy way was through the sea,
>   thy path through the great waters;
>   yet thy footprints were unseen.
> Thou didst lead thy people like a flock
>   by the hand of Moses and Aaron. (vv. 16–20)

The speaker refers to "thy people" (vv. 15, 20) and clearly reckons himself among that people. By that identification, the speaker participates in an extraordinary remembering and reconstruction of the world even in this moment of personal crisis. The speaker is able to move past his own initial doubt about the truth of the memory of the community. At the same time he is able and willing to subject his trouble to that powerful memory. His trouble is recontextualized and thereby transformed. Oddly and importantly, the psalmist does not return to the trouble of vv. 1–10. The psalm ends in trusting celebration. The normative memory has rhetorically comprehended the hurt of Here.

I do not suggest that the mere recital of the credo is an adequate pastoral resolution of personal hurt. But the juxtaposition of personal hurt (vv. 1–10) and communal memory (vv. 11–20) is powerful and suggests a mode of praise that is genuinely healing and salvific. The credo is located in the psalm so that it contextualizes pain in ways that transform.

The recited credo affirms an intergenerational reality which eases the focus of the present moment without denying any part of it. It proposes a model for the transformation of trouble that is larger and more powerful than my own inclinations. It offers a fresh "Thou" so that my "I" is redeemable. Israel knows that without this pain-entering "Thou," "I" cannot be transformed. The very recital permits a rereading of trouble that ends in the glad practice of praise. We may believe that the trouble persists for the speaker even after v. 20, but everything has been changed. The trouble has been set in the context of remembered praise.

The praise has power to transform the pain. But conversely the present pain also keeps the act of praise honest. Praise about old transformations by themselves may permit the old troubles to seem remote from the present moment. But the present reality of pain within which praise is done reminds Israel that this longstanding formulation of praise was articulated and utilized precisely in a context of pain, namely, the pain of slavery. Just as this praise initially was sung in the midst of trouble and oppression, so now it is peculiarly germane in the present pain. As praise recontextualizes pain, so pain refocuses praise.

The move from vv. 1–10 to vv. 11–20 is a characteristic step in Israel from a pained person to a glad community. That community in which the old memories are recited reiterates the conviction and assurance that God's *hesed* endures forever, even now, even with me, even in this pain. The recovery of the public history of pain transformed is repeatedly and astonishingly transformational in each new recital. That recital is able to say, "To him who led his people through the wilderness, for his steadfast love endures for ever" (Ps. 136:16).

That motif of God's sustenance in the wilderness is echoed in another historical recital in Psalm 78:19:

> They spoke against God, saying,
> "Can God spread a table in the wilderness?"[27]

The tradition is agreed in its mighty answer of yes. Yes, God can indeed spread a table in the wilderness (vv. 23–25):

> Yet he commanded the skies above,
>   and opened the doors of heaven;
> and he rained down upon them manna to eat,
>   and gave them the grain of heaven.
> Man ate of the bread of the angels;
>   he sent them food in abundance.

This credo memory of deliverance and nurture is drawn on by the speaker of Psalm 77 at the end of the canonical recall in this psalm (v. 20):

> Thou didst lead thy people like a flock
>   by the hand of Moses and Aaron.

It is indeed this canonical memory which now impinges upon the psalmist's recital of self-preoccupation and self-pity to contextualize and thereby transform. Everything depends on having the public, canonical memory available which becomes in this moment of pain a quite powerful, personal hope.

The Lament Psalm

A second subversive model of how pain is turned to praise-filled energy is the lament psalm.[28] The lament psalms are obviously a scandal in the church, because they cannot be prayed to a god who does nothing, and because they must not be prayed within a social system that cannot be changed or criticized. The lament psalms are unworkable and inappropriate in a situation dominated by idolatry and ideology. For that reason they have largely dropped out of the repertoire of the church. If we are to permit the church back into its pain, in order that the church may seriously praise, then we must recover the use of these lament psalms, or we must find some speech forms like them.

Westermann has seen that the structure of "plea-praise" which is characteristic of lament psalms is normative for Israel's prayer speech. Israel's praise characteristically arises in the context of lament answered and resolved. The lament cannot be answered and resolved by God, however, unless it is spoken. The possibility of genuinely liberated praise depends upon lament as its point of origin. The laments of Israel are regularly and everywhere addressed to God. In this speech Israel has already made a decision that pain and hurt must be addressed to God and it is this decision of faith which begins the process of transformation. To address God with such hurt is a bold theological act. It dares to draw the theological judgment that God is not as unapproachable as the "idolatry of praise" suggests, nor is the system as immune to criticism as the ideology of the system suggests.

The lament psalm is Israel's foremost word on pain and Israel's most daring theological act. It asserts:

- that pain is present, and that it can be articulated with candor. In this speech Israel exhibits its remarkable "knack for the Here."
- that pain can and must be addressed to God. It must be addressed to God because dysfunction in a covenanted world is God's proper business and God cannot be protected from the reality of trouble. The trouble can be addressed to God because the God of Israel is not the unapproachable god of the temple construction or royal ideology, but is the One whose entry into Israel's life happened in the cries of Exod. 2:23–25. Subsequent laments in Israel rely upon and appeal to the paradigmatic beginnings of Exodus 2.
- that the pain can be addressed to God in an imperative, an insistent hope that the trouble can be changed and it must be changed.[29] The boldness of the imperative reflects that Israel's notion of initiative and power is different from the splendid unapproachability of imperial gods. The covenant in Israel has greatly shifted the possibility of communication "from below" to which the "God above" must give heed. The imperatives addressed to God model a form of interaction in which the lesser party compels the greater party to act.

Israel knows that pain must be publicly processed. Israel articulates its pain publicly not simply as a cathartic activity, but in order to make the pain into the public business of God, and if of God, then of all managers of public business. Such speech requires power managers in heaven and on earth to deal with the hurt. Israel's speech about pain is both a powerful theological conviction and an elemental human insight. The theological conviction spoken against imperial religion (enshrined in most catechisms) is that God must attend to the faithful cries of the wretched. The elemental human insight is that hurting people will not receive help if they keep silent. In Israel's *speech of complaint,* Israel's *discernment of God* and Israel's *embrace of human reality* converge. Pain must be processed and not denied or siphoned off into guilt. When adequately processed, that is, when God is mobilized, the cry of wretchedness has reason to turn to praise and energy.

In Psalm 39, the psalmist has learned the costly, unbearable reality of keeping silent (vv. 1–3):[30]

> I said, "I will guard my ways,
>   that I may not sin with my tongue;
> I will bridle my mouth,
>   so long as the wicked are in my presence."
> I was dumb and silent,
>   I held my peace to no avail;
> my distress grew worse,
>   my heart became hot within me.
> As I mused, the fire burned;
>   then I spoke with my tongue.

We may wonder how and why this speaker guarded his tongue and bridled his mouth. It is most plausible that such silent faith was encouraged and valued by the idolatry of a god who may not be addressed and a system which must not be assaulted. The decision to speak from a "hot heart" (v. 3) is a decision to break the grip of the idolatry and the legitimacy of the ideology. Finally, when there is courage to speak, the psalmist asserts that God in the midst of trouble is a source of hope (vv. 7–8):

> And now, Lord, for what do I wait?
>   My hope is in thee.
> Deliver me from all my transgressions.
>   Make me not the scorn of the fool!

Speech breaks the despair. The speech out of despair moves toward and addresses God, the subject of hope. As silence leads to hopelessness, so speech invites the God of all hope to be present. Speech which mobilizes God is a bold move beyond hopelessness.

On the basis of that conviction, the poem ends with an appeal to God to break out of God's passivity and indifferent silence into rage and indignation on behalf of the speaker (v. 12):

> Hear my prayer, O Lord,
>   and give ear to my cry;
> hold not thy peace at my tears!
>   For I am thy passing guest.

The speaker kept silent and things only got worse. As long as the speaker kept silent, God kept silent as well. As the speaker finally erupts in rage and indignation, so it is urged that God should break God's silence and make a difference. The phrase "I held my peace" in v. 2 corresponds to the same petition in v. 12, "hold not thy peace." We are not told the outcome of this petition. We only know that Israel characteristically addressed such bold petitions to God. Israel sensed and believed in the transformative efficaciousness of such a prayer. When the petitioner breaks the silence of passivity, God may also break the silence of inactivity.

The world of lament speech thus is based on the premise that the speech of Israel draws God into the trouble. God will act and life will be restored. The psalm urges that God should not be silent, but should speak (and act) on behalf of the one in trouble. Psalm 39 does not tell us if God responded and broke the silence in response to the petition. But we find closely paralleled language in a comparable situation in Isa. 42:14–17. It is likely that this oracle on God's part is a response to a lament like Psalm 39.[31]

> For a long time I have held my peace;
>   I have kept still and have restrained myself. (Isa. 42:14a)

God concedes that God has been reticent too long. In relation to our critique of idolatry and ideology, the God who now finally speaks has been too long the complacent, indifferent god of the empire. But now, now in the midst of a poetic rendering of pain through the great memories of Israel,

> Now I will cry out like a woman in travail,
>   I will gasp and pant.
> I will lay waste mountains and hills,
>   and dry up all their herbage;
> I will turn the rivers into islands,
>   and dry up the pools.
> And I will lead the blind in a way that they know not,
>   in paths that they have not known
>   I will guide them.
> I will turn the darkness before them into light,
>   the rough places into level ground.
> These are the things I will do,
>   and I will not forsake them.
> They shall be turned back and utterly put to shame,
>   who trust in graven images,
>   who say to molten images,
>   "You are our gods." (Isa. 42:14b–17)

What a speech! It is a remarkable self-assertion of God who will now mobilize power to transform the world. The body of the speech (vv. 15–16) is a recital of strong first-person verbs of transformation. Everything will be inverted. This self-assertion is introduced in v. 14b with the entry of Yahweh into the action like a woman in labor, with exaggerated, abrupt, unstoppable action. There is nothing here of passivity, indifference, restraint. There is nothing here of an idol who cannot move, act, care, or respond. All of God's powerful birthing-energy is at work to form a new world. This recital of self-assertion is concluded in v. 17 with a dismissal of idols and of all those who trust in idols. If the prayer of Psalm 39 and the response of Isaiah 42 are held together, it is clear that it is the urging of Israel that moves this birthing God into action. Silence is broken by God only as silence is broken by Israel.

In Isaiah 42 there is a doxology that bespeaks enthronement (42:5–13) just before this poignant assertion. Israel is invited to sing a new song (42:10) not unlike the new song of enthronement we have already considered (Ps. 96:1).[32] In Isa. 42:8 Yahweh asserts that glory will not be shared with graven images (cf. Ps. 96:4–5), and in v. 9 "new things" are announced. But the enthronement, the "new things," and the defeat of the idols are not received from Yahweh apart from the grief and rage of Israel who breaks the cosmic silence of docility and passivity. As *the idols* are correlated with silence too long kept, the speech of hurt and then of praise is correlated with *this living God* who breaks the silence and fills the void with new song and new life.[33]

The situation between Israel and God is transformed because it becomes a situation of speaking and hearing and answering. Because, and only because, the trouble of the psalmist is brought to speech, it is injected into the ongoing life of Israel and Yahweh. The one addressed and evoked by the complaint is the one who has a long history of transformative intervention. While Yahweh is summoned to do a new thing, Yahweh is not asked to do a new kind of thing. Yahweh is asked, rather, to do yet again concretely what God does characteristically and best. But note well, the thing God is summoned to do and gladly does is not a heavenly hope about a Hereafter. This is a hope in the earth, in the Here, in the traffic of human activity, for Yahweh is a partner in a drama which is a real human drama of pain acknowledged and resolved. It is this very God who will not "abandon" (Isa. 42:16). This is the ultimate word of fidelity, and it is spoken among all the Virgils, Mats, and Burneys who imagine their common life is abandoned. The hope given in response to lament is not "thin comfort," which Burley perceived from the preacher.[34] It is now rich, full-bodied comfort (Isa. 40:1), available only because of daring complaint.

Songs of Thanksgiving

The individual songs of thanksgiving offer a third way in which Israel goes back behind hymns to the concrete Here of pain.[35] These songs may be the most immediately pertinent to our theme. They are songs in which individuals tell of actual troubles that have been resolved. They stay very close to Here. As is characteristic of such testimonies, we do not get detailed descriptions of the mechanics of resolution. Indeed, that is the reason that such things as healing, rescue, deliverance, even forgiveness must be spoken about liturgically and poetically. The transformation is always hidden, always a surprise, always a miracle, always a gift that resists and resents explanation. Liturgy is not a place for explanation, but for candor and for amazement.

> I was blind, now I see. (John 9:25)

> My son was dead, and is alive again;
> he was lost, and is found. (Luke 15:24)

> Instead of the thorn shall come up the cypress;
> instead of the brier shall come up the myrtle. (Isa. 55:13)

> A garland instead of ashes,
> the oil of gladness instead of mourning,
> the mantle of praise instead of a faint spirit. (Isa. 61:3)

We are here at the irreducible heart of evangelical faith. We do not know how the newness happens. There is something inscrutable and hidden about the ways in which God transforms. God's people are not able to give explanations. But they are capable of testimony about the possibility of new life. Israel's characteristic speech does not tone down the harshness or hurt of trouble. Israel's speech is honest acknowledgment of death, its power and its destructiveness: "blind, dead, lost, slaves, thorns, brier, ashes, mourning, faint spirit." The trouble is real, it is specific, it hurts. And it has been overcome! Trouble has been defeated and Israel must sing. Israel's world of new possibility is formed out of this astonished, specific singing. Israel sings about the transformation it receives but cannot explain.

The song of thanksgiving builds on the lament. The song of thanksgiving is the lament now recited from the other side, from the side of resolution, from the side of God's transformation. I remember how I complained. I remember what I complained about. I remember whom I addressed in my complaint. I remember what I said and the God to whom I said it. And I remember how God listened. I remember how I went public with my pain, to the throne and to the community of faith. I remember what a bold daring act it was. I remember how embarrassed I was and how intimidated the community was.[36] I remember how the conventional God did not seem approachable. But I spoke anyway, addressing a God for whom I yearned, but whom I did not know until the moment of my abrasive speech.

We may take Psalm 30 as illustrative of Israel's song of thanksgiving. In vv. 1–5 the psalm asserts the speaker's readiness to praise and thank Yahweh. Four times in these verses Yahweh is named. The speaker knows the name of the One to be addressed, the One who has acted. The unit of vv. 1–5 divides into four parts arranged in an envelope. Verse 1 stands by itself as a hymnic beginning:

> I will extol thee, O Lord,
>> because: thou has drawn me up,
>> thou hast not let my foes rejoice over me.

This formulation of praise is matched in vv. 4–5 by a second hymnic construction. In vv. 4–5 there is the double summons to sing praise, to give thanks, because,

> His anger is but for a moment,
>> and his favor is for a lifetime.
> Weeping may tarry for the night,
>> but joy comes in the morning.

This hymnic structure is intensely personal. It is sung by one who has known the transformation. There is no denial of how burdensome life has been. There really was anger from God, and it is not denied that God's anger might be appropriate. There was weeping—a troubled act of faith—through the night, perhaps remorse, perhaps self-pity. Then comes favor from the God who has been angry, then comes a joy after weeping tarried in the night.[37] There has been a transformation. The psalm narrates. It does not explain, indeed it does not even know how to explain. Nor does it care for such matters. It is enough to tell.

Between 30:1 and 30:4–5 is a double address to Yahweh:

> O Lord my God,
>   I cried . . . thou hast healed me.
> O Lord, thou hast brought up my soul from Sheol,
>   restored me to life.

The threefold actions of God—"heal, bring up, give life"—are all in response to "cry." The cry mobilizes God and brings a new world. All three verbs witness to a transformation which is beyond reason, beyond expectation, beyond explanation, wrought by Yahweh in response to Israel's cry.

The memory of the transformation becomes even more concrete: "To thee, O Lord, I cried" (Ps. 30:8). The speaker then reiterates what was said in the previous lament. The speaker quotes himself and has not forgotten the concreteness of pain nor the specificity of speech. The speaker remembers the candor and concreteness of what was said that moved God to hear and act (30:9–10):

> What profit is there in my death,
>   if I go down to the Pit?
> Will the dust praise thee?
>   Will it tell of thy faithfulness?
> Hear, O Lord, and be gracious to me!
>   O Lord, be thou my helper.

Verse 9 consists in three rhetorical questions that intend to motivate God. The questions are followed by a triple imperative: "hear, be gracious, be a helper." Finally Yahweh is twice more addressed insistently by name. The two verses (9–10) are a lament remembered and quoted, with an intense "knack for Here."

Psalm 30 makes an abrupt turn in v. 11. The abruptness is intensified by the absence of a conjunction:

> Thou hast turned for me my mourning into dancing;
> Thou hast loosed my sackcloth
>   and girded me with gladness.

The verb is strong: "turn." The address is direct: "Thou." Yahweh's decisive action is surprising. The more the transformation is reflected upon, the more inexplicable and wondrous it is; the more the turn wrought by God looms with cosmic significance. The transformation becomes a way to think about God's way elsewhere in the world, and Israel takes the change as a paradigm for God's characteristic way in the world. The conclusion of v. 12 utilizes the verbs "praise" (*zmr*) and "thank" (*ydh*), the same verbs used in v. 4. The psalm of thanksgiving in retrospect is shaped in celebration. But the speaker is honest about the complaint which evoked the transformation. Indeed, the transformation happened in and through and not without the complaint. The transformation evoked by complaint is the source of praise. The initial verb "extol," which is hymnic, receives its force from the specificity of the recital that follows.

It is noteworthy that in v. 4 the community of the faithful is summoned to praise. All are invited to doxology. That general communal invitation has its warrant and reason, however, in a previous transaction that was personal, concrete, and specific, which is told again for the benefit of and in the presence of the whole congregation. Out of such intimate personal reason Israel articulates a comprehensive summons. As the psalm moves from reason to summons, so songs of thanksgiving move from intimate, personal experience to comprehensive, communal celebration.

Psalm 30, which we have considered in detail, is representative of a special mode of speech in Israel (see also Psalms 40; 66:13–20; Jonah 2:2–9). These songs constitute a posture toward God quite in contrast to the generalizing mode of hymns of praise. They are much more specific and they are immediately in contact with the pain that was expressed in lament, and the recent transformation of that pain wrought by God. Thus they are the concluding expression of a sequence from trouble to complaint to divine intervention to responding thanksgiving. They express a history of trouble turned to joy. Each time they are sung, they invite Israel to participate in that entire history of transformation again. The practice of the history of transformation guards against an idolatry of a god who cannot be changed and an ideology that imagines the world is fixed and settled. The song of thanksgiving characteristically avoids the temptations to idolatry and ideology to which the hymn is susceptible, because it has memory and hope which always stay close to pain and rescue.

LITTLE STORIES OF HURT,
LITTLE SONGS OF GRIEF

The concreteness of the *credo recital*, the remembered pain of the *lament*, and the inscrutable transformation of the *song of thanksgiving* all move from remembered hurt and trouble to celebrated well-being and resolution. The speech form in each case carries that move. The rhetoric reenacts the transformation and makes the remembered transformation available again each time the psalm is recited. Indeed these modes of speech present a community whose characteristic mode of life is to be transformed, to have been transformed, and to still be transformed in time to come.[38] This community is under transformation in its past, its present, and its future. It is being transformed as long as it uses this transformative speech. It is the nature of the relation between this singing, confessing people and the God who is confessed and about whom Israel sings to be engaged together in the process of transformation. Israel's speech at its most candid and concrete is to articulate life with God in the process of transformation.

This mode of remembering and celebrating is in a distinctive way "a little story," a story sung "from below," a story sung by those who can remember being "little ones" whom the world has either crushed or disregarded.[39] The little story is characteristically rooted in hurt, amazed at well-being, astonished at the move from hurt to well-being. This little story is indeed a story! In each of these speech forms—credo, lament, and thanksgiving—Israel's way of thanks is to tell a story that moves from problem to resolution, from hurt to well-being.[40] The ones who sing and recite can remember when it was not like it is now, and can hope for when it will again not be like it is now. As the rhetoric carries the community through a transformation, so the form carries Israel repeatedly through its treasured past, amazed present, and promised futures. These forms keep Israel and Israel's faith in time and open to time, available for new time under God's transformative sovereignty. Thus these speech forms work against absolutizing the present and excessively legitimating present arrangements. Indeed these songs of transformation resist every attempt to freeze life in a certain mode, and subvert every pretense of timeless or absolute legitimacy. The "little story" of the "little ones" (which constitutes the primal data of Israel's faith and the primal material of Israel's world) thus always speaks against the Great Story of the royal establishment.[41]

The "Great Story," with its summons to praise without reason, its summons to a world without remembered legitimatization, does not cherish or value the remembered transformations. Indeed the remembered transformations are a threat to such a world. That Great Story expressed in hymns which lack reason wants to overcome time, to have no memories of hurt, to entertain no unexplained transformations, to celebrate no amazements that occur beyond administered reality. The Great Story wants to banish the "underneathness" of Israel's timefulness. In the language of Wendell Berry, the "Great Story" would like to relate to God apart from the claims of "time and sorrow." But such an avoidance of the claims of time and sorrow is inevitably idolatrous and ideological, is unavoidably false about human life and about the character of God. Such an avoidance of the claims of time and sorrow ends in despairing death. If hurt is not to be remembered and timefulness is not treasured, then there need be no threatening, destabilizing hope that "this world" will soon or late pass away. The Great Story would rather imagine ours is a "world without end."

The poignant, passionate, relentless, restless "little story" will not finally yield, will not ultimately defer, will not be silenced or censored. It will still have its awkward, disturbing, hope-generating say, right in the face of the great passionless story of absoluteness. Israel is uncompromisingly committed to saying its creed in the face of every empire, of singing its laments in the presence of every repressive, oppressive hurt, of shouting its songs of thanksgiving against every urbane hymn which puts the human world on hold. Israel will resiliently practice its speech which lives so close to the reality of its life that it cannot and will not live without its speech. The Israelite "does not think in the Hellenistic sense of the word; he cries out, he threatens, he orders, he groans, he exults,"[42] because it is in this irresistible, unadministered speech that Israel will be Israel, in the face of the nations who are embarrassed and even in the face of God who does not want to be disturbed. The kings keep managing the liturgy, but the managed liturgy cannot keep the lid on the abrasive, energizing reality of the gospel which is present and visible, and which must be told and sung and enacted.

In a dramatic way, language leads reality. Israel's credos, laments, and songs of thanksgiving reshape reality. That is why they are said and sung. The world cannot remain as it is when Israel is serious about its speech. The reshaping entails two decisive matters wrought in the singing and saying:

1. The idols who cannot act are abruptly displaced by the transformative God. In these speech forms Israel is doing its theological

work, redescribing, rearticulating, recharacterizing God. The stuff of God, the speech out of which God is dramatically offered, is no longer static, imperial adjectives; now it is the drastic verbs on the lips of little people, the verbs of "rescue, deliver, heal, release, redeem, snatch, feed, guide, give." God is not known generally but concretely.[43] God is not permitted an undisturbed administration, but now must be present to the transformation, in order to be the God known in this community. Fresh theology for Israel comes from recovering the reasons for praise among those who can anticipate transformation.

It is not a far move from Ps. 30:11,

> Thou hast turned for me my mourning into dancing;
> thou hast loosed my sackcloth and girded me with gladness,

to the Christology offered to John,

> the blind receive their sight, the lame walk, lepers are cleansed, and the deaf hear, the dead are raised up, the poor have good news preached to them. (Luke 7:22)

It is all of a piece. In such singing and reciting, Israel lingers no longer over the slow idols who celebrate the status quo, who sanction imperial power, who legitimate inequality for the sake of order. The recitations of Israel banish such false gods and make possible grateful trust in the living God.

2. The ideology which commands no allegiance is abruptly displaced by a conviction of possibility. The imperial theology had imagined that everything was settled. The way things are is the way they must be and will be. The power arrangements as we have them are exactly right. Present distributions of power are appropriate, legitimate, and everyone has a place. Present access to economic well-being or denial of access is ordained by God and by the rulers of this age, and it cannot be changed. The world as is, is to be celebrated and maintained.

Israel's characteristic speech refuses that world. The credo concerns the overthrow of imperial ideology and challenges the claims of the imperial gods. Just below the surface of the credo is the memory of that strange power in the night which caused a cry of distress "throughout all the land of Egypt, such as there has never been, nor ever shall be again" (Exod. 11:6). Terror came among the well-defended. The credo is the communal memory that no legitimated power is beyond the reach of the drive for freedom and justice and well-being that is on the loose in the world, and that comes like a thief in the night, even among the well-defended.

Israel's laments are an enactment of speech precisely against power arrangements which oppress and hurt and abuse and exploit. The enemies seem so strong. Ruthless neighbors seem so powerful. God seems so indifferent. The world appears to be powerfully ordered in unbearable ways. But Israel, gathered around an alternative vision of what is possible, will not be silent, will not be domesticated, will not end hopeless, but will speak. This speech of protest breaks the ideology, opens possibilities, watches while life is given, power is shared, and goods are redistributed. Israel watches and then thanks and celebrates, because the world is reorganized out beyond and over against the ideology which no longer exercises any compelling authority.

Israel's daring recitals, confessions, and songs have no respect for the silent god who does not care, nor for an indifferent system which has no compassion. Israel narrates such idols to defeat and celebrates the new God who transforms. Israel sings the closed system to delegitimated oblivion and enacts a dream of another way in the world, a way of well-being and justice. Israel makes these moves precisely in liturgy. In the liturgy Israel enacts a different world. That different world—which in the liturgy is only a verbal proposal—powers Israel to joy and freedom. That different world is unleashed in odd, awkward ways, not only among Jews, but among all sorts of people who stay close to pain, who live free in hope, who will not settle for the dead god of the empire or the closed system of the status quo. Israel will not stop its confessing, its groans, its gratitudes. And because Israel will not stop, the world is open and God is under way.

A NEW GOD SUNG TO REALITY

Out of such singing against idols, out of such confessing against ideology, Israel does indeed sing praise. Israel sings and will not stop singing. Israel will sing like no other primal religion in the history of religions. Israel will sing with abandonment, without restraint. Israel will sing because it has this odd One before whom to sing. Israel will sing because it has this inexplicable passion against suffering and it has learned that silence breeds suffering.

Israel will sing even at great cost and with great hope. We have thus far considered how doxology, even well intentioned, falls prey to and is co-opted by ideology and idolatry. But in the context of credo, lament, and song of thanksgiving, it does not follow that doxology inevitably becomes idolatry and ideology. We have seen reasons to be suspicious of many of Israel's songs of praise. But in the end, after the long season of suspicion, we hear Israel's faithful voice in song and doxology.

Israel must sing different hymns than the conventions of royal reality. Israel must sing praises that live close to credo, lament, and songs of thanksgiving. Israel's songs at their best are filled with transformative reasons so that the world made by the psalm is never far from the transformative ground and memory. Thus the doxology of faithful Israel is rooted in pain and astonished in liberation. This doxology is a singing against idolatry, a reciting against ideology. Israel sings about and treasures a God who continues to make and unmake, to create and destroy (Isa. 45:7), to fill the hungry with good things and send the rich empty away (1 Sam. 2:6–8; Ps. 113:7–8; Luke 1:52–53). Israel sings about and treasures a new world, a new social possibility in which swords will become plowshares, spears will turn to pruning hooks (Micah 4:3), in which you shall not plant and another eat (Isa. 65:21–22), in which everyone shall be content and none shall be afraid (Lev. 26:5–6). Israel's best doxology is not self-congratulation nor is it resignation. It is hope kept sharp by pain still present. It is praise kept honest by candid abrasiveness. It is celebration kept open for subversiveness. It is not self-satisfied endorsement of what is, but the insistence that God and the empire must be open, and must pay attention to what will be given out beyond pain into joy.[44]

The praise of Israel is deeply and uncompromisingly rooted in concreteness. But with that rootage secure, it takes off in flights of possibility.[45] The possibilities hoped by Israel seize initiative with God and force God to be engaged with Israel in transformative ways. Yet Israel's new possibilities which emerge in these songs are also derived from and permitted by this God who authorizes Israel's praise and who benefits from Israel's praise.

Israel sings boldly and courageously, with enormous nerve, in its address to Yahweh. It sings with resilient hope. But when pushed to the very extreme, Israel's own tongue is inadequate for the praise that finally must be addressed to Yahweh. Israel manages to

implement most of the songs of protest and praise which need to
be sung. At the extreme edge of its theological radicalness, however, Israel's praise fails. Thus, at the end of our analysis, I have
had one other thought about the extremity of praise. It is indeed
incongruous that in the end Israel is not quite up in the wonder,
eloquence, and extravagance appropriate to Yahweh. Finally, as
in Job 38—41, God must do the praise, for none but God finally
has a tongue adequate or a horizon sweeping enough to bring the
wonder of God to praise. Finally, there must be praise which
moves out beyond the excessive moral worry of Job and the moral
commitments of Israel. Finally, praise must be utterly disinterested, aimed at nothing other than the reality of God. Israel is
never able to do that fully, and so God alone takes up the full
doxology which moves beyond utility, beyond manipulation, beyond idolatry and ideology.

Karl Barth, in writing about the music of Wolfgang Amadeus
Mozart, has captured this sense of praise which bursts all bounds
of calculation and utility in a liberated, yielding articulation. Of
Mozart, Barth writes:

> Mozart's music is not, in contrast to that of Bach, a message, and not,
> in contrast to that of Beethoven, a personal confession. He does
> not reveal in his music any doctrine and certainly not him-
> self. . . . Mozart does not wish to *say* anything: he just sings and
> sounds. Thus he does not force anything on the listener, does not
> demand that he make any decisions or take any positions. . . . Nor
> does he *will* to proclaim the praise of God. He just does it.[46]

Mozart is a prime example of praise that must be sung by God
alone, because Israel is not able to be so free at the throne. That
the poet of Job creates the doxology and at the same time the
doxology is placed in the mouth of God suggests an overcoming of
the alienation which is the subject of much of Israel's prayer. The
overcoming of the alienation in the poem of Job, as in the Psalms,
only happens from God's side.[47]

But that is only at the end. All along the way Israel's praise is
wrought

- *through* ethical sensitivity,
- *through* the awareness of moral coherence,
- *through* indignation at injustice,
- *through* nervy insistence on righteousness in the world.

But in the end—only at the end—praise in Israel bursts out of such categories. In speaking of praise in such a way as abandonment and yielding, I may now have finally come to Psalm 150 which earlier I suggested was dangerously close to ideology. I suggest that the danger is that a psalm like Psalm 150 (which has no "reason") will be sung too soon. Israel can join God in God's full praise only at the end. Finally Israel with God imagines the world no longer under stress or in anguish, when God will be all in all.[48] Such affirmation is not Israel's first song, but it is Israel's last doxology which is a satisfied, obedient, delighted yielding.

On the matter of delighted yielding, the words of Isak Dinesen are helpful and suggestive. She takes three metaphors for a life of yielding delight: a *dream* which forsakes allegiance to the world as it is, a *ship* which no longer fights the water, a *dancer* who yields gracefully to the partner. She writes:

> For we have in the dream forsaken our allegiance to the organizing, controlling, rectifying forces of the world, the Universal Conscience. We have sworn fealty to the wild, incalculable creative forces, the Imagination of the Universe. . . .
> To the imagination of the world, we do not pray.[49] We call to mind how, when last we did so, we were asked back, quick as lightning, where we had been when the morning stars sang together, or whether we could bind the sweet influences of Pleiades. Without our having asked them for freedom, these free forces have set us free as mountain winds, have liberated us from initiative and determination, as from responsibility. They deal out no wages, each of their boons to us is a gift, baksheesh, and their highest gift is inspiration. A gift may be named after both the giver and the receiver, and in this way, my inspiration is my own, more even than anything I possess, and is still the gift of God.
> The ship has given up tacking and has allied herself to the wind and the current; now her sails fill and she runs on proudly, upon obliging waves. Is her speed her own achievement and her merit or the work and merit of outside powers? We cannot tell. The dancer in the waltz gives herself into the hands of her skilled partner; is the flight and wonder of the dance, now, her own achievement or his? Neither the ship nor the dancer, nor the dreamer, will be able to answer or will care to answer. But they will, all three, have experienced the supreme triumph of Unconditional Surrender.[50]

Dinesen clearly speaks in a mode different from that of ancient Israel. It is different from the adversarial element in covenant. But her break with moral balancing is not different from Job who also makes the break and whose tough faith is transformed into yielding glad celebration.[51] I find Dinesen's words suggestive because she is describing what happens at the end of serious covenantal transactions and not at the beginning. Her words concern the end resolution of the struggle of dancer and dance partner, of ship and sea. At the end of Israel's discourse with God (at the end and not at the beginning), at the end of the other side of idolatry defeated and ideology delegitimated, then it is exactly right to speak of the "triumph of Unconditional Surrender."

The phrase "triumph of Unconditional Surrender" is an oxymoron, for one speaks in the same phrase of triumph and surrender. That is exactly right in the act of praise, for praise concerns the strange power in willing yielding. The reason Israel can willingly yield is that the singing of Israel does not permit a maintained, reasoned distance. "The triumph of Unconditional Surrender" is a phrase that catches the central inversion of the gospel, as do the more familiar notions of gaining by losing (Mark 8:35), and the strange juxtaposition of wisdom and foolishness, strength and weakness (1 Cor. 1:25; 2 Cor. 12:9).

We with Israel speak yielding words to God. As we speak yielding words, we must accompany the words with active yielding. We with Israel find ourselves gladly yielding our very selves. Praise which comes at the end of credo recital, lament, and thanksgiving, praise which comes at the end of concrete hurt and candid petition is a very different kind of praise. This kind of praise which comes at the end of our discourse with God is not an escape. It permits us to live beyond hurt and trouble, because hurt and trouble have not been denied but fully faced in honest, bold, trusting speech.

Such praise is not abdication. It permits us to move in a welcome rush toward God's new possibility for us that emerges through remembering and singing. Such praise is not resignation. It affirms that the transformations are still under way and are yet to be given. Finally at the end, and not before, Israel sings—untroubled and untempted by idols now defeated, unfettered and uncompromised by ideology now exposed. Israel sings committed to the subversion of the subversive God, prepared for a social possibility that outruns all our fearful necessities. Such praise is a yielding to the One who wants us never to submit to despair or in despair, but to yield to the inchoate but hinted possibility, never to submit to the present at the cost of the future.

In such singing, it could be that even the king who presides over the liturgy may become child, creature, and heir of this remarkable alternative. Even the presiding officer may be freed for an instance of the calculations of benefactor, freed from the burdens of sponsor, freed from the demands of participation, and may become child, creature, and heir, unconditionally surrendering, astonished at the triumph in yielding, "lost in wonder, love and praise." But such yielding is possible only after the astonishing credos of transformation have been engaged, only after the hurting laments have been honestly and harshly spoken, only after the surprised songs of thanksgiving have been concretely enumerated. Then Israel may indeed be lost in wonder, love, and praise, may indeed surrender in a way that heaven and earth recognize the surrender to be a triumph. But it is not a triumph the world expects, for there is a yielding. Conversely it is not a yielding the conventional religious world of idolatry and ideology recognizes, for it is a hard, demanding yielding.[52]

THE PRAISE OF GOD AS
DUTY AND DELIGHT

We return finally to Sigmund Mowinckel's question which, I submit, has been too long misunderstood and misinterpreted. Is liturgy a world-creating act? Does worship make a world? The old dismissals of Mowinckel's questions, in my judgment, reflect a mode of scholarship and an intellectual milieu that were excessively positivistic, defensively Protestant, blatantly and naively historical-critical. Such an intellectual climate screened out important questions, which only now can be taken up again, as we move away from the seductions of reasonableness. The dismissal of Mowinckel is a dismissal occasioned by a fascination with objectivity that assumed that worship is an empty act of rational description. Such a notion, however, misses the power of reenactment, redemption, and reconstruction through which worship is fresh "making" by communal imagination and public construal.

Formally, the intent of my argument is to say yes to Mowinckel: the liturgy does indeed make a world. The action of worship is indeed and unavoidably constructive. It is constitutive sociologically, engaged in Peter Berger's "social construction of reality."[53] It is constitutive literarily as Amos Wilder understood, for imaginative literature does generate worlds in which we can live.[54] It is constitutive psychologically, as Robert Kegan, Roy Schafer, and Paul Pruyser have understood, for in such moments we are being formed, and formed again, and re-formed as persons.[55] It is constitutive theologically, as Gordon Kaufman proposes, for we are engaged in the articulation of God who is not known or available in this particular way until the speech of the gospel makes God available in a distinctive rendering of concrete speech.[56]

Mowinckel's hypotheses of dramatic, dynamic reality in cultic activity is not only formal, however. Beyond his own anthropological insights, there is a substantive theological dimension to this world-making. And this, I think, Mowinckel did not see clearly, for he was preoccupied with the commonalities shared by Israel with Mesopotamian culture. Mowinckel attended to cultural parallels but was not interested in theological specificity. Israel's world-making is not simply a replica of the great imperial liturgies of Babylon, even though there are important parallels. Israel's world-making is characteristically distinctive, polemical, and subversive.[57] Israel's world-making is counter world-making, counter to the empire and its oppression, counter to the imperial gods and the exploitative ordering of the regime. It is counter to conventional idolatry and routine ideology. Israel's liturgy at its best is not triumphalist, not self-serving of Zion, but it must "tell among the nations" that there is a new governance in heaven and in earth. In heaven the new governance has defeated the powers of death and oppression. On earth, the regimes of injustice and unrighteousness are placed in a final jeopardy by the new governance of Yahweh. To "tell among the nations" is not only a bold theological act but also is a telling among the nations of a new subversive psychology of human possibility and a sociology of covenantal alternative.

"Telling among the nations" about the new governance, which is what Israel does in praise, has extraordinary social and missional significance. That is why we sing,

> Proclaim to every people, tongue, and nation
> that God, in whom they live and move, is Love . . .[58]

That mission of "telling among the nations" (which is not Western, not imperialistic, not committed to an economic ideology) depends on faithful liturgy. Missional testimony to the nations cannot take

place until a new world of social possibility and theological governance is imagined, and that imagining is primarily liturgical.[59]
When imagined, the new governance may be enacted. Until imagined, the new governance will not and cannot be enacted. Without
that bold and faithful act of imagination, we are consigned to old
governances which are predictably idolatrous about heaven and
ideological about earth.

Faithful energy for life in the world depends on the liturgic
offer of another world of possibility and permission, presided over
by another authority, the one known in credos recited, in laments
resolved, in songs of thanksgiving sung. The God of the doxology
will order the world anew! But the God of the doxology can only
be the transforming God of surprising credo, honest lament, and
astonishing thanksgiving.

Mowinckel has understood in a scholarly, critical way what Moses
and Miriam already understood. A life alternative to Pharaoh and
alternative to the gods of Pharaoh depends on alternative, subversive praise, and on the particular subject to whom praise is sung.
Through that powerful, passionate, pain-informed praise, Israel

- *hosts the living, transforming God* in the face of the idols,
- *envisions a world of truth, righteousness, and equity* in the
  face of a powerful, hostile ideology,
- *invites and evokes genuine covenanted persons* in the face of
  regimented automatons or rootless, defenseless, self-sufficient
  persons,
- *legitimates the urgent practice of justice* against all the cover-
  ups of fear and the denials of uncritical order,
- *watches the powerful emergence of a missional community* in
  the face of a human community nearly voiceless and passionless in despair.

Israel's praise is a dangerous, joyous witness of a different world,
a world "this age" does not suspect, permit, or credit. No wonder
the rulers of this age want to stop the singing, or pollute it with
ideology and managed slogans! But Israel has not stopped singing
and Yahweh has not stopped governing, enthroned on the praises
of Israel (Ps. 22:3).

Against the deathliness of idolatry and the falsehood of ideology, Israel sings another world to reality. The subject of Israel's
songs is Yahweh who works wonders in the earth, wonders marked

by justice, equity, and righteousness. The outcome of Israel's praise is another world marked by justice, mercy, and peace. Israel sings out of a long memory of transformations, out of a passionate hope for "all things new." Israel always sings this song up from concrete transformations to a new, coherent, authorized world. It is my judgment that in Western Christianity, so long self-assured and legitimate, our primary pastoral task is to sing back down to the specificity of hurt, to the amazement of healing, to the miracle of transformation.

NB.

Such praise is indeed our duty and our delight, the ultimate vocation of the human community, indeed of all creation. Yes, all of life is aimed toward God and finally exists for the sake of God. Praise articulates and embodies our capacity to yield, submit, and abandon ourselves in trust and gratitude to the One whose we are. Praise is not only a human requirement and a human need, it is also a human delight. We have a resilient hunger to move beyond self, to return our energy and worth to the One from whom it has been granted. In our return to that One, we find our deepest joy. That is what it means to "glorify God and enjoy God forever."

Notes

PREFACE

1. For a summary of recent scholarship concerning intratextual exegesis, see Patrick D. Miller, Jr., *Interpreting the Psalms* (Philadelphia: Fortress Press, 1986).

2. See Martin J. Buss, "The Study of Forms," in *Old Testament Form Criticism*, ed. J. H. Hayes (San Antonio: Trinity University Press, 1974), 1–56.

3. For a review of Hermann Gunkel's understanding of *Sitz im Leben* and critical attempts to move beyond Gunkel, see Rolf Knierim, "Old Testament Form Criticism Reconsidered," *Interpretation* 27 (1973): 435–68, esp. 463–66; and Martin J. Buss, "The Idea of Sitz im Leben—History and Critique," *Zeitschrift für die alttestamentliche Wissenschaft* 90 (1978): 157–70.

4. The history of ministerial "professionalism" and its gains and costs have been well explicated several times by Robert Lynn.

5. I use the term "surplus" in the way suggested by Paul Ricoeur (*Interpretation Theory: Discourse and the Surplus of Meaning* [Fort Worth: Texas Christian University Press, 1976]).

6. The categories of "therapeutic" and "managerial" for sociological assessment of American life have been well explicated by Robert N. Bellah et al. in *Habits of the Heart: Individualism and Commitment in American Life* (Berkeley and Los Angeles: University of California Press, 1985). Apparently they are categories which he in turn appropriated from Alasdair MacIntyre's *After Virtue: A Study in Moral Theory* (Notre Dame, Ind.: University of Notre Dame Press, 1984).

7. On the work of the pastoral office in resymbolizing, see Gail Ramshaw-Schmidt, *Christ in Sacred Speech: The Meaning of Liturgical*

Language (Philadelphia: Fortress Press, 1986); and Elaine Ramshaw, *Ritual and Pastoral Care* (Philadelphia: Fortress Press, 1987).

8. On this battle for the heart and mind of the community, see Amos N. Wilder, *Jesus' Parables and the War of Myths: Essays in Imagination in Scripture* (Philadelphia: Fortress Press, 1982).

9. I have explored this curious and powerful inversion in the prophetic traditions of Israel in *Hopeful Imagination: Prophetic Voices in Exile* (Philadelphia: Fortress Press, 1986).

1. PRAISE AS A CONSTITUTIVE ACT

1. See Geoffrey Wainwright, "The Praise of God in the Theological Reflection of the Church," *Interpretation* 39 (1985): 39.

2. On the theological vocation of praise, see Daniel W. Hardy and David F. Ford, *Praising and Knowing God* (Philadelphia: Westminster Press, 1985), 50 and passim.

3. Karl Barth (*Church Dogmatics* [Edinburgh: T. & T. Clark, 1960], III/3:264–88) makes petition the center of Christian prayer. But on pp. 264–65 he shows how petition is framed, before and after, by praise and thanksgiving.

4. Ibid., 4:75.

5. Ibid., 80.

6. Ibid., 564.

7. Stanley Hauerwas, ("The Gesture of a Truthful Story," *Theology Today* 42 [1985]: 181–89) comments on the cruciality of "truthful gestures." I take praise to be a truthful gesture made on earth, for the sake of heaven.

8. Gerhard von Rad, *Old Testament Theology* (New York: Harper & Row, 1962), 1:356–418.

9. Claus Westermann, *The Praise of God in the Psalms* (Richmond: John Knox Press, 1965), 22.

10. Sigmund Mowinckel, *Psalmenstudien*, 6 vols. (Amsterdam: Schippers, 1961).

11. Sigmund Mowinckel, *The Psalms in Israel's Worship*, 2 vols. (Nashville: Abingdon Press; Oxford: Basil Blackwell & Mott, 1962).

12. Mowinckel, *Psalmenstudien*, vol. 2: *Das Thronbesteigungsfest Jahwäs und der Ursprung der Eschatologie* (Amsterdam: Schippers, 1961 [1922]).

13. On the work of Gunkel, see Aubrey Johnson, "The Psalms," in *The Old Testament and Modern Study*, ed. H. H. Rowley (Oxford: Clarendon Press, 1951), 162–81; Ronald Clements, *One Hundred Years of Old Testament Interpretation* (Philadelphia: Westminster Press, 1976), 79–82; and John H. Hayes, *Introduction to Old Testament Study* (Nashville: Abingdon Press, 1979), 291–317. For an English translation of Gunkel's introduction to his analysis of the Psalms, see Hermann Gunkel, *The Psalms: A Form-Critical Introduction* (Philadelphia: Fortress Press, 1967). Regrettably, the remainder of the book remains untranslated.

14. On Mowinckel's contribution, see Johnson, "The Psalms," 189–207; Clements, *One Hundred Years*, 82–95; and Hayes, *Introduction*, 299–317.

15. See Aubrey Johnson, *Sacral Kingship in Ancient Israel* (Cardiff: University of Wales Press, 1967).

16. Mowinckel, *Das Thronbesteigungsfest*, 226–27 and passim.

17. On the meaning of myth in the context of cult, see Sigmund Mowinckel, *Religion und Kultus* (Göttingen: Vandenhoeck & Ruprecht, 1953), 94–98.

18. Johnson ("The Psalms," 192–96), summarizes the characteristic criticisms of Otto Eissfeldt, Lazlo I. Pap, and Norman Snaith.

19. It is exceedingly important that Israel's most elemental rendering of the "gospel" of Yahweh's kingship is on the lips of liberated slave women. The power of that kingship as social reality shapes Israel's singing in a decisive way as world-making "from below." Yahweh's kingship is given a specific nonnegotiable social location. Miriam and her sisters are processing Israel's shared experience through a particular set of metaphors, that of an alternative governance. Miriam is engaged in world-making for a very particular world. For a contemporary parallel of world-making "from below," see Eugene Genovese, *Roll, Jordan, Roll* (New York: Random House, 1976). Note esp. the subtitle, "The World the Slaves Made." See also his earlier book, *The World the Slaveholders Made* (New York: Pantheon Books, 1969).

22. J. H. Eaton, *Kingship and the Psalms* (London: SCM Press, 1976), and *Vision in Worship* (London: SPCK, 1981).

23. For an introduction to the sociological and anthropological aspects of cult, see James D. Shaughnessy, ed., *The Roots of Ritual* (Grand Rapids: Wm. B. Eerdmans, 1973).

24. See the comments of Westermann in *The Praise of God*, 20–22, which effectively bracket out Mowinckel's concern for cult.

25. Gunkel's intent of course was not narrowly formal or literary. See Martin J. Buss, "The Study of Forms," in *Old Testament Form Criticism*, ed. John H. Hayes (San Antonio: Trinity University Press, 1974), 39–54, for a full appreciation of Gunkel's comprehensive social interest.

26. Mowinckel, *Das Thronbesteigungsfest*, 19.

27. Ibid., 21.

28. Ibid., 22.

29. Mowinckel, *The Psalms in Israel's Worship* 1:17.

30. Ibid., 18.

31. On the epistemological crisis, see Langdon Gilkey, *Society and the Sacred* (New York: Crossroad, 1981). In a very different mode, see the comments of Theo. Wilvliet in *A Place in the Sun* (Maryknoll, N.Y.: Orbis Books, 1985), 25–41, on the epistemological break reflected in liberation hermeneutics.

32. On the shift in scholarly method, see Robert Polzin, *Moses and the Deuteronomist* (New York: Seabury Press, 1980), chap. 1. That shift is well reflected in the various articles in the first issue of *Ex Auditu* (1985).

33. As a compelling example of constituting an alternative world by action, see Jonathan Schell, "A Better Today," *The New Yorker* (Feb. 3, 1986): 47–67. In characterizing the world-creating life of Adam Michnik, Schell says,

> Its simple but radical guiding principle was to start doing the things you think should be done, and to start being what you think society should become. Do you believe in freedom of speech? Then speak freely. Do you love the truth? Then tell it. Do you believe in an open society? Then act in the open. Do you believe in a decent and humane society? Then behave decently and humanely.

34. This chemist, R. Garth Kidd, at the University of Western Ontario, suggests that the great physicists of recent time, e.g., Planck and Einstein, finished their major analytical work by the age of thirty, and spent the remainder of their scholarly lives reflecting on the dimension of amazement appropriate to the design of the world yet to be done.

35. On the notion of continuing creation, see Langdon Gilkey, *Maker of Heaven and Earth* (Garden City, N.Y.: Doubleday & Co., 1959), 257 and passim; and Jürgen Moltmann, *God in Creation* (San Francisco: Harper & Row, 1985), 206–14.

36. On the "image of God" as the way in which human persons participate in God's creative activity, see Wolfhart Pannenberg, *Anthropology in Theological Perspective* (Philadelphia: Westminster Press, 1985). Note esp. chaps. 4, 7, and 8 on the interplay of imagination, formation of culture, and development of institutions under the rubric, "The Shared World."

37. Peter L. Berger and Thomas Luckmann, *The Social Construction of Reality* (Garden City, N.Y.: Doubleday & Co., 1966).

38. Ibid., 21.

39. Ibid., 51.

40. Ibid.

41. Berger and Luckmann write of "reality" the way Mowinckel does "world," in quotation marks. They say, "The philosopher is driven to decide where the quotation marks are in order and where they may safely be omitted, that is, to differentiate between valid and invalid assertions about the world. This the sociologist cannot do. Logically, if not stylistically, he is stuck with the quotation marks" (ibid., 2). See Alfred Schutz and Thomas Luckmann, *The Structures of the Life-World* (Evanston, Ill.: Northwestern University Press, 1973), for a normative characterization of the notion of "life-world."

42. Peter L. Berger, *The Sacred Canopy* (Garden City, N.Y.: Doubleday & Co., 1969), 40–41.

43. On recent study of narrative and its importance for theology, see David Tracy, *The Analogical Imagination* (New York: Crossroad, 1981), 275–87. See esp. his comprehensive note (p. 296 n. 81).

44. See James Barr, *The Scope and Authority of the Bible* (London: SCM Press, 1980), esp. chaps. 1 and 3.

45. See esp. Paul Ricoeur, *Essays in Biblical Interpretation*, ed. Lewis S. Mudge (Philadelphia: Fortress Press, 1980).

46. On the significance of Wilder's work on these matters, see Dominic Crossan, *A Fragile Craft: The Work of Amos Wilder* (Chico, Calif.: Scholars Press, 1981). Of Wilder's own work, see "The Word as Address and the Word as Meaning," in *The New Hermeneutic*, ed. James M. Robinson and John B. Cobb, Jr. (New York: Harper & Row, 1964), 198–218; and *Early Christian Rhetoric* (Cambridge: Harvard University Press, 1971 [1964]).

47. Amos N. Wilder, "Story and Story-World," *Interpretation* 37 (1983): 353–64.

48. Ibid., 358.

49. Ibid., 360.

50. On social chaos, normlessness, and anomie, see Berger, *Sacred Canopy*, chap. 3 and passim; and Robert Merton, *Social Theory and Social Structure* (Glencoe, Ill.: Free Press, 1957), chaps. 4 and 5.

51. Wilder uses the word "recital" ("Story and Story-World," 359).

52. Ibid., 361. The word "real" is in quotes.

53. Ibid., 362.

54. David J. A. Clines, *I, He, We, & They* (Sheffield: JSOT Press, 1976).

55. Ibid., 60–64.

56. David J. A. Clines, *The Theme of the Pentateuch* (Sheffield: JSOT Press, 1978).

57. Ibid., 102.

58. Ibid., 104.

59. Ibid., 105.

60. Ibid., 117–18.

61. Gerhard von Rad, "The Form-Critical Problem of the Hexateuch," in *The Problem of the Hexateuch and Other Essays* (New York: McGraw-Hill, 1966), 1–78.

62. See Norman K. Gottwald's schematic summary of the matter, *The Tribes of Yahweh: A Sociology of the Religion of Liberated Israel, 1250–1050 B.C.* (Maryknoll, N.Y.: Orbis Books, 1979), 102–3.

63. Robert Kegan, *The Evolving Self* (Cambridge: Harvard University Press, 1982), 11.

64. Ibid., 17–18.

65. Ibid., 18.

66. Ibid., 64.

67. Roy Schafer, *Language and Insight* (New Haven: Yale University Press, 1978).

68. Ibid., 16–17.

69. Ibid., 18.

70. Paul W. Pruyser, *The Play of Imagination* (New York: International Universities Press, 1983).

71. Ibid., 63–64. Perhaps the dramatic structure of the poem of Job shows the range and juxtaposition of these worlds. The friends articulate the *real* world. Job may be a voice of *autism*, for he stands at the center of his world. The resolution of the poem (in the Whirlwind speeches and in

Job's response) may be a movement to the third *illusional* alternative. On this third "intermediate" world, see also Ralph L. Underwood, "The Presence and Absence of God in Psychoanalytic and Theological Perspectives," paper read to the American Academy of Religion, Nov. 24, 1985, p. 11 and passim.

72. Pruyser, *Play of Imagination*, 65. See also Walter Brueggemann, "The Third World of Evangelical Imagination," *Horizons in Biblical Theology* 8, no. 2 (1986): 61–84.

73. Ibid., 167–68.

74. Gordon D. Kaufman, *God the Problem* (Cambridge: Harvard University Press, 1972); *The Theological Imagination* (Philadelphia: Westminster Press, 1981); and *Theology for a Nuclear Age* (Philadelphia: Westminster Press, 1985).

75. On rendering God, see Dale Patrick, *The Rendering of God in the Old Testament* (Philadelphia: Fortress Press, 1981). Note esp. his utilization of the insights of Hans Frei.

76. See esp. his *Theology for a Nuclear Age*.

77. Ibid., 32.

78. Kaufman, *God the Problem*, 85.

79. Kaufman, *Theological Imagination*, 185.

80. As one would expect, Kaufman is severely criticized by theological conservatives. See Clark H. Pinnock, "How I Use the Bible in Doing Theology," in *The Use of the Bible in Theology/Evangelical Option*, ed. Robert K. Johnston (Atlanta: John Knox Press, 1985), 24–25. In the same volume, however, Robert K. Johnston ("Introduction: Unity and Diversity in Evangelical Theology," 6–7), quoting David Wells, writes, "In the one understanding of contextualization, the revelatory trajectory moves only from authoritative Word into contemporary culture; in the other, the trajectory moves both from text to context and from context to text. . . ." "Increasingly, evangelicals are opting for the second of these modes—an 'interactionist' approach. . . ." When it is recognized that theology is a two-way interaction between text and context, we are not so far removed methodologically from Kaufman.

81. Clearly, many of the "historical reconstructions" of Jesus are in fact projections of those who do the reconstruction. See the magisterial summary of Albert Schweitzer, *The Quest of the Historical Jesus* (New York: Macmillan Co., 1968).

82. Kaufman, *Theological Imagination*, 151.

83. Ibid., 154. Kaufman places "humanize" and "relativize" in italics as his programmatic dialectic.

84. Indeed, Kaufman (*Theological Imagination*, 127) concedes that there is "a point where contemporary theology must—unavoidably—live out of tradition." See Kaufman's own appeal to the tradition in "Some Theological Emphases of the Early Swiss Anabaptists," *Mennonite Quarterly Review* 35 (1951): 75–99.

85. Kaufman (*Theological Imagination*, 139) says of myth, "A myth, in its depiction, interpretation, and explanation of the meaning and problems of human existence, finds it essential to make reference to *another world*

than that of everyday life. . . ." For our purposes it is important that the phrase "another world" is italicized. His point seems very close to that of Mowinckel.

86. See Bernhard W. Anderson, *Creation in the Old Testament* (Philadelphia: Fortress Press, 1984), 14–21; Moltmann, *God in Creation*, 86–93; and idem, "Schöpfung aus Nichts," in *Wenn nicht jetzt, wann dann? Aufsätze für Hans-Joachim Kraus zum 65. Geburtstag,* ed. Hans-Georg Geyer et al. (Neukirchen-Vluyn: Neukirchener Verlag, 1983), 259–67. Moltmann's statement indicates how the constructive work of systematic theologians proceeds in categories other than those permitted an exegete.

87. Amos N. Wilder (*Jesus' Parables and the War of Myths: Essays in Imagination in Scripture* [Philadelphia: Fortress Press, 1982]) has argued that each such world of literary creation competes with other worlds and so polemizes against them.

88. See Sallie McFague, *Metaphorical Theology* (Philadelphia: Fortress Press, 1982).

89. Karen Lebacqz, *Professional Ethics: Power and Paradox* (Nashville: Abingdon Press, 1985), 116–17.

90. Ibid., 119–20.

2. THE "WORLD" OF ISRAEL'S DOXOLOGY

1. The linkage between world-construction and the character of Yahweh is mediated through the canon. The canon functions as the normative articulation of both the character of Yahweh and the world of Israel. The normative function of the canon for theology, I believe, is the real concern of Brevard S. Childs's *Introduction to the Old Testament as Scripture* (Philadelphia: Fortress Press, 1979), but that aspect of the canon does not receive very clear articulation by him.

2. Thomas Green ("Congregational Education" [unpublished paper, 1986]) has suggested that liturgy is not only "the work of the people," but also "God-work" and "priest-work." Green understands liturgy as "public service."

3. The important work on the credo recitals generated by Gerhard von Rad can be handled in fresh ways to see the recitals as the connection between shared experience and world-construction. Valid world-making can be done only out of the materials that the community shares in its common experience. Otherwise, the world constructed is an ideological imposition.

4. Sigmund Mowinckel, *Psalmenstudien,* vol. 2: *Das Thronbesteigungsfest Jahwäs und der Ursprung der Eschatologie* (Amsterdam: Schippers, 1961 [1922]), 3 and passim.

5. Paul Hanson ("Zechariah 9 and the Recapitulation of an Ancient Ritual Pattern," *Journal of Biblical Literature* 92 [1973]: 37–59) has shown how this same sequence recurs in later texts which move in the direction of apocalyptic. Following Frank Cross, his argument is that

the persistent ancient sequence of the myth again becomes visible in a situation of social crisis.

6. For a detailed analysis of the creation theme in relation to Yahweh's possession of the world in psalms like Psalm 96, see Eckart Otto, "Schöpfung als Kategorie der Vermittlung von Gott und Welt im Biblischer Theologie," in *Wenn nicht jetzt, wann dann? Aufsätze für Hans-Joachim Kraus zum 65. Geburtstag,* ed. Hans-Georg Geyer et al. (Neukirchen-Vluyn: Neukirchener Verlag, 1983), 53–68.

7. See Peter Stuhlmacher, *Das paulinische Evangelium* (Göttingen: Vandenhoeck & Ruprecht, 1968), 109–53, for a detailed analysis of the term.

8. This sequence of texts assumes that Second Isaiah derives from the enthronement psalms. Hans-Joachim Kraus (*Die Königsherrschaft Gottes im Alten Testament* [Tübingen: J. C. B. Mohr (Paul Siebeck), 1951]), following Gunkel, proposes a different relation between the two.

9. On the formulation of Yahweh as "maker of heaven," see Norman Habel, "Yahweh, Maker of Heaven and Earth," *Journal of Biblical Literature* 91 (1972): 321–37.

10. It is commonly assumed that Psalm 29 lives close to the common liturgic pattern of the Near East and has been transformed for Israelite use only in the most surface ways. See Frank M. Cross, *Canaanite Myth and Hebrew Epic* (Cambridge: Harvard University Press, 1973), 151–56. It is often noticed that Psalm 96 has transformed the tradition of Psalm 29 so that the summons to praise is not addressed to the sons of gods, but to the families of the peoples. Psalm 96 characteristically moves Israel closer to reflection concerning the earthly, worldly dimension of its faith, a dimension in which the gospel of God's rule over the other gods is acutely at issue for Israel.

11. See Sigmund Mowinckel, *The Psalms in Israel's Worship,* 2 vols. (New York: Abingdon Press, 1962), 1:109–16.

12. On the problematic of relating the dramatic to the ontological, see Jose Miranda, *Being and Messiah* (Maryknoll, N.Y.: Orbis Books, 1977). Jerome Bruner (*Actual Minds, Possible Worlds* [Cambridge: Harvard University Press, 1986] 46) says of this issue, ". . . it is far more important, for appreciating the human condition, to understand the ways human beings construct their worlds (and their castles) than it is to establish the ontological status of the products of these processes." To be sure, theology cannot go all the way with Bruner, but his point is well taken for this element in our argument.

13. Jürgen Moltmann (*Theology of Hope* [New York: Harper & Row, 1967], 95–138) has most clearly shown what is at stake in this matter. James M. Robinson ("The Historicality of Biblical Language," in *The Old Testament and Christian Faith,* ed. Bernhard W. Anderson [New York: Harper & Row, 1963], 150–58) has gone very far in appropriating Heidegger's categories of "unveiling" as a way to understand revelation through language. The contrast between Moltmann and Robinson on this point is drastic. The dynamic understanding of real event in cult (which I am urging) is that, in the cult, something new is wrought. It is not a mere unveiling

of what has always been. Robinson's utilization of Heidegger moves in the direction of Gnosticism, and finally negates any historical *novum*.

14. On the actual power of reenactment, see Mircea Eliade, *The Myth of the Eternal Return* (Princeton: Princeton University Press, 1954). On pp. 159–62, Eliade notes the peculiar problematic of biblical faith in relation to the matter of reenactment.

15. The notion of all of creation singing together is perhaps articulated in Hosea 2:21–22, with the use of the verb "answer." The poetic image suggests that all parts of creation are responding to each other antiphonally. This motif is expressed in "Joy to the World." When heaven and earth receive the new king, "fields and floods, rocks, hills, and plains repeat the sounding joy." To understand creation as an accented chorus of praise pushes us to a dramatic (as distinct from ontological) articulation of creation.

16. It may be for this reason that apocalyptic literature employs the motif of labor pains and birth for the coming of the new age which comes abruptly and not gradually. See Rom. 8:22. That abruptness is expressed in Isa. 43:19:

> Behold, I am doing a new thing;
> now it springs forth, do you not perceive it?

The metaphor is of a new growth; new reality sprouts abruptly.

17. See Cross, *Canaanite Myth and Hebrew Epic*, 121–44; and Patrick D. Miller, Jr., *The Divine Warrior in Early Israel* (Cambridge: Harvard University Press, 1973), 113–17.

18. See Bernhard W. Anderson, "The Song of Miriam Poetically and Theologically Considered," and Walter Brueggemann, "A Response to 'The Song of Miriam' by Bernhard Anderson," in *Directions in Biblical Hebrew Poetry*, ed. Elaine R. Follis (Sheffield: JSOT Press, 1987), 285–302; and Gail R. O'Day, "Singing Woman's Song: A Hermeneutic of Liberation," *Concordia Theological Monthly* 12 (1985): 203–10.

19. It is exceedingly important that Israel's most elemental rendering of the "gospel" of Yahweh's kingship is on the lips of liberated slave women. The power of that kingship as social reality shapes Israel's singing in a decisive way as world-making "from below." Yahweh's kingship is given a specific nonnegotiable social location. Miriam and her sisters are processing Israel's shared experience through a particular set of metaphors, that of an alternative governance. Miriam is engaged in world-making for a very particular world. For a contemporary parallel of world-making "from below," see Eugene Genovese, *Roll, Jordan, Roll* (New York: Random House, 1976). Note esp. the subtitle, "The World the Slaves Made." See also his earlier book, *The World the Slaveholders Made* (New York: Pantheon Books, 1969).

20. See James Muilenburg, "A Liturgy of the Triumphs of Yahweh," in *Studia Biblica et Semitica: Vriezen Festschrift* (Wagenignen: H. Veenman & Zonen, 1966), 233–51.

21. On the continuing unsettling potential of this tradition in every new time as a generator of revolutionary thought and action, see Michael Walzer, *Exodus and Revolution* (New York: Basic Books, 1985).

22. In the initial announcement of the exodus (Exod. 3:8), the nations to be overcome are already in purview. To be sure, the list of nations in 3:8 is not the same as in the Song of Moses, but the various lists all bear witness to the common agenda. The list of nations is, in any case, paradigmatic and is not to be taken with historical specificity.

23. On the revolutionary power of dance in the face of oppression, see the remarkable statement of Elie Wiesel, *The Jews of Silence* (New York: Holt, Rinehart & Winston, 1966), chap. 6, entitled "A Night of Dancing." Wiesel writes (pp. 62–63):

> A little later I went up to talk with her. Would she speak to a stranger? She would. Not afraid? No, not tonight. And other nights? Let's stick to tonight. She was a humanities major at the university. She spoke Yiddish, she said, with her grandfather, sometimes with her parents, and occasionally even with friends when they were alone. Was she religious? Far from it; never had been. Her parents had been born after the Revolution, and even they had received an antireligious education. What did she know about the Jewish religion? That it was based on outdated values. And about the Jewish people? That it was made up of capitalists and swindlers. And the state of Israel? That it was aggressive, racist, and imperialist. Where had she learned all this? From textbooks, government pamphlets, and the press. I asked her why she insisted on remaining Jewish. She hesitated, searching for the proper word, then smiled. "What does it matter what they think of us . . . it's what we think that counts." And she added immediately, "I'll tell you why I'm a Jew. Because I like to sing."
>
> The songs they sang were mostly products of the nineteenth century. The most popular was a Yiddish folk song, "Come let us go together, all of us together, and greet the bride and groom." But they had updated the lyrics, substituting for the last phrase, "Come let us greet the Jewish people," or "the people of Israel," or "the God of Israel and His Torah."
>
> One group of students had formed a human pyramid. The young man at the apex was yelling defiantly, "Nothing can help them! We shall overcome them!" His audience roared back, "Hurrah! Hurrah!"
>
> More cheers came from a nearby group that was celebrating the holiday in a manner decidedly Russian, tossing one of their number into the air. Five times, six, seven. Higher, higher. A girl pleaded with them to stop, but they paid no attention. Eight times, nine, ten. Nothing would happen. Nothing did. A carpet of outstretched hands was waiting to catch the hero upon his return from on high. "Hurrah! Hurrah!"
>
> This is how Russian soldiers celebrated their victory over the Germans, and how the Jews celebrate their triumph over despair.
>
> "What does anyone in America or Israel care if my passport is stamped 'Jewish'? It doesn't matter to me, and it doesn't matter to these young people here tonight. So stop protesting about things that don't bother us. We have long since ceased being ashamed of our

Jewishness. We can't hide it anyway. Besides, by accepting it we've managed to turn obedience to the law into an act of free choice."

24. On unpermitted dance as a point of engagement with "transcendence" that has revolutionary potential, see Younghak Hyun, "A Theological Look at the Mask Dance in Korea," in *Minjung Theology* (Maryknoll, N.Y.: Orbis Books, 1981), 47–54.

25. O'Day ("Singing Woman's Song") has paid special attention to the role and voice of women as the appropriate way Israel articulates Yahweh's freedom.

26. On liturgy and theology to which the "others" do not have access, see Walter Brueggemann, "II Kings 18—19; The Legitimacy of a Sectarian Hermeneutic," *Horizons in Biblical Theology* 7 (1985): 1–42.

27. Note the report that, during the Christmas season of 1985, the South African government prohibited Christmas carols among restless blacks, because such carols generated revolutionary energy. See "Christmas in South Africa," *The St. Louis Post-Dispatch* (Dec. 27, 1985), section B, p. 2. The South African police agent said, "Carols were too emotional to be sung in a time of national arrest . . . candles have become revolutionary symbols . . ."

28. On this psalm and its combination of liturgic and narrative dimensions, see Cross, *Canaanite Myth and Hebrew Epic*, 133–40.

29. Note that the verb "skip" (*rkd*) is the same as in Ps. 29:6.

30. On the power of language and its theological function in Second Isaiah, see Richard J. Clifford, *Fair Spoken and Persuading* (New York: Paulist Press, 1984); and Walter Brueggemann, *Hopeful Imagination: Prophetic Voices in Exile* (Philadelphia: Fortress Press, 1986).

31. On recent studies of the canonical shape of Isaiah and its implications for Second Isaiah, see Childs, *Introduction*, 325–38; and Ronald E. Clements, "The Unity of the Book of Isaiah," *Interpretation* 36 (1982): 117–29; and idem, "Beyond Tradition-History: Deutero-Isaiahic Development of First Isaiah's Themes," *Journal for the Study of the Old Testament* 31 (1985): 95–113.

32. The power of the language is not to describe but, in the context of speaking and healing, to effect what is said. On the effective power of such language, see Paul Ricoeur, *Essays on Biblical Interpretation*, ed. Lewis S. Mudge (Philadelphia: Fortress Press, 1980).

33. See Christopher R. North, *The Second Isaiah* (Oxford: Clarendon Press, 1964), 221–22.

34. On the focus on the city of Jerusalem in the tradition of Isaiah, see William J. Dumbrell, "The Purpose of the Book of Isaiah," *Tyndale Bulletin* 36 (1985): 111–28. See also J. J. Schmitt, "The Motherhood of God and Zion as Mother," *Revue Biblique* 92 (1985): 557–69.

35. Civil disobedience as practiced by Israel is a systemic "withdrawal" from the empire, a withdrawal that means the behavioral nullification of economic expectations and political requirements, but also a withdrawal from the epistemological claims of the empire and a nullification of its modes of speech and power. On the theme of withdrawal as a social strategy, see Norman K. Gottwald, *The Tribes of Yahweh: A Sociology of*

the Religion of Liberated Israel, 1250–1050 B.C. (Maryknoll, N.Y.: Orbis
Books, 1979), 326, 408. Gottwald acknowledges his indebtedness to
Mendenhall on this particular point. "Withdrawal" is a decisive notion for
the entire hypothesis of internal revolution.

36. Worth noting is the juxtaposition of Psalms 114–115, which are
intentionally linked in LXX. Whereas Psalm 114 is about the power of
Yahweh to transform, Psalm 115 is a dismissal of the other gods, who are
powerless. This juxtaposition is congruent with the central claim of the
enthronement theme: that Yahweh is acknowledged to have power, and
that acknowledgment effectively delegitimates the other gods, who lack
comparable power.

37. On this notion, see Guy Davenport, *Geography of Imagination* (San
Francisco: North Point Press, 1981).

38. The metaphor of "home" is useful for our theme, not only for the
ancient world, because "homelessness" is an apt metaphor for our present
circumstance in the midst of modernity. See Peter Berger, *The Homeless
Mind* (New York: Random House, 1973).

39. Bruner (*Actual Minds, Possible Worlds*, 54) concludes:

Aristotle in the Poetics (II 9) puts the conclusion well:
"The Poet's function is to describe, not the thing that has happened,
but a kind of thing that might happen, i.e., what is possible as being
probable or necessary . . . and if he should come to take a subject
from actual history, he is nonetheless a poet for that, since some
historic occurrence may very well be in the probably once-possible
order of things; and it is in that aspect of them that he is their poet."
Perhaps that is why tyrants so hate and fear poets and novelists and
yes, historians. Even more than they fear and hate scientists, who
though they create possible worlds, leave no place in them for possible alternative perspectives on those worlds.

40. On imaginative acts out beyond the visible world, see Paul Pruyser,
The Play of Imagination (New York: International Universities Press,
1983). Pruyser terms such acts "illusional." Israel's liturgy, in this sense,
stakes everything on "the future of an illusion."

41. On the polemical character and function of praise, see Robert
Martin-Achard, "A Propos de la Theologie de l'Ancien Testament," *The-
ologische Zeitschrift* 35 (1979): 63–71.

3. DOXOLOGY AT THE EDGE OF
IDEOLOGY: THE KING OF
MAJESTY AND MERCY

1. On this tension, see Gary A. Herion, "The Social Organization of
Tradition in Monarchic Judah" (diss., University of Michigan, 1982). On
pp. 51–63 and passim, Herion contrasts the "great tradition" and the
"little tradition." The Jerusalem liturgy appeals to the "little traditions"
of transformation, but it has been so co-opted that in the doxologies of
Israel, only the "great tradition" is visible and powerful.

2. By "revelatory" and "inspired" I do not mean to invoke scholastic or classical notions of inspiration and revelation. I mean rather that fresh disclosures of open possibility from God were mediated to Israel precisely in these liturgies of pain and transformation. To "disclose" and "reveal" is to make clear that the world is not closed and settled as dominant rationality wants to claim. It is this new openness that Israel's liturgies characteristically mediated.

3. This is the basic issue with which Frank M. Cross (*Canaanite Myth and Hebrew Epic* [Cambridge: Harvard University Press, 1973]) is concerned. See Patrick D. Miller, Jr., "Israelite Religion," in *The Hebrew Bible and Its Modern Interpreters,* ed. D. A. Knight and G. M. Tucker (Philadelphia: Fortress Press, 1985), 201–38, for a carefully nuanced discussion of the problem. See my discussions of this tension in "A Shape for Old Testament Theology, I: Structure Legitimation," and "A Shape for Old Testament Theology, II: Embrace of Pain," *Catholic Biblical Quarterly* 47 (1985): 28–46, 395–415, respectively. The "common theology" of the ancient Near East is both indispensable and inadequate for Israel.

4. Northrop Frye (*The Critical Path* [Bloomington: University of Indiana Press, 1971], 34–55) shrewdly notices that Israel shares a common "myth of concern," but that Israel also gave special attention to a revolutionary "myth of freedom" which is in tension with the "myth of concern." Moreover, biblical faith concentrated on its central myth and subordinated all other factors to it. This mythic drive toward monotheism, in our categories, means that all aspects of life are brought under the rule of this single liberating sovereign. Frye recognizes that the intent of Israel's faith cannot be explained in terms of common religious categories. On the monotheizing tendency of the Old Testament, see James A. Sanders, *From Sacred Story to Sacred Text* (Philadelphia: Fortress Press, 1987) 21, 147.

5. Rainer Albertz (*Persönliche Frömmigkeit und offizielle Religion* [Stuttgart: Calwer Verlag, 1978]) has noticed and described the stark difference between the religion of the temple (*Grosskult*) and the more intimate religious practice of family and tribe.

6. On the alternative claim of Israel's faith, see Miller, "Israelite Religion," 212–18. Miller draws special attention to "the claim of exclusive worship by Yahweh, and the aniconic requirement" (p. 212). For an exposition of this aniconic requirement as it bears upon Israel's life, see Walter Brueggemann, "Old Testament Theology as a Particular Conversation: Adjudication of Israel's Socio-Theological Alternatives," *Theology Digest* 32 (1985): 303–25.

7. On this text, see Patrick D. Miller, Jr., and J. J. M. Roberts, *The Hand of the Lord* (Baltimore: Johns Hopkins Press, 1977).

8. This matter is evidenced in 1 Samuel 7—15, in the complicated debate about kingship in Israel. That debate was not simply about institutional matters, but about the delicate relationship between faith and social power.

9. See my analysis of Solomonic use of the tradition in "The Social Nature of the Biblical Text for Preaching," in *Preaching as a Social Act*, ed. Art Van Seters (Nashville: Abingdon Press, forthcoming).

10. That old and powerful memory of hurt and rescue shows up in Christian theology as crucifixion and resurrection. But that also turns out, in its common form, to be mostly too radical for liturgies which in fact intend to support the royal enterprise. That the combined memory is too radical is evident in the practical decision of the American church to focus on Easter (rescue), but to minimize the importance of the season of passion (hurt).

11. It is exceedingly important that for Israel the theophanic experience occurs not only in the context, but also for the purpose of the liberation of slaves. Israel has little interest in theophany per se. Samuel Terrien (*The Elusive Presence* [New York: Harper & Row, 1978], 109–19) gives insufficient attention to the context which evokes the theophany. When the theophany can be separated from its social intention, it becomes a convenient vehicle for established and establishment religion. Such an approach to theophany always minimizes the experience which wells up. When theophanic memories are held in a vacuum, the "presence" is made available for sponsorship.

12. The current situation of the Catholic Church in Nicaragua is a fine example of this tension. The difficult conversation is between the church that supports the revolution and the established church which is largely allied with the Vatican in its critique of liberation theology. See Conor Cruise O'Brien, "God and Man in Nicaragua," *The Atlantic Monthly* (August 1986): 50–72.

13. See John M. Lundquist, "What is a Temple? A Preliminary Typology," in *The Quest for the Kingdom of God*, ed. H. B. Huffmon, F. A. Spina, and A. R. W. Green (Winona Lake, Ind.: Eisenbrauns, 1983), 205–19.

14. Aubrey Johnson, *Sacral Kingship in Ancient Israel* (Cardiff: University of Wales Press, 1955), 102–44. J. H. Eaton, *Kingship and the Psalms* (Naperville, Ill.: Alec R. Allenson, n.d.), 109–34. John M. Halligan ("The Role of the Peasant in the Amarna Period," in *Palestine in Transition*, ed. David Noel Freedman and David Frank Graf [Sheffield: Almond Press, 1983]) comments on the social conflict between the king and the landed aristocracy over the claims of land (p. 19):

> The landed aristocracy also provided a permanent power source of opposition to the king. Therefore it was necessary to surround the lord-peasant relationship with a ceremony to lessen the edge of the single interest, profit. In addition, ceremony relieved a constant anxiety of rulers everywhere: it underwrote their claim to legitimacy. Through ritual the regent may assume the power and glory of the gods or the absent Pharaoh by acting out the myths of fertility for his peasants. Festivals give occasion for the normal state of the society to be put aside to ease the oppressive tension. The Canaanites regulated the critical moments of life from birth to the grave by customs designed to separate the participants from historical time and place them for a period in mythical time.

Halligan does not have an intentional interest in liturgy as a form of social control, but it is impossible to miss the implications of his comments in that direction. What interests us in particular is the judgment that the king claimed power "by acting out the myths."

15. Johnson, *Sacral Kingship*, 126. I have intentionally used the language of "humiliation and exaltation" to suggest a connection to Phil. 2:5–11 and the christological issues which Christians probe through these texts.

16. The reading of social reality from the perspective of the marginal is one not often noticed in critical scholarship, but it is a perspective that surely operates in the texts. Robert R. Wilson (*Prophecy and Society in Ancient Israel* [Philadelphia: Fortress Press, 1980]) has called attention to the work of the prophets who function at the periphery of society among the people who "lack status and social power" (p. 38). Harvey H. Guthrie (*Theology as Thanksgiving* [New York: Seabury Press, 1981], 16–25) has suggested that worship among "outsiders" and in the "temple-palace complex" yield very different hymnodies. A dramatic example of a "sponsored liturgy" which has a grotesque dimension is the narrative by Margaret Atwood, *The Handmaid's Tale* (Boston: Houghton Mifflin, 1986). On pp. 88–89, the Commander makes good "use" of Genesis materials and the Beatitudes for the strange social order he embodied.

17. For a very old and suggestive parallel of liturgy as political benefit, see Peter Machinist, "Literature as Politics: The Tukulti-Ninurta Epic and the Bible," *Catholic Biblical Quarterly* 38 (1976): 455–82.

18. The connections between the mandate of Gen. 2:15 to "tend and care" and the expectation of the kings in the Davidic line hardly need argument. David as a shepherd (cf. 2 Sam. 5:2; Jer. 23:1; and esp. Ezekiel 34) and those who came after him are to tend and care for the earth and for the community.

19. Thus, for example, in Ps. 96:5, the gods are "idols," which means they "could not." The liturgy functions to delegitimate their false claims.

20. Norman K. Gottwald ("Social History of the United Monarchy," [Society of Biblical Literature Seminar Papers, Dec. 20, 1983]) has argued that the monarchy was developed to guard and maintain a monopoly of production which had already begun to appear.

21. I suggest that Deut. 17:14–20 reflects this concern. That provision in the mouth of Moses provides that the king should regularly read the torah, i.e., should submit to it and be shaped by it. Submission to the torah is closely related to being shaped by the liturgy which is an enactment of the central claims of torah.

22. On the polarity, see Claus Westermann, *The Psalms: Structure, Content and Message* (Minneapolis: Augsburg, 1980), 90–92.

23. According to conventional source analysis, these texts and this motif are assigned to the Priestly tradition. See Claus Westermann, "Die Herrlichkeit Gottes in der Priesterschrift," in *Wort—Gebot—Glaube*, ed. Hans Joachim Stoebe (Zurich: Zwingli, 1970), 227–49.

24. According to conventional source analysis, these texts and this motif are assigned to the Yahwist tradition.

25. On the salvation oracles, see Edgar W. Conrad, *Fear Not Warrior* (Chico, Calif.: Scholars Press, 1985); and Claus Westermann, "Sprache und Struktur der Prophetie Deuterojesajas," in *Forschung am Alten Testament* (Munich: Chr. Kaiser, 1964), 117–24.

26. Westermann, "Sprache und Struktur," 124–44.

27. It is congenial to my argument that the royal psalms are elements in world-building, and that such world-building lives very close to ideology. The conventional treatment of the royal psalms, in my opinion, indicates how the point is missed if, methodologically, the wrong questions are asked. Conventional scholarship has been preoccupied with historical-critical questions and has therefore missed the social critical questions that must be asked.

28. David Jobling ("Deconstruction and the Political Analysis of Biblical Texts: A Jamesonian Reading of Psalm 72" [Society of Biblical Literature Seminar Paper, 1986]) has recently provided a suggestive reading of Psalm 72 in terms of a critical social analysis.

29. It is often and rightly observed that Ps. 96:7–9 (which we have earlier considered in detail with reference to "gospel") is parallel to the old doxology of Ps. 29:1–2, except that the praise is now rendered on earth and not in heaven among the gods. The move from Psalm 29 to Psalm 96 shows the process of liturgy moving decisively into Israel's public life.

30. On this theme as it was utilized in the traditions generated by the Jerusalem establishment, see Hans Walter Wolff, "The Kerygma of the Yahwist," in *The Vitality of the Old Testament Traditions*, by Walter Brueggemann and Hans Walter Wolff (Atlanta: John Knox Press, 1975), 41–66.

31. For the resilience of the memory in the liturgy derived from David, see Walter Brueggemann, *David's Truth in Israel's Imagination and Memory* (Philadelphia: Fortress Press, 1985), chap. 4.

32. See Walter Brueggemann, "'Vine and Fig Tree': A Case Study in Imagination and Criticism," *Catholic Biblical Quarterly* 43 (1981): 188–204, for a comparable critique.

33. See Glendon E. Bryce, *A Legacy of Wisdom* (Lewisburg, Pa.: Bucknell University Press, 1979), chaps. 6 and 7. Cf. Eric W. Heaton, *Solomon's New Men* (London: Thames & Hudson, 1974).

34. On the social function of horses in the royal apparatus, see Walter Brueggemann, *Revelation and Violence: A Study in Contextualization* (Milwaukee: Marquette University Press, 1986).

35. See Jon Douglas Levenson, *Theology of the Program of Restoration of Ezekiel 40—48* (Missoula, Mont.: Scholars Press, 1976), 55–107.

36. Josiah, at least according to Jer. 22:13–17, is an important exception to this generalization.

37. Jeremiah 22:13–19 contains both a heavy critique of such self-serving kingship and a statement on the proper function of kings.

38. On the core tradition, see Walter Harrelson, "Life, Faith, and the Emergence of Tradition," in *Tradition and Theology in the Old Testament*, ed. Douglas A. Knight (Philadelphia: Fortress Press, 1977), 11–30.

39. R. N. Whybray (*The Second Isaiah* [Sheffield: JSOT Press, 1983], 30–34) takes Psalm 117 as a model for hymn more generally.

40. Note that the word "make" is in quotes (see my discussion in the first chapter of the quotes used by sociologists). In such a use I mean to bracket out the ontological question and deal with the dramatic forming power of liturgic usage.

41. Frank Crüsemann, *Studien zur formgeschichte von Hymnus und Danklied in Israel* (Neukirchen-Vluyn: Neukirchener Verlag, 1969).

42. On the credo as normative for Israel's world, see Gerhard von Rad, "The Form-Critical Problem of the Hexateuch," in *The Problem of the Hexateuch and Other Essays* (New York: McGraw-Hill, 1966), 1–78. Note the powerful social function of this recital as it has been presented by Norman K. Gottwald in *The Tribes of Yahweh: A Sociology of the Religion of Liberated Israel, 1250–1050 B.C.E.* (Maryknoll, N.Y.: Orbis Books, 1979), 63–114.

43. Von Rad ("Form-Critical Problem of the Hexateuch," 67) judges this inclusion of creation faith to be relatively late in the development of the tradition.

44. On the character and function of songs of thanksgiving, see Westermann, *The Psalms*, 73–83, and esp. Guthrie, *Theology as Thanksgiving*, 6–12 and passim.

45. G. E. Wright's most mature expression of these matters, though not his best, is in *The Old Testament and Theology* (New York: Harper & Row, 1969), his Sprunt Lectures.

46. Erhard Gerstenberger (*Der bittende Mensch* [Neukirchen-Vluyn: Neukirchener Verlag, 1980]), and Albertz (*Persönliche Frömmigkeit*) have shown how the context of petition and thanks tends to be the family crises of birth and death.

47. Both Gerstenberger and Albertz have proposed that the life-setting of such complaints concern the *Kleinkult,* the intimate, less formal worship of the clan or village, which is quite in contrast to the great formalized worship of the temple.

48. William H. Gass (*Habitations of the Word* [New York: Simon & Schuster, 1985] 10) articulates some of this painful specificity:

> But life is not all eloquence and adulation: life is wiping the baby's bum; it is a bad case of croup; it is quarrels with one's spouse; it is disappointment, distraction, indignities by the dozen; it is the death of friends, wife, son, and brothers, carried off like fluff in the wind; it is alien evenings, cold stairwells, frosty sheets, lack of love; for what does the great spirit need that touches the body but the touch of the body, as oratory needs silence, and revolution peace? We are nourished by our absences and opposites; contraries quench our thirst.

49. On this agenda for the Psalms, see Walter Brueggemann, "From Hurt to Joy, from Death to Life," *Interpretation* 28 (1974): 3–19.

50. I do not assume that a study of Old Testament praise leads automatically or necessarily to the New Testament or to Christology. I mean only that for baptized Christians that is where it leads. The same history of

praise leads in a different but not dissimilar direction for Jews. Cf. Paul van Buren, *Discerning the Way* (New York: Seabury Press, 1980).

51. On trust in such transformative impossibilities, see Walter Brueggemann, "'Impossibility' and Epistemology in the Faith Tradition of Abraham and Sarah (Gen. 18:1–15)," *Zeitschrift für die alttestamentliche Wissenschaft* 94 (1982): 524–25; and Patrick D. Miller, Jr., *Interpreting the Psalms* (Philadelphia: Fortress Press, 1986), 73–78.

4. DOXOLOGY WITHOUT REASON:
THE LOSS OF ISRAEL'S
WORLD OF HOPE

1. On the data for the notion of guilds of temple singers, see Sigmund Mowinckel, *The Psalms in Israel's Worship* (Nashville: Abingdon Press, 1962), 2:84–103.

2. The claim of "abiding" is especially indicated in the word "forever," e.g., in the temple hymn of dedication (1 Kings 8:12–13) and in David's prayer in response to the divine oracle (2 Sam. 7:24–29). The term "forever" is characteristically used to make this claim in such contexts.

3. Clear recent examples of liturgy "from below," which jeopardizes established order, come from societies in the midst of fundamental upheaval. In Nicaragua, the religious crisis concerns the established church in deep conflict with the church of the revolution, on which see Conor Cruise O'Brien, "God and Men in Nicaragua," *The Atlantic Monthly* (August 1986): 50–72. The crisis in South Africa is even more blatant. In a news report of a meeting led by Andries Truernicht, leader of the conservative party, it is reported that he "prayed, sang patriotic hymns and donated cans of food for distribution to underprivileged white children." In the same week, a news story on the acquittal of 142 black women squatters who were arrested by the government reports that "the women sang and danced, and one said, 'It's another victory for us.'" The contrast between "patriotic songs" and "the women sang and danced" is an example of the contrast between controlling liturgies "from above" and threatening liturgies "from below."

4. For a graphic imaginative picture of the king giving such advice to his public voices, see Stefan Heym, *The King David Report* (New York: G. P. Putnam's Sons, 1973).

5. Patrick D. Miller, Jr., *Interpreting the Psalms* (Philadelphia: Fortress Press, 1986), 70 n. 9.

6. On praise as an act of "overflow," see Daniel W. Hardy and David F. Ford, *Praising and Knowing God* (Philadelphia: Westminster Press, 1985).

7. Robert Jay Lifton (*The Broken Connection* [New York: Basic Books, 1983 (1979)]) has offered a remarkable analysis of the importance of vitality and the emergence of violence in pursuit of vitality when vitality has been lost. See esp. chap. 12, and his programmatic statement: ". . . there is also recourse to violence as a quest for something on the

order of vitality" (p. 248). Lifton's work is important for our topic, for it suggests a connection between praise and public policy.

8. The test of how these remembered transformations function as critique and as possibility is found in what kinds of churches engage in such concrete recitals. It is clear in the contemporary church that where the church is "settled" in culture, these remembered transformations disappear from the horizon.

9. The metaphor of "horn" characteristically means power or victory. More precisely it may well refer to the king in light of v. 11, but that in part depends on one's dating and placement of the psalm.

10. Claus Westermann, *The Praise of God in the Psalms* (Richmond: John Knox Press, 1965), 22 and passim.

11. See Harvey H. Guthrie, *Theology as Thanksgiving* (New York: Seabury Press, 1981), 10 and passim.

12. On this psalm, see Miller, *Interpreting the Psalms*, 65–67, and note esp. his citation of Walter Beyerlin.

13. The opening verbs of the various stanzas lack specificity. In vv. 10 and 23 the verb is a participle and likely should be corrected in v. 4 to correspond. The fourth verb in v. 17 is a noun, but is characteristically modified to conform to the pattern. See, e.g., Hans Joachim Kraus, *Psalmen 2* (Neukirchen-Vluyn: Neukirchener Verlag, 1961), 736.

14. In a rebuke to a focus on the concrete social pain caused by unemployment, President Reagan asked, "Is it news if some guy in South Succotash loses his job and gets interviewed?" (reported in *The Washington Post* [March 18, 1982] section A, p. 1). The news does not concern individuals, but making of national policy.

15. A summary of the hypothesis of the "Solomonic Enlightenment" as formulated by Gerhard von Rad and Kurt Galling, together with a critique, is offered by James L. Crenshaw in *Studies in Ancient Israelite Wisdom* (New York: Ktav, 1976), 16–20. While von Rad may have claimed too much for the notion, I do not believe the matter can be dismissed as easily as Crenshaw proposes.

16. See R. N. Whybray, *The Intellectual Tradition in the Old Testament* (New York: Walter de Gruyter, 1974); and Robert Gordis, *Poets, Prophets, and Sages* (Bloomington: Indiana University Press, 1971), chap. 6.

17. Unfortunately, it is not always possible to identify the differences in verb forms from English translation. But the distinctions I am making are clear enough in Hebrew.

18. See the splendid analysis of this psalm by Anthony R. Ceresko, "Psalm 149: Poetry, Themes (Exodus and Conquest), and Social Function," *Biblica* 67 (1986): 177–94. My conclusion that the psalm calls Israel to do the action that Yahweh might otherwise undertake is paralleled by the last sentence of Ceresko's, "But it was Israel's 'acting' (*'ish*, vv. 7–9) in the Conquest which turned that possibility into a reality."

19. For a summary of the current status of "creation theology," see the fine collection of essays edited by Bernhard W. Anderson, *Creation in the Old Testament* (Philadelphia: Fortress Press, 1984), and esp. the article

by H. H. Schmid, "Creation, Righteousness, and Salvation: 'Creation Theology' as the Broad Horizon of Biblical Theology" (pp. 102–17). For a perceptive and judicious response to the recent emphasis on creation and with particular respect to Schmid, see Henning Graf Reventlow, *Problems of Biblical Theology in the Twentieth Century* (London: SCM Press, 1986), 164–78. Reventlow seems more aware of the potential problematic of such an accent than some other scholars who make certain theology a central emphasis. Rolf P. Knierim ("The Task of Old Testament Theology," *Horizons in Biblical Theology* 6 [1984]: 25–57) has struggled significantly with creation as a theme in Old Testament theology. He rightly relates it to the theme of God's righteousness, but I am not certain that he has done so with sufficient critical sensitivity.

20. See the heavy and dread-filled satire on this theme in Margaret Atwood, *The Handmaid's Tale* (Boston: Houghton Mifflin, 1986), 88–89 and passim. The mandates of creation (particularly "be fruitful") are employed in this fictional scenario to justify an abusive social practice and authoritarian regime. Because of the popular allusion to Bible and religion, it seems apparent that Atwood is commenting on the use of religion for the sake of legitimating present social order.

21. Karl Marx formulated this most succinctly, "The ruling ideas of each age have ever been the ideas of its ruling class." Cf. David McLellan, *The Thought of Karl Marx* (London: Macmillan & Co., 1971), 46. Michel Clevenot (*Materialist Approaches to the Bible* [Maryknoll, N.Y.: Orbis Books, 1985]) has most intentionally worked out this thesis with reference to the Bible. While I do not want to overstate the matter, it gives one pause that a century ago, the creation texts were used by serious people to keep blacks in "their created place," even as parallel arguments are now used in some quarters with reference to the social location of women. While we may conclude that such use is misguided, nonetheless such texts on "order" lend themselves readily to such use.

22. See esp. H. H. Schmid, "Creation, Righteousness, and Salvation," and more fully, idem, *Gerechtigkeit als Weltordnung* (Tübingen: J. C. B. Mohr [Paul Siebeck], 1968).

23. On the relation between economics and epistemology, see George E. Mendenhall, "The Shady Side of Wisdom: The Date and Purpose of Genesis 3," in *A Light Unto My Path*, ed. Howard N. Bream et al. (Philadelphia: Temple University Press, 1974), 319–34.

24. On energy as related to a healthy, human world, see Lifton, *The Broken Connection*, 115–24. His general argument is that energy for life derives from being "connected" in a human world. Where the connections are broken, there death gains power. In the categories of Lifton's analysis, one can conclude that liturgy is to keep the world "connected," so that there may be energy for life.

25. For a survey of a primary trajectory of these terms in relation to God, see Phyllis Trible, *God and the Rhetoric of Sexuality* (Philadelphia: Fortress Press, 1978), chap. 1. More specifically on *ḥesed*, see Katharine Doob Sakenfeld, *Faithfulness in Action* (Philadelphia: Fortress Press, 1985).

26. Hans Walter Wolff ("'Wissen um God' bei Hosea als Urform von Theologie," in *Gesammelte Studien zum Alten Testament* [Munich: Chr. Kaiser, 1964], 182–205) has made it clear that *ḥesed* and *'emeth* have specific content as a memory of Yahweh's saving deeds which are the basis of covenant bonding. When that "knowledge" is lost, the relation and the bonding will disappear. Wolff asserts concerning our terms, "Treue Verbundenheit (*'emeth* und *ḥesed*) ist die Verhaltungsweise, die den Gottestaten und der Gottesgabe in 'Bund' und 'Lehre' entspricht." In his commentary, *Hosea* (Philadelphia: Fortress Press, 1974), concerning *ḥesed*, Wolff writes, "For Hebrew thought, these existential components are inseparably bound to the cognitive functions, all of them in turn belonging to the structure of *da'ath*" (pp. 120–21). It is the "reason" in praise that keeps the cognitive element available and compelling. Where the "reason" no longer mediates the cognitive basis, an existential feeling of bonding cannot be sustained. The loss of the concreteness about the language and the tradition is surely what Hosea and Jeremiah mean by "forgetting."

27. Norman K. Gottwald has written in various places on the social organization of the royal world in Israel. See his succinct summary of his social analysis, *The Hebrew Bible: A Socio-Literary Introduction* (Philadelphia: Fortress Press, 1985), 323–25. My point here is that it requires a certain liturgical legitimation to sustain such a social organization that is in deep tension with Israel's foundational memory.

28. Jon D. Levenson (*Sinai and Zion* [New York: Winston Press, 1985], 56–70) has provided a shrewd and discerning analysis of Israel's polemic against the other gods. I am not sure, however, that he has articulated what is theologically at stake for Israel. On a contemporary suggestion about idolatry, see David Bakan, *On Method: Toward a Reconstruction of Psychological Investigation* (New York: Jossey-Boss, 1967). He suggests that in complacent science, idolatry is "being stuck" on an answer, rather than a restless pursuit of the search. It is "the loss of the sense of search, of the sense of freshness of the experience" (p. 154). On the contemporary theological issue of idolatry, see Pablo Richard et al., *The Idols of Death and the God of Life* (Maryknoll, N.Y.: Orbis Books, 1983), 36–37.

29. The social function of such concrete transformations remembered in exile greatly illuminates why Second Isaiah appeals to the exodus tradition. It is not only the appeal to old tradition, but the very specific tradition which undermines the rationality of the empire which depends on imperial gods. See Bernhard W. Anderson, "Exodus and Covenant in Second Isaiah and Prophetic Traditions," in *Magnalia Dei: The Mighty Acts of God*, ed. Frank Moore Cross, Werner E. Lemke, and Patrick D. Miller, Jr. (Garden City, N.Y.: Doubleday & Co., 1976), 339–60.

30. In spite of a great deal of attention to historical-critical problems related to this text, it is increasingly clear that the materials of Isaiah 36—37 need to be treated from a literary-canonical and therefore theological perspective. That is, these chapters are an assertion about the true character of Yahweh, even if "the world" (of Assyria and of Israel) does

not comprehend. On the theological character of the assertions made in the text, see Ronald Clements, *Isaiah and the Deliverance of Jerusalem* (Sheffield: University of Sheffield Press, 1980), esp. 90–108. See also Walter Brueggemann, "II Kings 18—19: The Legitimacy of a Sectarian Hermeneutic," *Horizons in Biblical Theology* 7 (1985): 1–42.

31. These terms—departure, withdrawal, homecoming, keeping of promises—constitute an unlikely catalogue with very different references. Thus, "departure" refers to Exodus, "homecoming" to the end of exile, "keeping promises" to the main claims of Deuteronomy, whereas "withdrawal" is a term that has gained usage only as a result of the sociological analyses of Mendenhall and Gottwald. All of these terms, however, point to the same characteristic intervention of Yahweh which permits transformation and inversion.

32. On the continuing radical function of this narrative, see Michael Walzer, *Exodus and Revolution* (New York: Basic Books, 1985). In a very different idiom, see the address by Laura Geller, "Living Well Is Not the Best Revenge" (commencement address at Brown University). She speaks of the Jewish memory of the exodus as "my second language" that maintains freedom and perspective midst "cynicism, careerism, or individualism."

33. On the interface of pain and political power, see the extraordinary study of Elaine Scarry, *The Body in Pain* (New York: Oxford University Press, 1985).

34. Ernest W. Nicholson (*God and His People* [Oxford: Clarendon Press, 1986], 193–217) has well understood the connection characteristically made between the rule of God and the rule of the king: "The structures and institutions of society were believed to reflect the order willed by the gods, and were thus understood as being divinely legitimated" (p. 195). See his critique of "state ideology" and its relation to creation theology.

35. The equation of God's rule and the present order is the reason that the contemporaries of Amos so welcomed the coming of "the Day of the Lord," and it is Amos's sense of the incongruity of the two that is the basis of his warning and critique (cf. Amos 5:18–20). The theological equation made by Amos's contemporaries is not unrelated to their social practice. On the latter, see Bernhard Lang, "The Social Organization of Peasant Poverty in Biblical Israel," *Journal for the Study of the Old Testament* 24 (1982): 47–63. The social analysis and religious critique must be seen as interrelated.

36. In making the contrast between Sinai and Zion as I am making it, I am aware that my interpretation contradicts that of Harmut Gese, *Vom Sinai Zum Zion* (Munich: Chr. Kaiser, 1974), in which he has been followed by Peter Stuhlmacher, "The Law as a Topic of Biblical Theology," in *Reconciliation, Law, and Righteousness: Essays in Biblical Theology* (Philadelphia: Fortress Press, 1986), 110–33. I am not at all sure what is meant concretely by "Zion torah." I am not sure how to assess this contradiction, as I am impressed by and have learned much from the construct of

Gese and Stuhlmacher. Yet serious social criticism I believe requires the conclusions I have drawn. Clearly we are not at the end of our conversation. If "law" is understood as "covenant law," then one cannot so easily celebrate the "end of the law," for the kings of Israel in their own way wanted the end of the law. The move from such social analysis to the theological insights of Gese and Stuhlmacher is not an easy or obvious one.

37. The social practice and social ideology of the Jerusalem establishment benefited greatly from such uncritical doxology. On the implications of the urban ideology, see Frank S. Frick, *The Formation of the State in Ancient Israel* (Decatur, Ga.: Almond Press, 1985); David Noel Freedman and David Frank Graf, eds., *Palestine in Transition* (Sheffield: Almond Press, 1983); Lang, "Social Organization of Peasant Poverty"; and Hans Walter Wolff, "Micah the Moreshite—The Prophet and His Background," in *Israelite Wisdom,* ed. John Gammie et al. (Missoula, Mont.: Scholars Press, 1978), 77–84.

38. See the carefully nuanced statement of Patrick D. Miller, Jr., "Faith and Ideology in the Old Testament," in *Magnalia Dei,* ed. Cross et al., 464–79. I am using the term "ideology" more pejoratively than does Miller. For a shrewd statement on the contemporary issues related to ideology, see R. C. Lewontin, Steven Rose, and Leon J. Kaim, *Not in Our Genes* (New York: Pantheon Books, 1984), 30–32, in their attack on E. O. Wilson's biological determinism as ideology. They conclude: "Why, then are they given such serious attention? It is because, in contemporary Western society, science as an institution has come to be accorded the authority that once went to the church. When 'science' speaks—or rather when its spokesmen (and they generally are men) speak in the name of science—let no dog bark. 'Science' is the ultimate legitimator of bourgeois ideology" (p. 31). What Lewontin, Rose, and Kaim ascribe to Wilson's science is, I suggest, parallel to the function of ideology in the royal liturgy.

39. Even though the narratives have been silenced, they continue to live and function in communities of the oppressed. It is for that reason that Rubem Alves (*Tomorrow's Child; Imagination, Creativity, and the Rebirth of Culture* [New York: Harper & Row, 1972], 182–205) has urged that, in a totalitarian state, the most important educational work is to tell the young the tales of transformation and possibility, because, sooner or later, those stories will generate energy, courage, and action. The narratives finally refuse to be silenced.

40. See George E. Mendenhall, "The Monarchy," *Interpretation* 29 (1975): 155–70; and Nicholson, *God and His People,* 198–201.

41. Lifton (*The Broken Connection*) has characterized such loyal conformists who become so numbed that they are unable to notice, or discern, or criticize. It is ironic that Lifton's most frightening example of such conformism happens in the name of science, for which Edward Teller stands as the paradigm.

42. Ibid., 293–301. Such "totalism" has no symbols whereby to enter-

tain either ambiguity or alternative. "There is the overall assumption that there is just one valid mode of being—just one authentic avenue of immortality—so that an arbitrary line is drawn between those with a right to exist and those who possess no such right" (p. 298).

43. Andre Neher, *The Exile of the Word* (Philadelphia: Jewish Publication Society of America, 1981), 31.

44. See D. W. Winnicott, *The Maturational Processes and the Facilitating Environment* (London: Hogarth Press, 1965). See also the important use made of Winnicott by Lifton, *The Broken Connection;* and Paul Pruyser, *The Play of the Imagination* (New York: International Universities Press, 1983), 57–72. See my own use of Winnicott's categories in "The Costly Loss of Lament," *Journal for the Study of the Old Testament* 36 (1986): 57–71.

45. Winnicott (*The Maturational Processes,* 145) concludes, "The mother who is not good enough is not able to implement the infant's omnipotence and so she repeatedly fails to meet the infant's gesture. Instead she substitutes her own gesture which is to be given compliance by the infant. This compliance on the part of the infant is the earliest stage of the False Self, and belongs to the mother's inability to sense her infant's need."

46. See Brian W. Kovacs, "Is There a Class-Ethic in Proverbs?" in *Essays in Old Testament Ethics,* ed. James L. Crenshaw and John T. Willis (New York: Ktav, 1974), 171–87; and Mendenhall, "The Shady Side of Wisdom."

47. Gerhard von Rad (*Wisdom in Israel* [Nashville: Abingdon Press, 1972], 65) has observed that in the wisdom traditions (to which Psalms 10 and 14 are related) "foolishness" is "practical atheism." That is, this atheism is not a denial of God, but inattention to God's ordering of creation.

48. It is worth noting that the word "moved" (*môṭ*) in v. 6 is the same word applied to Zion in Ps. 46:5. The "fool" only claims for himself what royal ideology claimed for Zion. Both claims, one condemned and one transmitted as high theology, are a denial of the freedom of God and the risk of history.

49. On the unfaithful options of blind submission and self-sufficient autonomy, see Walter Brueggemann, "The Third World of Evangelical Imagination," *Horizons in Biblical Theology* 8, no. 2 (1986): 61–84.

50. I intend to play on Joseph Heller, *Something Happened* (New York: Alfred A. Knopf, 1974). The ironic title communicates for 353 pages that in fact nothing happens. That is finally the "message" of the book.

51. See *The Broken Connection,* where Lifton quotes Winnicott who speaks of "snapping of the thread of continuity of the self" (p. 127), and where Lifton reports James's quote of Tolstoy: "I felt . . . that something had broken within me on which my life had always rested, that I had nothing left to hold on to, and that morally my life had stopped . . ." (p. 371).

52. Ibid., 366–68.

53. Norman K. Gottwald (*The Tribes of Yahweh: A Sociology of the*

Religion of Liberated Israel, 1250–1050 B.C.E. [Maryknoll, N.Y.: Orbis Books, 1979]) has most fully and programmatically shown what this means for penetrating the original self-understanding of Israel.

54. See the telling contemporary example of the banishment of abrasive questions by John Robert McFarland, "Looking for the Gospel at a Gospel Concert," *The Christian Century* 103 (1986): 579–81.

55. This is a fair characterization of the society reported by Robert Bellah et al. in *Habits of the Heart: Individualism and Commitment in American Life* (Berkeley and Los Angeles: University of California Press, 1985).

56. The trade-off of violence for vitality, for which Lifton provides a theoretical base, is evident in the domestic violence in our society and in the religious venom supporting the arms race. It is mind-boggling to suggest that one root of these developments is the inadequacy of "world-making" in liturgy which fails to mediate vitality. Scarry (*The Body in Pain*) studies the ways in which the violence of war and torture "unmakes" worlds, even as it "unmakes" language.

57. Vincent Crapanzano (*Waiting: The Whites of South Africa* [New York: Random House, 1985]) has chronicled the desperate, empty, hopeless waiting of whites in South Africa and the way in which such waiting brutalizes all the parties—the powerful and the powerless.

5. DOXOLOGY INSIDE THE "CLAIMS OF TIME AND SORROW"

1. On pastoral leadership as world-making, see Karen LeBacqz, *Professional Ethics: Power and Paradox* (Nashville: Abingdon Press, 1985), 116–17 and passim; and chap. 1, p. 28 above.

2. On this theme in Jeremiah, see Walter Brueggemann, *Hopeful Imagination: Prophetic Voices in Exile* (Philadelphia: Fortress Press, 1986), 9–47.

3. Ibid., 9–47, on Jeremiah; and 90–130, on Second Isaiah.

4. The loss of the credo is crucial for the life of Israel. Deuteronomy warns against forgetting (8:11, 18; cf. Hos. 2:13). Jeremiah 2:6–7 (in the same tradition) specifically notes that Israel "did not say" the credo. When the community no longer recites the memory, it becomes hopeless, and it succumbs to the power of ideology and the seduction of idolatry. Memory is an important defense against faithlessness in Israel, and it is the credo which sustains and articulates the memory.

5. Robert Bellah ("Biblical Religion and Social Science in the Modern World," *NICM Journal for Jews and Christians in Higher Education* 63 [1982]: 8–22) has nicely and succinctly characterized the rationality that precludes the very dimensions of faith that are crucial to our humanness.

6. This is an allusion to the current advertising slogan of the *Wall Street Journal,* that it is the "diary of the American dream." On the American dream and the critique of Reinhold Niebuhr which is crucial for American theology, see Douglas Hall, "The Cross and Contemporary Culture,"

in *Reinhold Niebuhr and the Issues of Our Time,* ed. Richard Harris (Grand Rapids: Wm. B. Eerdmans, 1986), 188 and passim.

7. See the acute analysis of shame and embarrassment by Gabriele Taylor, *Praise, Shame, and Guilt: Emotions of Self-Assessment* (New York: Oxford University Press, 1985), esp. 67–71.

8. Dorothee Soelle, *The Strength of the Weak* (Philadelphia: Westminster Press, 1984), 90.

9. William B. Yeats, "Crazy Jane Talks with the Bishop," in *Oxford Anthology of English Poetry,* ed. Howard Foster Tawry and William Thorp, 2d ed. (New York: Oxford University Press, 1956).

10. Our theme urges us to draw attention to Wendell Berry's writing more generally. See also his essays in *The Unsettling of America: Culture and Agriculture* (New York: Avon Books, 1977), and *The Gift of Good Land* (San Francisco: North Point Press, 1981). While Berry is impatient with and critical of conventional, formal church religion, his writings live very close to the claims and themes of biblical faith. Indeed, his writings may be viewed as a deep and long lament over the death of the land.

11. Wendell Berry, *A Place on Earth* (San Francisco: North Point Press, 1983).

12. Ibid., 97.

13. Ibid., 94.

14. The phrase "desperate hope of hope" is a peculiar phrase and I have wondered if Berry did not mean "hint of hope," but the double use of hope is surely correct and is reminiscent of "hope against hope" in Rom. 4:18.

15. Berry, *A Place on Earth,* 95.

16. Ibid., 100.

17. Freud has understood that guilt is frequently an ideological way of handling pain. On the rationalization of hurt toward guilt, see Paul Ricoeur, *The Symbolism of Evil* (Boston: Beacon Press, 1967), 100–150.

18. On the need for a critical "counter-vocabulary," see James L. Farrell, "Speaking of Nuclear War; A Semantic Defense Initiative," *The Christian Century* 103 (1986): 939–42.

19. On the production of ideological violence in a culture that has empty, formal, controlling relationships without a human dimension, see Robert J. Lifton, *The Broken Connection* (New York: Basic Books, 1983), esp. 283–387.

20. *No Exit* is the title of a play by Jean-Paul Sartre (*No Exit and Three Other Plays* [New York: Vintage Books, 1955]). I would not agree with Sartre's existential subjectification of despair, but he has used the expression and written the play to communicate the debilitating power of utter hopelessness. Lifton has best understood the "psychic numbness" which comes from a loss of humanizing symbolization. See *The Broken Connection,* 130, 366 and passim, and *The Life of the Self* (New York: Basic Books, 1983), 78–81 and passim.

21. Gerhard von Rad, *The Problem of the Hexateuch and Other Essays* (New York: McGraw-Hill, 1966), 1–78. This essay became programmatic

for von Rad's subsequent two-volume theology of the Old Testament which explicated the theme of historical recital.

22. G. Ernest Wright, *God Who Acts: Biblical Theology as Recital* (London: SCM Press, 1952).

23. See the review and sympathetic assessment of Werner E. Lemke, "Revelation through History in Recent Biblical Theology," *Interpretation* 36 (1982): 34–46. Lemke is more positive than many other scholars might be but argues the point well and candidly.

24. On the cruciality of the theme of crying and being heard in Israel's faith and the pivotal importance of Exod. 2:23–25 for Israel's faith, see Walter Brueggemann, *Hope Within History* (Atlanta: John Knox Press, 1987), 16–20.

25. See Walter Brueggemann, "Psalm 77: The 'Turn' from Self to God," *Journal for Preachers* 6 (1983): 8–14.

26. On the cruciality of finite verbs which refer to specific events and identifiable occurrences, see chap. 4. Israel's concreteness is jeopardized in any move away from finite verbs.

27. On this theme, see David Noel Freedman, "The Twenty-Third Psalm," in *Michigan Oriental Studies in Honor of George G. Cameron,* ed. Louis L. Orlin (Ann Arbor: Dept. of Near Eastern Studies, University of Michigan, 1976), 139–66.

28. On the lament, see the foundational work of Claus Westermann, *The Praise of God in the Psalms* (Richmond: John Knox Press, 1965); the derivative work of Patrick D. Miller, Jr., *Interpreting the Psalms* (Philadelphia: Fortress Press, 1986), 48–63; and Walter Brueggemann, *The Message of the Psalms* (Minneapolis: Augsburg, 1984), 51–77.

29. See Erhard Gerstenberger, "Der klagende Mensch," in *Probleme biblischer Theologie,* ed. Hans Walter Wolff (Munich: Chr. Kaiser, 1971), 64–72; and Moshe Greenberg, *Biblical Prose Prayer* (Berkeley and Los Angeles: University of California Press, 1983), 1–18. An impressive example of this use of lament psalms is given in the novel by Carolyn Chute, *The Beans of Egypt, Maine* (New York: Ticknor & Fields, 1985). This is a narrative about a poor, socially marginal family that has no social power and is helpless in brutal ways. Chute has her characters at many crucial places in their helplessness recite lament psalms which we are to understand not only as statements of hopelessness but also as statements of desperate hope. See, for example, pp. 180–81.

30. See my general comments on this psalm, "The Costly Loss of Lament," *Journal for the Study of the Old Testament* 36 (1986): 57–71; and the detailed analysis of Robert Alter, *The Art of Biblical Poetry* (New York: Basic Books, 1985), 67–73.

31. This possible correlation between lament and divine response (Isa. 41:14) is an example of the kind of correlations on which Joachim Begrich ("Das priesterliche Heilsorakel," in *Gesammelte Studien zum Alten Testament* [Munich: Chr. Kaiser, 1964], 217–31) established his magisterial hypothesis about lament and salvation oracle. However, as nearly as I can determine, Begrich does not mention this particular case.

32. In chap. 2, I have dealt with Psalm 96 as a primary example of enthronement liturgy which is the enactment of the gospel. Second Isaiah makes use of and appeals to the longstanding and quite familiar liturgy of enthronement in relating the claims of the liturgy to his specific situation. The liturgy provides a "world" through which specific experiences of life may be perceived and lived differently.

33. On the silence and speech of God, see Andre Neher, *The Exile of the Word* (New York: Jewish Publication Society of America, 1981).

34. On "thin" comfort, see the phrase used by Berry, p. 132 above. That comfort is nicely contrasted to the evangelical comfort of Second Isaiah which is "thick."

35. See Claus Westermann, *The Psalms: Structure, Content and Message* (Minneapolis: Augsburg, 1980), 73–83. It is important that for these psalms, Westermann uses the suggestive theme, "Individual Psalms of Narrative Praise." The emphasis on narrative is congruent with our general argument. Westermann sees that thanks consists in the retelling of the particular story of transformation. On the function of thanksgiving in the liturgical life of Israel and the church, see Harvey H. Guthrie, Jr., *Theology as Thanksgiving* (New York: Seabury Press, 1981).

36. On the work and function of complaint by the individual in a community of "rehabilitation," see Erhard Gerstenberger, *Der bittende Mensch* (Neukirchen-Vluyn: Neukirchener Verlag, 1980).

37. Among the more dramatic articulations of the massive reversal characteristically wrought by Yahweh is Isa. 54:7–10. See my exposition of this text in *Hopeful Imagination*, 115–22.

38. George A. Lindbeck (*The Nature of Doctrine* [Philadelphia: Westminster Press, 1984]) has stressed the decisive importance of language for faith. Israel's mode of speech decisively shapes the possibilities and limitations of Israel's mode of life.

39. On the critical function of "the little story" in the face of "The Great Story," see Gary A. Herion, "The Social Organization of Tradition in Monarchic Judah" (diss., University of Michigan, 1982), and his derivative study, "The Role of Historical Narrative in Biblical Thought: The Tendencies Underlying Old Testament Historiography" *Journal for the Study of the Old Testament* 21 (1981): 25–57. See my comments on "little story" and "Great Story" in chap. 3.

40. See Walter Brueggemann, "From Hurt to Joy, from Death to Life," *Interpretation* 28 (1974): 3–19.

41. One of the important differences between the "little story" and the "Great Story" is that the former is concrete and the latter tends to as much abstraction as possible. In commenting on the concreteness of the little story which constitutes the gospel, Luise Schottroff (in the preface to Luise Schottroff and Wolfgang Stegemann, *Jesus and the Hope of the Poor* [Maryknoll, N.Y.: Orbis Books, 1986], vi) writes that "The reality of human beings' lives must be grasped as concretely as possible. 'Humankind' as an anthropological quantity, timeless and abstract, should no longer appear in biblical interpretation." The contrast between "as

concretely as possible" and "timeless and abstract" determines whether one attends to the little story of unnoticed persons, or only to the great claims of the great. Schottroff is concerned with "oppressed persons, the unemployed, Jews, women, children, the sick" who have been "'disqualified' from being key figures in the biblical milieu."

For a more philosophical analysis of the same problem of the concrete and abstract in theological method, see Joseph Stephen O'Leary, *Questioning Back: the Overcoming of Metaphysics in Christian Tradition* (New York: Winston Press, 1985). O'Leary regards Augustine as the chief model of those who accommodate "every dimension of the biblical metaphorical and anthropomorphic language about God into a metaphysical order" (p. 169). His argument is based in the recognition that "Indeed, the narrative and doxological texture of the Bible itself and the nature of the Hebrew tongue never allow any of these notions to become as stabilized as they do when grasped in terms of being by Western thinkers. . . . Thus the overcoming of metaphysics is the first step in the Western journey to an open dialogue with other traditions" (p. 172). It is telling for our general argument that it is the "narrative and doxological texture" of the Bible that is crucial. Our argument is that the narrative quality of doxology is nonnegotiable in the world of Israel's praise, and when it ceases to be concrete narrative, it moves toward idolatry and ideology. Thus the philosophical argument of O'Leary and the sociological awareness of Schottroff and Stegemann converge on the matter of little story and Great Story.

42. Ricoeur, *The Symbolism of Evil*, 53.

43. This tradition thus protests against the reduction of God to the imperial categories of omniscience, omnipotence, and omnipresence which betray the God of the narrative. The God which is enthroned in the hymns of the empire is remote from the narratives of transformation. Such "stable" theology is not without political interest and function. O'Leary has seen the conflict, but has not explored the political implication nor the human cost.

44. In this sense the eschatological interpretation of the Psalms by Brevard S. Childs (*Introduction to the Old Testament as Scripture* [Philadelphia: Fortress Press, 1979], 517–18) is correct, though I take the eschatological dimension of this speech in a sociological sense that Childs would perhaps not accept.

45. The possibilities are both formed by human initiative in the face of God, and at the same time derived from and permitted by God. This odd, dual source of hope is not unlike the odd, dual source of evil as explicated by Ricoeur. Ricoeur (*The Symbolism of Evil*, 257–58) argues that evil is part of human choice and it is "already there." Cf. also pp. 311, 324. Evil is "committed" and "suffered" (p. 324). In a similar way, human possibility is "committed" and "received."

46. Karl Barth, *Wolfgang Amadeus Mozart* (Grand Rapids: William B. Eerdmans, 1986), 37–38.

47. On this new coming-together, Barth writes of Mozart's music:

"This is perhaps because Mozart's sacred music, too, is heard to originate in a region from which vantage point God and the world are certainly not to be judged identical but which does allow church and world (these also not to be interchanged) to be recognizable and recognized in their merely relative difference, in their ultimate togetherness: both emanating from God, both going back to God" (pp. 39–40). On Barth and Mozart, see Theodore A. Gill, "Barth and Mozart," *Theology Today* 43 (1986): 403–11.

48. The Speech of the Whirlwind in Job functions like a theodic resolution of the problem of Job. See Donald E. Gowan, "God's Answer to Job: How Is it an Answer?" *Horizons in Biblical Theology* 8, no. 2 (1986): 85–102. In their offer of an overriding resolution to Job's moral incongruity, the Whirlwind speeches function in a way parallel to the great doxologies in the Book of Revelation. On the latter, see Fred B. Craddock, "Preaching the Book of Revelation," *Interpretation* 40 (1986): 270–82. At its most passionate, biblical faith has no alternative to praise.

49. This is the difference between prayer and praise, on which see Theodore W. Jennings, Jr., *Life as Worship; Prayer and Praise in Jesus' Name* (Grand Rapids: Wm. B. Eerdmans, 1982). Dinesen will not call this yielding prayer, but it surely is something akin to praise.

50. Isak Dinesen, *Out of Africa and Shadows on the Grass* (New York: Random House, 1985), 476–77.

51. Norman C. Habel (*The Book of Job* [Philadelphia: Westminster Press, 1985]) has understood the resolution of the poem in a subtle, ironic way as an acknowledgment of Yahweh's splendid rule without the crushing of Job. Certain elements of the cosmic design in the Whirlwind speech "seem to exist for celebrative rather than pragmatic reasons. They point to the aesthetic, the playful and comic in Yahweh's design. . . . Thus the double resolution of the plot corresponds to the two-part structure of Job's answer. Yahweh's integrity is preserved by Job's confession; Job's integrity is vindicated by Yahweh's face-to-face encounter with the hero. Job's suit can therefore be dropped and normal relations restored" (pp. 533, 579). The resolution seems much like Dinesen's image of ship and sea. The ship must yield to the sea as Job has yielded, but the ship in the process is taken seriously and valued, as is Job.

52. Job's yielding is hard and relentless, his triumph is fragile and penultimate. The subtlety of his yielding and triumph is not unlike that of Jacob in Gen. 32:22–32, so nicely characterized by Frederick Buechner as "Magnificent Defeat" (*The Magnificent Defeat* [London: Chatto & Windus, 1967], 10–18).

53. See chap. 1, under "Sociological Understandings" and nn. 37, 41, 42.

54. See chap. 1, under "Literary Understandings" and nn. 45, 46, 47, 54, 56. A wonderful case of literature as world-making is suggested in the statement of Anais Nin (*In Favor of the Sensitive Man and Other Essays* [New York: Harcourt Brace Jovanovich, 1976], 12) quoted by William H. Shurr ("Mysticism and Suicide: Anne Sexton's Last Poetry," *Soundings* 48

[1985]: 349): "Why one writes is a question I can answer easily, having so often asked it of myself. I believe one writes because one has to create a world in which one can live. I could not live in any of the worlds offered to me—the world of my parents, the world of war, the world of politics. I had to create a world of my own, like a climate, a country, an atmosphere in which I could breathe, reign, and recreate myself when destroyed by living. That, I believe, is the reason for every work of art."

55. See chap. 1, under "Psychological Understandings" and nn. 63, 67, 70, 71.

56. See chap. 1, under "Theological Understandings" and nn. 74, 75. On the distinctiveness of concrete speech for the faithful rendering of world and of God, see Lindbeck, *The Nature of Doctrine*, chap. 6 and passim; and with more textual specificity, Dale Patrick, *The Rendering of God in the Old Testament* (Philadelphia: Fortress Press, 1981).

57. See Ricoeur, *The Symbolism of Evil*, 269 n. 25, on the recognition that everything is borrowed, but that everything is radically transformed. Ricoeur is here concerned with the materials for New Testament Christology, but the same acknowledgment is to be made of Israel's world-making. It is the radical transformation of the borrowed materials due to Israel's pain and healing that is decisive for Israel's praise.

58. The tone of the hymn and its intent is missional and conversionary, but it is not sectarian or triumphalist.

59. On liturgical, sacramental imagination, see Jack Seymore, Robert T. O'Gorman, and Charles R. Foster, *The Church in the Education of the Public* (Nashville: Abingdon Press, 1984), 134–53.

Scripture Index

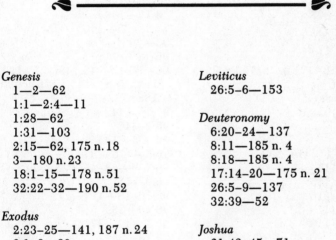